Teaching Language \
in the Classroom

Bringing together the varied and multifaceted expertise of teachers and linguists in one accessible volume, this book presents practical tools, grounded in cutting-edge research, for teaching about language and language diversity in the ELA classroom. By demonstrating practical ways teachers can implement research-driven linguistic concepts in their own teaching environment, each chapter offers real-world lessons as well as clear methods for instructing students on the diversity of language. Written for pre-service and in-service teachers, this book includes easy-to-use lesson plans, pedagogical strategies and activities, as well as a wealth of resources carefully designed to optimize student comprehension of language variation.

Michelle D. Devereaux is Associate Professor of English Education at Kennesaw State University, USA.

Chris C. Palmer is Associate Professor of English at Kennesaw State University, USA.

Teaching Language Variation in the Classroom

Strategies and Models from
Teachers and Linguists

Edited by Michelle D. Devereaux
and Chris C. Palmer

Routledge
Taylor & Francis Group

NEW YORK AND LONDON

First published 2019
by Routledge
52 Vanderbilt Avenue, New York, NY 10017

and by Routledge
2 Park Square, Milton Park, Abingdon, Oxon, OX14 4RN

Routledge is an imprint of the Taylor & Francis Group, an informa business

© 2019 Taylor & Francis

Library of Congress Cataloging-in-Publication Data
A catalog record for this title has been requested

ISBN: 978-1-138-59794-5 (hbk)
ISBN: 978-1-138-59795-2 (pbk)
ISBN: 978-0-429-48667-8 (ebk)

Typeset in Bembo
by Newgen Publishing UK

Visit the eResources page: www.routledge.com/9781138597952

We dedicate this book to all the K-12 teachers, linguists, and university educators who have been working to create a more equitable education system by studying language ideologies and variation and by promoting a richer understanding and appreciation of linguistic diversity.

Contents

List of Contributors   x

Foreword   xi
ANNE CURZAN

Acknowledgments   xiv

*Introduction: Teaching Language Variation and
Ideologies—Questions and Strategies*   xv
MICHELLE D. DEVEREAUX AND CHRIS C. PALMER

How to Use This Book   xxv

Part 1: Teachers' Perspectives   1

1 "Word Crimes" and Linguistic Ideology: Examining
   Student Ideas about Language in the English Language
   Arts Classroom   3
   AMY L. PLACKOWSKI

2 Prescriptive and Descriptive Lenses: How a Teacher Worked
   with Local Linguists to Develop a Language Ideologies Unit   11
   ANDREW BERGDAHL

3 Profiling, Prejudice, and Prestige: Language Ideologies
   across Contexts   18
   STACY ISHIGAKI AREVALO

4 "Working With" Instead of "Pushing Against": Meeting
   Testing Standards while Teaching Language Ideologies   25
   MIKE WILLIAMS

5 "Mr. D, Is This, Like, a Real Word?" Stories of a Linguist
   in a High School English Classroom   32
   JOHN A. DAMASO

6 Linguistics in an English Language Arts Class: Elevating
   Language Awareness   39
   BETH KEYSER

7 Using Music to Bridge Language Diversity   47
   JILLIAN RATTI

8 Power, Society, and Identity: Language and Life in a
   Ninth-Grade English Classroom   54
   HOLLY HOOVER

9 Language Awareness in Education: A Linguist's Response
   to Teachers   61
   WALT WOLFRAM

Part 2: Linguists' Perspectives   67

10 Principles to Navigate the Challenges of Teaching English
   Language Variation: A Guide for Nonlinguists   69
   MIKE METZ

11 Teaching Linguistic Diversity as the Rule Rather than
   the Exception   76
   ANNE LOBECK

12 *DARE*(ing) Language Ideologies: Exploring Linguistic
   Diversity through Audio Data and Literature in
   Secondary Language Arts Courses   84
   KELLY D. ABRAMS AND TRINI STICKLE

13 Bringing Critical Language Pedagogy to the Middle
   School Social Studies Classroom: Lessons for Standard
   English Learners   93
   JESSICA HATCHER AND JEFFREY REASER

14 Grammar in the Spanish/English Bilingual Classroom:
   Three Methods for Teaching Academic Language   101
   MARY HUDGENS HENDERSON

15 Attitude Change Is Not Enough: Changing Teacher
    Practice to Disrupt Dialect Prejudice in the Classroom   109
    REBECCA WHEELER

16 Extending the Conversation: Two Teachers' Response
    to Linguists   120
    SUZANNE LOOSEN AND TEAIRA MCMURTRY

Part 3: Collaborations between Teachers and Linguists   127

17 Using Digital Resources to Teach Language Variation
    in the Midwest   129
    AMANDA SLADEK AND MATTIE LANE

18 How Power Reveals and Directs Teacher Language
    Ideologies with High-Achieving African American Students
    in a Secondary English Classroom   138
    TANJI REED MARSHALL AND CHRYSTAL SEAWOOD

19 Sustained Linguistic Inquiry as a Means of Confronting
    Language Ideology and Prejudice   147
    KRISTIN DENHAM AND DAVID PIPPIN

20 "Standard" English, "Classic" Literature: Examining
    Canonical and Linguistic Ideologies in *Huck Finn*   157
    JEANNE DYCHES AND CAMERON GALE

    Index   165

Contributors

Kelly D. Abrams, University of Wisconsin-Madison, Wisconsin
Stacy Ishigaki Arevalo, Eastside College Preparatory School, California
Andrew Bergdahl, Stoneleigh-Burnham School, Massachusetts
Anne Curzan, University of Michigan, Ann Arbor, Michigan
John A. Damaso, Brophy College Preparatory, Arizona
Kristin Denham, Western Washington University, Washington
Michelle D. Devereaux, Kennesaw State University, Georgia
Jeanne Dyches, Iowa State University, Iowa
Cameron Gale, West Des Moines Community Schools, Iowa
Jessica Hatcher, NC State University, North Carolina
Holly Hoover, Kennesaw Mountain High School, Georgia
Mary Hudgens Henderson, Winona State University, Minnesota
Beth Keyser, Superior High School, Montana
Mattie Lane, West High School, Iowa
Anne Lobeck, Western Washington University, Washington
Suzanne Loosen, Milwaukee Public Schools, Wisconsin
Teaira McMurtry, Milwaukee Public Schools, Wisconsin
Mike Metz, University Of Missouri, Missouri
Chris C. Palmer, Kennesaw State University, Georgia
David Pippin, Young Achievers Science and Math Pilot School, Massachusetts
Amy L. Plackowski, Hudson High School, Massachusetts
Jillian Ratti, McMinn County High School, Tennessee
Jeffrey Reaser, NC State University, North Carolina
Tanji Reed Marshall, Virginia Polytechnic Institute and State University, Virginia
Chrystal Seawood, Washington Leadership Academy, Washington, DC
Amanda Sladek, University Of Nebraska at Kearney, Nebraska
Trini Stickle, Western Kentucky University, Kentucky
Rebecca Wheeler, Christopher Newport University, Virginia
Mike Williams, Joseph Wheeler High School, Georgia, and Dundalk High School, Maryland
Walt Wolfram, NC State University, North Carolina

Foreword

Anne Curzan, University of Michigan, Ann Arbor, Michigan

By the time students get to secondary and college classrooms, many of them have very strong feelings about "grammar." Some of them shudder when they hear the word; they have decided that they "aren't good at grammar" or that it is just rote drills and memorization. They assume there is a right way to use language and they haven't mastered it—or they don't want to. For some students, perhaps especially those coming from communities where nonstandard varieties or languages other than English are spoken, their experiences being told that they speak or write "incorrectly" may have shaken their confidence in their rhetorical skills and made them less willing to speak up (in class or on paper); this is not a good place from which to learn. Other students have identified themselves as the ones who "really know grammar" and enjoy being the people who help friends edit their essays. They are invested in the idea that there is a right way to use language, which they have taken the time and interest to master. It can be hard to let go of the surety that there are clear-cut answers to usage questions.

All of these perspectives can impede learning about how language actually works in a language arts classroom. Readers will notice that I have phrased the goal as "learning about how language actually works" as opposed to "learning grammar." Whether we think of "grammar" narrowly as a set of prescriptive usage rules for formal writing or more broadly as a set of descriptive rules or patterns for how we create words and sentences, "grammar" is only one piece of the puzzle when it comes to understanding language. Let's work from the premise that students should study how human language works in the same way that they study geology, biology, chemistry, history, and government; after all, there is nothing more distinctively human than language. To do this, we need to be open to rethinking the language arts curriculum such that it still helps students master what they need for standardized evaluations but also contextualizes this information within the broader, richer picture of an ever-changing and always variable language.

This volume, with contributions by secondary teachers and linguists, valuably approaches this situation in two ways. First, the authors show how to expand our understanding of "teaching grammar" in secondary schools to encompass exploration of language structure (e.g., phonology, morphology, syntax), dialect variation, language change, and language authority. And *exploration* is a key term in that sentence, to which I will return. Second, many of the essays in this volume discuss how to foreground language ideologies or the commonsense beliefs people hold about language such that both teachers and students can challenge ideas about what people mean by "right" and "wrong" when we speak and write.

Let's start with the focus on exploration. One of the things I love about this volume is that the classroom approaches and activities engage students' curiosity about the language they see and hear around them, as well as the language they encounter in literature. Human beings are really interested in language: taking it apart, playing with it, learning more about how it works. We see boundless creativity and play in the slang that young people create, the novel rhyming schemes in hip-hop, and the many word games that younger and older people alike play in their spare time. Many people also have lots of questions about language: where words and phrases come from, why people in different regions or social groups speak differently, how words get into dictionaries, why English spelling is so irregular, how words exert their power, what texting is doing to English. With questions like these to explore, how could teaching language ever be boring?

My concern has been that the way we teach language in school—whether in secondary or college writing classrooms—can take the questions and the fun out of it. Yet the fun is exactly what can inspire students to dig in and pay attention to the nuances of usage, which is what effective speakers and writers do. In my experience, for example, the best way to inspire students to master the conventions of formal, standard English is to allow them to explore usage questions *as questions*. Let's debate the Oxford comma or rules about singular *they* or the status of *ain't* in formal writing.

This volume is a gem because it has experienced secondary teachers and linguists in conversation about how to teach in a linguistically informed and engaging way. Here we have explanations of how these professionals have approached teaching different aspects of language and language ideology, based on their backgrounds in linguistics, as well as tested classroom plans. Linguists have much to learn from these essays about how to make linguistics more accessible for K-12 classrooms and how to design introductory linguistics courses to be more helpful for teachers in training. And secondary teachers (as well as teachers of younger students) can find information here that may inspire them to experiment with new approaches in their classrooms as early as tomorrow, because experienced teachers are laying out in detail how to do so—and why. These teachers also know that for a classroom plan to be realistically implementable at scale it must not only be interesting and fit within the time allowed for a class, but it should also link to various state standards: in this way, linguistically informed approaches can be integrated into the curriculum as opposed to being an add-on in a curriculum that has little or no space for add-ons.

One of the real challenges of teaching a linguistically informed curriculum is trying to understand and address the previously held beliefs that students bring with them to the classroom—and that in some cases we as teachers may at least partially share. On the flip side of this challenge, though, there lies an opportunity: as contributions to this volume suggest, students are interested in talking about these beliefs and open to questioning them if they can see how this will help them reach their goals.

The consistent focus on language ideology also distinguishes this volume. Students are not blank slates when they enter our classrooms, and we as teachers are not neutral conveyors of linguistic information. As teachers, we need to realize that subtle changes in how we talk about language can have a significant impact on how students experience language difference and language change. If we move away from words like "right" and "wrong" or "correct" and "incorrect" and provide more subtle answers about linguistic choices and their effects, we have shifted the entire ideological footing of the conversation. If we adopt the language of repertoires where everyone's goal is to increase their linguistic repertoire as much as possible, suddenly the students coming to the class with language varieties other than the standard variety, as well as other languages, are empowered: they have the potential to be even more versatile as speakers and writers than those without that linguistic knowledge already under their belt. As I often say to students, the person with the biggest linguistic repertoire—and the knowledge about how to deploy it effectively in speech and writing—wins.

I understand that it can feel time-consuming to adopt this new approach to teaching language as it eschews quick and easy answers. But with the kinds of pedagogy described in this volume, the information has a better shot at sticking with students in a meaningful way. I believe firmly that in language arts and writing classrooms, we should be allowing students to explore language and how it works in speech, writing, and signing; and in this context we can help students master and think critically about a set of usage rules that govern formal, edited prose. This kind of close attention to the details of language—which requires reflection on purpose and audience and linguistic choices—is a key ingredient of effective writing. I hope that teachers and students will find that this volume empowers them to talk with each other about language in a shared spirit of investigation, attentiveness, and pleasure in speakers' and writers' creativity with words.

Acknowledgments

This volume is indebted to the community of scholars and teachers who, for the past several decades, have been thinking, teaching, and researching about the educational implications of language variation. This project grew out of conversations we had about teaching language variation and ideology with our own pre-service and in-service teachers in our educational linguistics courses at Kennesaw State University, and we must thank them for their thoughtful engagement with the topic, which, in turn, continued to spur our own thinking and questioning.

Our initial research began with a couple of simple questions (which revealed their complexity as we really dug into them): What are the most practical ways to teach language variation and ideologies in schools? And how can we get linguists and teachers to talk about these issues even more with one another? We are grateful to Anne Curzan and the American Dialect Society for accepting our application to speak about our preliminary ideas at their 2016 panel on teaching, and to Jeffrey Reaser for inviting us to present and develop these ideas further at the Linguistic Society of America panel at the 2016 National Council of Teachers of English conference. The insights from our students and from the scholars and teachers at these panel sessions—as well as the constant encouragement from our friend and colleague Darren Crovitz—provided the spark that ignited our conception of this book.

We are particularly thankful to several anonymous reviewers for their helpful comments in revising the content and structure of the volume, and to Kennesaw State University and Routledge for their support of scholarship about teaching. This volume would not have been possible without the steady guidance by Routledge's editorial team, particularly Karen Adler, Emmalee Ortega, and Siobhan Murphy. Finally, thanks to our families—in particular our spouses, George Koulouris and Paul Padur—for their help through many stages of this project.

Introduction

Teaching Language Variation and Ideologies— Questions and Strategies

Michelle D. Devereaux and Chris C. Palmer,
Kennesaw State University, Georgia

English language arts (ELA) teachers have the complicated task of teaching *language.* And while linguistics isn't in every teacher preparation program, teachers still walk into classrooms where language varieties prosper, both in the literature they teach and in the speech and writing of their students.

When we welcome in-service and pre-service teachers into our linguistics classrooms at the university, and when we get into the messy world of English language variation and the beliefs associated with it, teachers begin questioning how to navigate the spaces of power, place, and people that are inherently part of language and language ideologies:

> This is where I'm conflicted. How do I nurture my students' love and pride for their own dialect and then tell them that they must speak and write Standard English in the "real world" if they want to succeed?
>
> (Jennifer, pre-service English teacher)

> The more I push the "Standard" on my students, the more I take away part of their identity. So what do I do? I don't want ... my students struggling with feelings of isolation, but I also want them to be successful.
>
> (Katie, in-service English teacher)[1]

Whether or not teachers are trained in linguistics, they may still grapple with issues like Jennifer and Katie discuss above. So what's to be done?

Curricula are full. Standardized tests matter (a lot). Standards, expectations, and mandates still trickle down to classrooms across the country. And many teachers and linguists aren't having critical conversations about language in ways that matter to, and that fully grapple with, the constraints of the modern ELA classroom.

In this edited volume, we invite the voices of both teachers and linguists to share how they teach language, language variation, and language ideologies. There are so many good ideas being generated by linguists and educators, but not enough spaces for them to share and test those ideas. More to the point, when teachers learn about language varieties and language ideologies, they often find themselves saying things like, "These are great ideas, but where do I have time and space in my

---

1 The voices and perspectives of pre-service and in-service teachers in this chapter were gathered from an IRB-approved research study of our educational linguistics courses. All names have been changed.

classroom to incorporate them?" Linguists often wonder, "I have a lot to say about how language works in my educational linguistics course, but how do I really know what teachers need to know?" This book serves as one forum for conversations among teachers and linguists. And it presents models not only for incorporating language variation and ideology in ELA classes but also for collaboration between teachers and linguists.

What Do We Mean by *Language Variation* and *Language Ideologies*?

In our daily lives, we typically recognize that different varieties of English coexist in our culture. ("Do you really say *pop* for soft drinks? I say *soda*, and my new roommate calls them all *cokes!*") When linguists talk about *language variation*, they're describing a social fact: different groups of speakers tend to use language in systematically distinct ways. There are patterns to women's speech that tend to differ from men's; younger generations commonly create and use slang that older generations don't; people from highly educated or upper-class backgrounds in cities such as Boston and New York may pronounce their *r*'s differently than socioeconomically disadvantaged individuals from those same cities.

One of the greatest sources of variation arises from differences in regional and ethnic varieties of American English. Regional dialects are associated with groups of speakers who live in particular geographical areas. In fact, linguists have discovered a number of distinct varieties in the continental U.S., including (but certainly not limited to) the different Englishes of the West, the South, the Midland/Midwest, the St. Louis corridor, Western Pennsylvania, the mid-Atlantic, New York City, and Eastern New England (Labov, Ash, & Boberg, 2005). Language variation is also apparent in the non-continental regions of the U.S. as well, such as Alaska, Hawaii, and the various territories.[2]

In addition to regional varieties, ethnic varieties describe dialects often spoken by members of different ethnic groups, including (but certainly not limited to) African American English, Chicanx English, and Korean American English. It's important to note that not all members of an ethnic group speak a variety associated with that group, and that ethnic varieties themselves can vary by region (e.g., there are differences between the African American English spoken in Detroit and in Atlanta).

Most ethnic and regional varieties are considered to be nonstandard in our society, particularly in contrast to a variety known as "Standard American English" (SAE). SAE is perhaps best understood as a variety associated more with writing than speaking, one that is most valued and favored by institutions and individuals in positions of mainstream power, including corporations, the government, the media, editors, publishers, and schools and universities. It is less a logical system of rules than it is a hodgepodge of conventions deemed favorable by these institutions and individuals, who tend to value and promote the least stigmatized variants in English (e.g., using *aren't* rather than *ain't*, or *you* rather than *y'all*). To complicate matters further, institutions often adopt differing standards (e.g., the different rules for citations as outlined in the style guides of the American Psychological Association

2 For more on language variation and ideology in Alaska, see Stone (2019); for Hawaii, see Lippi-Green (2012).

Box 0.1 Key facts about Standard American English

1. Standard American English (SAE) is a variety of the English language. It is not *the* English language, but only one among many varieties, such as African American English, Chicanx English, and Southern English.
2. SAE is associated more often with formal, written English used in academic and professional contexts than with spoken varieties of the language. Even so, spoken varieties are often compared to and judged against written SAE, and some language authorities do attempt to enforce standards for spoken English.
3. SAE is *not* an inherently better variety of English than other varieties, but it is often perceived as better because it is valued by individuals and institutions in positions of mainstream power.
4. The codified rules of SAE are arbitrary. Indeed, the conventions of non-standard dialects are sometimes more systematic than the conventions of SAE (see Tables 0.1 and 0.2).
5. SAE is not considered appropriate in all contexts. For example, if you were watching a football game with friends and asked them "To whom did the quarterback just throw the ball?," you might get a few odd looks.

---

or the Modern Language Association); and standards tend to differ among global English varieties (compare the standard American spelling of *theater* and *center* to British *theatre* and *centre*). Box 0.1 summarizes some of the most important facts to remember about SAE.[3]

The standard variety would not have the status it does without an associated set of beliefs—namely, *standard language ideology*—which holds that SAE is an inherently better variety of English than all other varieties (Lippi-Green, 2012). Linguists tend to approach this issue with a different perspective, grounded in (what we might call) a *linguistic diversity ideology*: all varieties of language have value, whether they are deemed nonstandard or standard, and no single variety is inherently better than another.

This is not to say that linguists don't value the standard; many linguists, in fact, think the standard can play an important role for bridging communication between speakers of different varieties. The problem with standard language ideology is that in our culture—and certainly in our classrooms—it creates a social hierarchy of language, where nonstandard varieties (and speakers) are given less value and social esteem than SAE. For our students, this can be damaging; standard language ideology tends to set up a binary, either/or choice: *choose the standard or choose your home variety*. And, faced with this choice, most students will pick home over school.

Another (somewhat ironic) complication for the classroom is that there doesn't seem to be a single, agreed-upon term to refer to a standard variety of English. There are different regional standard Englishes around the globe, of course. But

---

3 *Standard English* can be a messy concept to discuss with students. For a helpful overview of Standard English, particularly in U.S. contexts, see Curzan and Adams (2012, pp. 36–38). For additional illustration of the difficulties in defining it—including examples from Englishes outside the U.S.—see Trudgill (1999).

even when referring to the American standard variety, there are multiple names for it (as can be observed in the different chapters of this book)—often with different patterns of capitalization: e.g., *standard English, Standard American English, standardized (American) English, Mainstream English*. Teachers will want to consider which labels to introduce in their classroom, as different labels will convey different ideas about language to students. Moreover, teachers should share with their students the power of labeling. Students can learn the value of linguistic diversity more deeply when teachers take time to ask why particular labels are used—and which labels students think *should* be used—in their classroom (e.g., Which is a better descriptor: *mainstream English, academic English*, or *Standard American English*? Why might we call this variety "African American English" rather than "Ebonics"?).

This technique of engaging students in questions of language variation and ideology has been shown to have benefits; in fact, some research has found that students may be more willing to learn SAE when language ideologies are explicitly addressed in the classroom (Godley, Carpenter, & Werner, 2007; Kirkland & Jackson, 2009). Ultimately, we cannot understand language variation without also understanding how all speakers, including students in ELA classrooms, are pressured to negotiate their use of standard and nonstandard language varieties.

Key Themes for the Secondary Classroom

When we first started emailing with Suzi Loosen, one of our master teachers who writes a response in Part 2 of this volume, she asked us an important question: "What are some of the key ideas that you have in mind when you talk about teaching language variation and/or ideology?" Although we've been teaching these topics for years, Suzi's question forced us to consider what we believe are the key themes related to language varieties and their associated ideologies. We share these here so that our framing of these topics in the rest of this volume is clear.

Language Changes over Time and across Populations

It is a fact that language changes over time and varies across regions and peoples. And there's nothing inherently good or bad about those changes beyond what our society accepts or stigmatizes. We should remember, though, that what we accept or stigmatize also changes over time (as culture changes). Think about words that have become taboo relatively recently (e.g., *retarded*) or were formerly taboo or disfavored but are now somewhat unremarkable (e.g., saying "That sucks!" about mild annoyances). Or consider the word *nice*, which was first borrowed into English hundreds of years ago as an insult, then over time became a compliment, and probably now is so bleached of meaning that it is neither. (Think of how often we say "he's nice" or "that's nice" when we really can't think of anything else to say.)

All Language Varieties Show Evidence of Systematic Structure

All nonstandard dialects are as structurally patterned and rule-governed as SAE; in some respects, they can be *more* logical and consistent than SAE. Just compare the regular use of *ain't* in some varieties of American English, illustrated in

Table 0.1 Use of (nonstandard) *ain't* for each subject pronoun

I **ain't** workin'.	We **ain't** workin'.
You **ain't** workin'.	Y'all **ain't** workin'.
She/He/It **ain't** workin'.	They **ain't** workin'.

Table 0.2 Standard American English contractions of the verb BE + *not* for each subject pronoun

I **???** working.	We **aren't** working.
You **aren't** working.	You **aren't** working.
She/He/It **isn't** working.	They **aren't** working.

Table 0.1, with the equivalent contractions for the verb BE + *not* in SAE, illustrated in Table 0.2.

It should be immediately evident that the pattern for *ain't* is much more consistent than its equivalents in SAE.[4] It's also hard to see any ways in which the SAE pattern is more logical than the use of *ain't*: there isn't even an equivalent contraction of the verb BE + *not* that can be used after *I* in Standard American English![5]

SAE shows signs of consistent patterns and structure in other respects (e.g., certain prescriptive rules for using punctuation). But it is important to acknowledge the systematic qualities of nonstandard varieties and avoid assumptions about the standard variety being the most logical, consistent, or best form of language.

Language Use Is Complicated by Power, Society, and Identity

Language use (both standard and nonstandard) is intimately tied up in each person's identity and social relationships. And language use always reflects power dynamics among people. If a seventh-grader saw an epic food fight in the lunchroom, her story would sound very different when she told her friend than when she told the principal—that's because both contexts call on different identities, social relationships, and power dynamics. Schools, and, more specifically, classrooms might be the best place to see these relationships and dynamics in action, which is why we should give these conversations ample space there.

All Varieties of English Can Be Tools to Use Purposefully and with Awareness

When students learn the conventions of SAE, they gain access to mainstream power structures that traditionally employ those conventions. At the same time,

4 While some language purists may consider all contractions "nonstandard," we argue that contractions are an important part of informal registers of Standard English.
5 Note that all of the following contractions after *I* are considered unacceptable in SAE: *I aren't working*, *I isn't working*, and *I ain't working*. Instead, SAE uses a completely different contraction pattern with the first-person pronoun, in which the verb BE rather than *not* is contracted: compare *I'm not working* (*am* is contracted to *'m* and attached to *I*) to *You aren't working* (*not* is contracted to *n't* and attached to *are*).

students should feel that they and others can embrace and use their home, non-standard varieties, since those varieties are preferred or may be more accepted than SAE in many social spaces. We should empower our students by expanding their knowledge of different language varieties—i.e., by expanding their linguistic repertoires. We can achieve this by teaching them about the structure of standard and nonstandard varieties as well as the social contexts in which they matter, while discussing and problematizing the social hierarchies in which different varieties have been placed.

Important Issues to Negotiate

In the past, academics—linguists and pedagogues alike—have called for instructors to teach linguistic concepts in the secondary English classroom. Decades of research prove such instruction effective, and academics continue to compile and review this work (Pearson, Conner, & Jackson, 2012; Smith, 2016; Wheeler, 2016). These academics research, review, and theorize what will work for secondary students who speak multiple dialects in the modern American classroom; however, as so many note, these research-proven strategies are not widely and consistently implemented in the everyday classroom by the everyday teacher.

True change doesn't happen quickly, and rarely without grappling with important issues inherent in teaching language variation and ideologies. Below we discuss these issues, which have emerged in our linguistics courses designed for in-service and pre-service teachers, and how these issues relate to language, classrooms, and the players in those classrooms.

Authority

When we teach our in-service teachers about language and authority, most are amazed to learn that society views them as "language mavens"—people who have "the authority to tell us what constitutes proper and improper usage, especially in written language" (Curzan & Adams, 2012, p. 33). Our discussions about language mavens lead into discussions of their students as authorities and experts on their own language varieties, which begin to unravel previous assumptions about power, people, and language. Pre-service and in-service teachers in our classes begin grappling with standard language ideology, multicultural awareness, and students' relationships with language. All of these concepts are wrapped up in authority. Who has the authority to name which variety is right and in what context? Is this authority shared among people in different groups and with different language varieties? How do our students have authority and power over their language use and knowledge? How do these various power dynamics manifest in classrooms, and do these manifestations support the tenets of democracy and equality?

Canon

We praise those teachers who work to diversify the canon in ELA classrooms and acknowledge the ways in which the literary canon has recently expanded to include a greater range of writers from diverse backgrounds. But efforts to diversify the canon must include language as well—otherwise, we undermine the very message of diversification. That is, when SAE is the only linguistic option given attention or value, students internalize the message that perhaps diversity doesn't matter as much as we say it does. And since language reflects identity, we're also telling students that some identities don't matter as much as others. At the same time, when they take standardized tests, and after they graduate, students will be judged for their knowledge of the mainstream linguistic canon—i.e., their knowledge of SAE. So how can teachers make space in their classes to diversify the linguistic repertoire of the classroom—to expand the linguistic canon—while ensuring comfort and mastery of the conventions of Standard Written English?

Purpose

The first year Michelle taught language ideologies to in-service teachers, one of them raised her hand and asked, "So what does all of this matter? We tell our students that there are language varieties, and you have a variety, and it is wonderful and wrapped up in your identity and community and the power you have there, but, at the end of the day, students still have to pass the test. They still have to get a job. So why should I waste my time on this?" This question opens both teachers and linguists to important considerations: How do we teach language variation and ideologies not for their own sake but with a sense of purpose? What can students *do* with this information on language diversity in both academic and non-academic contexts? How can incorporating this linguistic material enhance the teaching of other materials and support other class objectives?

Practicality

Teachers face pressures and parameters that structure each day in their classrooms, from students to parents to administrators to districts. So often, they are asked to include "just this one more thing" in an already full curriculum. Teachers and linguists must *integrate* instruction related to language variation and ideologies rather than simply *adding* more material to be taught. So how can lessons on or discussions of language variation and ideology reinforce the reading and writing assignments that already exist in the curriculum? How can we support adaptations to the curriculum instead of additions? How can we be more conscious of such practical considerations when identifying important linguistic concepts for the classroom?

We understand that we have posed more questions than solutions in this section; however, these are the questions that teachers face each time they are asked to teach language variation and ideologies in their classrooms. These are the questions that both teachers and linguists must grapple with in order to find ways to *integrate* critical language instruction into the everyday English classroom. A central goal of this introductory chapter is to promote further discussion among teachers and linguists about the critical questions we have outlined above. A central goal of this volume is for each of its chapters to answer at least some part of one or more of these questions, and to identify further challenges and solutions for teachers and linguists to consider.

Conclusion

Teachers know teaching and linguists know language. We hope this volume creates a space where all of these experts can actively explore effective ways to teach language variation and ideology. Teachers can benefit from linguists' insights on recent theories, technological developments, and research-based findings about language variation, ideologies, and instruction of both. Linguists can benefit from teachers' insights on what has been working in everyday classrooms and what pedagogical ideas need improvement. Linguists also need to hear about the constantly shifting world of teaching as new standards are required and new mandates are passed down from both state and federal levels.

We don't see this volume as the final word on these matters. Instead, we see it as a widening floor for ongoing conversation among teachers and linguists, as they learn together and reflect together on how to create a more equitable education system for all of our students.

Further Reading

Below we list other books, publications, websites, and professional organizations that may help guide teachers' and linguists' thinking about linguistic instruction in schools. Some books are textbooks, while others are practitioner-focused; some websites are about pedagogy, while others are designed to help users learn more about language. While the list below is certainly not exhaustive, these resources have helped shape our thinking as we consider how to best bridge language and pedagogy.

Books

Brown, D. W. (2009). *In other words: Lessons on grammar, code-switching, and academic writing.* Portsmouth, NH: Heinemann.

Charity Hudley, A. H. & Mallinson, C. (2011). *Understanding English language variation in U.S. schools.* New York, NY: Teachers College Press.

Charity Hudley, A. H. & Mallinson, C. (2013). *We do language: English language variation in the secondary English classroom.* New York, NY: Teachers College Press.

Crovitz, D., & Devereaux, M. D. (2017). *Grammar to get things done: A practical guide for teachers anchored in real-world usage.* London and New York, NY and Urbana, IL: Routledge and NCTE.

Curzan, A., & Adams, M. (2012). *How English works: A linguistic introduction* (3rd ed.). Glenview, IL: Pearson.

Denham, K., & Lobeck, A. (2013). *Linguistics for everyone: An introduction* (2nd ed.). Boston, MA: Wadsworth Cengage Learning.

Devereaux, M. D. (2015). *Teaching about dialect variations and language in secondary English classrooms: Power, prestige, and prejudice.* London and New York, NY: Routledge.

Reaser, J., Adger, C. T., Wolfram, W., & Christian, D. (2017). *Dialects at school: Educating linguistically diverse students.* London and New York, NY: Routledge.

Tamasi, S., & Antieau, L. (2015). *Language and linguistic diversity in the U.S.: An introduction.* London and New York, NY: Routledge.

Wheeler, R. S., Swords, R. (2006). *Code-switching: Teaching standard English in urban classrooms.* Urbana, IL: NCTE.

Wheeler, R. S., & Swords, R. (2015). *Code-switching lessons: Grammar strategies for linguistically diverse writers*. Sun Prairie, WI: Ventris Learning.

Young, V. A., Barretta, R., Young-Rivera, Y., & Lovejoy, K. B. (2014). *Other people's English: Code-meshing, code-switching, and African American literacy*. New York, NY: Teachers College Press.

Edited Collections

Delpit, L., & Dowdy, J. K. (Eds.). (2002). *The skin that we speak: Thoughts on language and culture in the classroom*. New York, NY: The New Press.

Denham, K., & Lobeck, A. (Eds.). (2010). *Linguistics at school: Language awareness in primary and secondary education*. Cambridge: Cambridge University Press.

Moore, C., & Palmer, C. C. (Eds.). (2019). *Teaching the history of the English language*. New York, NY: MLA.

Scott, J. C., Straker, D. Y., Katz, L. (Eds.). (2009). *Affirming students' right to their own language: Bridging language policies and pedagogical practices*. London, New York, NY and Urbana, IL: Routledge and NCTE.

Journals

"Teaching American speech," an annual pedagogical section of the journal *American Speech*.

Websites

Abrams, K., Stickle, T., & Walton-Hanley, J. (n.d.). *Discovering DARE*. Retrieved from https://discoveringdare.wordpress.com

Charity Hudley, A., & Mallinson, C. (n.d.) *Valuable voices*. Retrieved from https://charityhudleymallinson.com

Denham, C. (2014). *Exploring language: Daily language investigations in English language arts*. Retrieved from www.explorelanguage.org

McCulloch, G. (n.d.). *All things linguistic*. Retrieved from https://allthingslinguistic.com

McCulloch, G., & Gawne, L. (n.d.). *Lingthusiasm*. Retrieved from https://lingthusiasm.com

Metz, M. (2017). *Resources for teachers in culturally and linguistically complex classrooms*. Retrieved from www.metzteaching.com/resources-for-teachers.html

Wolfram, W., & Reaser, J. (2018). *The language and life project at NC State*. Retrieved from https://languageandlife.org

Professional Organizations

American Dialect Society
Conference on English Education
The Linguistic Society of America: Language in the School Curriculum (LiSC)
National Council of Teachers of English

References

Curzan, A., & Adams, M. (2012). *How English works: A linguistic introduction*. Glenview, IL: Pearson.

Godley, A. J., Carpenter, B. D., & Werner, C. A. (2007) "I'll speak in proper slang": Language ideologies in a daily editing activity. *Reading Research Quarterly, 42*(1), 100–131.

Kirkland, D. E., & Jackson, A. (2009). Beyond the silence: Instructional approaches and students' attitudes. In J. C. Cobb, D.Y. Straker, & L. Katz (Eds.), *Affirming students' right to their own language* (pp. 132–150). London and New York, NY: Routledge.

Labov,W.,Ash, S., & Boberg, C. (2005). *The atlas of North American English: Phonetics, phonology, and sound change.* Berlin: Mouton de Gruyter.

Lippi-Green, R. (2012). *English with an accent: Language, ideology, and discrimination in the United States* (2nd ed.). London and New York, NY: Routledge.

Pearson, B. Z., Conner, T., & Jackson, J. E. (2012). Removing obstacles for African American English-speaking children through greater understanding of language difference. *Developmental Psychology, 49*(1), 31–44.

Smith, P. (2016). A distinctly American opportunity: Exploring non-standardized English(es) in literacy policy and practice. *Reading, Writing, and Language, 3*(2), 194–202.

Stone, J. C. (2019). Developing local approaches to the HEL course: An Alaskan example. In C. Moore & C. C. Palmer (Eds.), *Teaching the History of the English Language* (pp. 154–162). New York, NY: MLA.

Trudgill, P. (1999). Standard English: What it isn't. In T. Bex & R. J. Watts (Eds.), *Standard English: The widening debate* (pp. 117–128). London and New York, NY: Routledge.

Wheeler, R. S. (2016). "So much research, so little change": Teaching Standard English in African American classrooms. *Annual Review of Linguistics, 2*(3), 367–390.

How to Use This Book

The chapters in this volume have been ordered purposefully so that the book can be read from beginning to end—each chapter adds to the discussions of those that come before and after it. However, there are also chapters across the parts of this volume that can be grouped by various topics. Below we offer a summary of each chapter and then list chapters that foreground discussion of specific topics. Finally, we provide a list of lesson plans and other teaching materials appearing in the volume or on its related eResources site.

Chapter Summaries

Part I: Teachers' Perspectives

Part 1 highlights the voices of secondary teachers, inviting them to share how they already teach language and language ideologies in their classrooms. Each teacher provides a lesson plan at the end of their chapter to demonstrate what their practice looks like. These educators represent a wide variety of schools and regions in the country, including public and private schools from the West Coast, Southwest, Southeast, and New England.

"Word Crimes" and Linguistic Ideology: Examining Student Ideas about Language in the English Language Arts Classroom

Amy L. Plackowski, Hudson High School, Massachusetts

Amy L. Plackowski offers core questions that should be grappled with in any language study curriculum and shares specific activities she does in her own classroom, including discussion of examples from audiovisual media and pop culture.

Prescriptive and Descriptive Lenses: How a Teacher Worked with Local Linguists to Develop a Language Ideologies Unit

Andrew Bergdahl, Stoneleigh-Burnham School, Massachusetts

Andrew Bergdahl outlines a unit on descriptive and prescriptive attitudes toward language that he put together with guidance from linguists he contacted at his local university.

Profiling, Prejudice, and Prestige: Language Ideologies across Contexts

Stacy Ishigaki Arevalo, Eastside College Preparatory School, California

Stacy Ishigaki Arevalo describes a unit that covers the topics of dialect, register, code-switching, and linguistic profiling with texts such as Zora Neale Hurston's *Their Eyes Were Watching God*.

"Working With" Instead of "Pushing Against": Meeting Testing Standards while Teaching Language Ideologies

Mike Williams, Joseph Wheeler High School, Georgia, and Dundalk High School, Maryland

Mike Williams describes how a school-wide symposium on the N-word began his journey toward teaching language in critical ways, such as discussing language choices in "Dry September" by William Faulkner, while still meeting the required standards.

"Mr. D, Is This, Like, a Real Word?" Stories of a Linguist in a High School English Classroom

John A. Damaso, Brophy College Preparatory, Arizona

John A. Damaso provides a series of vignettes—from teaching traditional literature (e.g., *The Great Gatsby*) to discussing language with dictionaries, flashcards, games—outlining the strategies and challenges of balancing his dual role as a language authority in the classroom (both linguist and English teacher).

Linguistics in an English Language Arts Class: Elevating Language Awareness

Beth Keyser, Superior High School, Montana

Beth Keyser shows how she uses word parts (i.e., morphology) and word groupings (i.e., syntax and grammar) to teach students the sense, the order, and the possibilities of the English language.

Using Music to Bridge Language Diversity

Jillian Ratti, McMinn County High School, Tennessee

Jillian Ratti describes a different kind of diversity in her East Tennessee high school and shares how a March Madness-style unit incorporates music to build upon the language diversity in her classroom.

Power, Society, and Identity: Language and Life in a Ninth-Grade English Classroom

Holly Hoover, Kennesaw Mountain High School, Georgia

Holly Hoover shares her journey as a new teacher learning how to approach language ideologies in her classroom and describes how she now pairs language-ideology instruction with Shakespeare's *Romeo and Juliet*.

Language Awareness in Education: A Linguist's Response to Teachers

Walt Wolfram, NC State University, North Carolina

Walt Wolfram considers the common ways language variation and ideologies have been addressed in the teachers' chapters in Part 1, discusses the teaching profiles of the teachers who have undertaken this work, and concludes with potential ideas for expanding on this work in the future.

Part 2: Linguists' Perspectives

Part 2 features linguists sharing instructional ideas for teachers, moving beyond the theory of *why* to *how* to teach language and language ideologies. The authors address various practical considerations for implementing these ideas, as well as the purposes and benefits that a focus on language variation and ideology can have for both students and teachers.

Principles to Navigate the Challenges of Teaching English Language Variation: A Guide for Nonlinguists

Mike Metz, University of Missouri, Missouri

Mike Metz, emphasizing that teachers do not need to be experts in linguistics, outlines several guiding principles for teaching language variation and provides several examples of how these principles can be applied to the various strands of ELA.

Teaching Linguistic Diversity as the Rule Rather than the Exception

Anne Lobeck, Western Washington University, Washington

Anne Lobeck discusses how she uses prescriptive and descriptive grammar to teach language variation and language ideologies in her linguistics course for pre-service teachers.

DARE(ing) Language Ideologies: Exploring Linguistic Diversity through Audio Data and Literature in Secondary Language Arts Courses

Kelly D. Abrams, University of Wisconsin-Madison, Wisconsin, and Trini Stickle, Western Kentucky University, Kentucky

Kelly D. Abrams and Trini Stickle discuss several activities that ask students to wrestle with linguistic prejudice by analyzing written/literary and oral/real-life representations of dialect.

Bringing Critical Language Pedagogy to the Middle School Social Studies Classroom: Lessons for Standard English Learners

Jessica Hatcher and Jeffrey Reaser, NC State University, North Carolina

Jessica Hatcher and Jeffrey Reaser discuss their work in a social studies classroom where they incorporated sociolinguistic information and employed critical language pedagogy; these lessons can be easily adapted to ELA classrooms in secondary education settings.

Grammar in the Spanish/English Bilingual Classroom: Three Methods for Teaching Academic Language

Mary Hudgens Henderson, Winona State University, Minnesota

Mary Hudgens Henderson describes how tools such as linguistic inquiry and contrastive analysis can help students explore nonstandard varieties of Spanish and how they can help students distinguish differences in the writing conventions of English and Spanish.

Attitude Change Is Not Enough: Changing Teacher Practice to Disrupt Dialect Prejudice in the Classroom

Rebecca Wheeler, Christopher Newport University, Virginia

Rebecca Wheeler details step-by-step classroom methods to analyze the written vernacular patterns common in communities speaking African American Vernacular English, demonstrating how one might take tangible steps to break the cycle of dominant language ideology in U.S. classrooms.

Extending the Conversation: Two Teachers' Response to Linguists

Suzanne Loosen and Teaira McMurtry, Milwaukee Public Schools, Wisconsin

Suzanne Loosen and Teaira McMurtry address the challenges and solutions described by the linguists in Part 2, discuss prerequisites needed to implement their recommendations, and consider how linguists and teachers can collaborate toward these solutions.

Part 3: Collaborations between Teachers and Linguists

The third part of this volume presents four pairs of teacher–linguist collaborators. In each case, the teacher and linguist have worked together to design lessons for the ELA classroom, with each pair co-writing a chapter that offers practical strategies for teaching linguistic variation and/or ideology.

Using Digital Resources to Teach Language Variation in the Midwest

Amanda Sladek, University of Nebraska-Kearney at Nebraska, and Mattie Lane, West High School, Iowa

Amanda Sladek and Mattie Lane provide strategies for using digital resources to teach dialectal variation; they also discuss adaptations each instructor made to this material, accounting for student needs, core curriculum standards, larger pedagogical goals, and other contextual/institutional factors at the high school and university levels.

How Power Reveals and Directs Teacher Language Ideologies with High-Achieving African American Students in a Secondary English Classroom

Tanji Reed Marshall, Virginia Polytechnic Institute and State University, Virginia, and Chrystal Seawood, Washington Leadership Academy, Washington DC

Tanji Reed Marshall and Chrystal Seawood explore the relationship between teachers' language ideologies and the dynamics of power that impact instructional decision-making and delivery with high-achieving African American students.

Sustained Linguistic Inquiry as a Means of Confronting Language Ideology and Prejudice

Kristin Denham, Western Washington University, Washington, and David Pippin, Young Achievers Science and Math Pilot School, Massachusetts

Kristin Denham and David Pippin explain how they teach linguistics through scientific inquiry, demonstrating how syllable instruction can help students better understand and respect the nuances of both language use and language varieties.

"Standard" English, "Classic" Literature: Examining Canonical and Linguistic Ideologies in Huck Finn

Jeanne Dyches, Iowa State University, Iowa, and Cameron Gale, West Des Moines Community Schools, Iowa

Jeanne Dyches and Cameron Gale draw on models grounded in participatory action research and discuss the planning and implementation of lessons around *Huck Finn* that help students understand the power dynamics that permeate language practices and canonical traditions.

Topics

Selected chapters have been organized below into topical groups, demonstrating how different courses of study might use this book. These groupings are meant to be a rough guide rather than an exhaustive listing of all topics covered and of all chapters touching on each topic. (Readers who don't see a topic they have in mind are encouraged to use the index to seek out other topical threads among chapters.) The primary goal here is to demonstrate how instructors may envision using this volume for different types of courses, units, activities, or other classroom ideas.

Literature

Arevalo (pp. 18–24)
Williams (pp. 25–31)
Damaso (pp. 32–38)
Keyser (pp. 39–46)
Hoover (pp. 54–60)
Abrams and Stickle (pp. 84–92)
Sladek and Lane (pp. 129–137)
Dyches and Gale (pp. 157–164)

TV, film, music, and media

Plackowski (pp. 3–10)
Bergdahl (pp. 11–17)
Arevalo (pp. 18–24)
Ratti (pp. 47–53)
Metz (pp. 69–75)
Abrams and Stickle (pp. 84–92)
Hatcher and Reaser (pp. 93–100)
Sladek and Lane (pp. 129–137)

Grammar and grading

Keyser (pp. 39–46)
Lobeck (pp. 76–83)
Hudgens Henderson (pp. 101–108)
Wheeler (pp. 109–119)

Prescriptive versus descriptive approaches

Plackowski (pp. 3–10)
Bergdahl (pp. 11–17)
Wolfram (pp. 61–66)
Metz (pp. 69–75)
Lobeck (pp. 76–83)
Loosen and McMurtry (pp. 120–125)

Race and ethnicity

Arevalo (pp. 18–24)
Williams (pp. 25–31)
Hoover (pp. 54–60)
Abrams and Stickle (pp. 84–92)
Wheeler (pp. 109–119)
Loosen and McMurtry (pp. 120–125)
Reed Marshall and Seawood (pp. 138–146)
Dyches and Gale (pp. 157–164)

Geography and region

Plackowski (pp. 3–10)
Keyser (pp. 39–46)
Ratti (pp. 47–53)
Abrams and Stickle (pp. 84–92)
Hatcher and Reaser (pp. 93–100)
Sladek and Lane (pp. 129–137)
Denham and Pippin (pp. 147–156)

Multilingual education and English as a second language

Arevalo (pp. 18–24)
Hoover (pp. 54–60)
Hatcher and Reaser (pp. 93–100)
Hudgens Henderson (pp. 101–108)
Denham and Pippin (pp. 147–156)

Linguistic areas[1]

Damaso (pp. 32–38)

• Lexicon

Keyser (pp. 39–46)

• Morphology
• Syntax

Metz (pp. 69–75)

• Syntax

Lobeck (pp. 76–83)

• Morphology
• Syntax

Abrams and Stickle (pp. 84–92)

• Phonology
• Morphology
• Syntax
• Lexicon

Hatcher and Reaser (pp. 93–100)

• Phonology
• Morphology
• Lexicon

Hudgens Henderson (pp. 101–108)

• Morphology

Wheeler (pp. 109–119)

• Morphology
• Syntax

---

1 All chapters in this volume include some discussion of sociolinguistic concepts.

Loosen and McMurtry (pp. 120–125)

- Phonology
- Morphology
- Syntax
- Language acquisition

Denham and Pippin (pp. 147–156)

- Phonology
- Morphology

Lesson Plans and eResources

Below we list the titles of the lesson plans included in this volume and on the eResources site (www.routledge.com/9781138597952). But the eResources site has more than just lesson plans: the contributors have included teacher notes, student handouts, PowerPoints, assignment sheets, and rubrics to help guide teachers toward integrating language variation and ideology instruction in their classrooms. Recommended grade levels have been provided for those lessons in the book, but readers should note that all lessons are adaptable for different grades.

Plackowski

This volume (pp. 7–9): "'Word Crimes'—Examining Linguistic Prescriptivism and Attitudes about Language," designed for tenth to twelfth grade
eResources: "Bilingualism Mind Map"; "Etymology Paper"; "Language Autobiography"; "Perceptual Dialectology Assignment"

Bergdahl

This volume (pp. 15–16): "Identifying Prescriptivism and Descriptivism," designed for tenth grade
eResources: Web Resources to Teach Linguistic Concepts

Arevalo

This volume (pp. 22–23): "Even Presidents Code-Switch: Exploring Language Variation," designed for ninth to twelfth grade
eResources: "Lesson 1: Survey—Opinions About Dialects"; "Lesson 1: Teacher Notes, Definitions"; "Lesson 2: American Dialects, 'Broken English,' and Reading Eye Dialect"; "Lesson 2: *New York Times* Dialect Quiz Assignment"; "Exit Slip, Dialect Unit"

Williams

This volume (pp. 28–30): "Is It Ever Alright to Say *It*? The N-Word in Context," designed for eleventh to twelfth grade

Damaso

This volume (pp. 36–37): "Daisy and Jordan Snapchatting on the Couch: Updating the Language of *The Great Gatsby*," designed for eleventh grade

Keyser

This volume (pp. 44–45): "Morphology—Application in Literature," designed for ninth grade

Ratti

This volume (pp. 51–53): "The Tournament of Songs—Match 1," designed for ninth to tenth grade
eResources: "Tournament of Songs, Complete Assignment Packet"

Hoover

This volume (pp. 58–59): "Party Perspective," designed for ninth grade
eResources: "Juliet's Language and Identity"

Wolfram

eResources: "eResources for Teaching Language Variation and Ideology"

Abrams and Stickle

eResources: "Comparing Literary and Authentic Dialects of the Southeast U.S.: Florida 'Cracker'"

Loosen

eResources: "Linguograms"

McMurtry

eResources: "'I Can Go to the Bafroom?': Communicative Disconnection and Cultural Clashes in the Classroom"; "Steve Harvey and Language Ideologies"; "The Missing A: Psychological Consequences of Overt Correction"; "Beliefs about Language: A Continuum"

Sladek and Lane

This volume (pp. 134–136): "Exploring Regional Dialects," designed for eleventh to twelfth grade and first-year college composition
eResources: "Code-Switching and *To Kill a Mockingbird*"; "Annotated Bibliography of Digital Resources"

Reed Marshall and Seawood

This volume (pp. 143–145): "The Language of Testing," designed for ninth to twelfth grade

Denham and Pippin

This volume (pp. 153–155): "Parsimonious Pig Latin," designed for all grades eResources: "Parsimonious Pig Latin, Teacher Notes"; "Linguistic Problem Set: Pig Latin"; "Lushootseed Reduplication"

Dyches and Gale

eResources: "PowerPoint, Canonical and Linguistic Ideologies in *Huck Finn*"; "PowerPoint, Student Handout"; "Full Interview Transcript"

Devereaux and Palmer

eResources: "Lesson Plan Template"

Part I

Teachers' Perspectives

"Word Crimes" and Linguistic Ideology

Examining Student Ideas about Language in the English Language Arts Classroom

Amy L. Plackowski, Hudson High School, Massachusetts

"Of course there's such a thing as correct grammar. I may not always use it, but I know it exists," one student said.

"I finally learned the difference between *their*, *they're*, and *there* when somebody shamed me on Twitter," another student admitted.

"When I hear someone with a Southern accent, I immediately assume they're at least a little bit racist," acknowledged another.

Despite varied levels of fluency with Standard Written English, high school students, perhaps like the population at large, tend to be prescriptivists at heart—that is, they believe there is a "correct" way to talk and write and that any other type of language use is incorrect, substandard, or even an indicator of unintelligence. Even students who struggle with learning standard written grammar, or who speak nonstandard varieties of English, often believe that there are good Englishes and bad Englishes. Informal surveys taken by linguistics students in high school reveal that this attitude is perpetuated by parents, peers, media, and even other teachers.

That's why the essential questions that students examine in my linguistics elective—all of which can be explored in language-focused units in English Language Arts (ELA) classes at multiple levels—are the following: What attitudes and beliefs do you have about language? How did those attitudes develop? and How do those attitudes and beliefs influence your worldview? Students engage in a broad study of language, with topics that include the elements of language (phonology, syntax, pragmatics, etc.), language acquisition, language change, and language variation. Whatever the topic of study, the discussion always returns to these essential questions, promoting self-reflection as well as a greater respect for language variety. By teaching about the social, historical, and economic forces that help drive language change, my hope is to promote the type of compassionate critical thinking essential to living in a diverse society.

For many students, the ideology of prescriptivism has been so ingrained—by their parents and other adults, by the media, and by their teachers and peers—that they rarely question it. To begin their examination of these attitudes, students complete an "opinionnaire" addressing attitudes about language on the first day of class (see lesson plan). After discussing their answers, I play the "Weird Al" Yankovic song "Word Crimes" and draw out a discussion about the attitudes expressed in the song (Yankovic, 2013, track 5). I ask if they've heard similar attitudes elsewhere, and we explore where these attitudes might come from. This activity can pave the way for further discussions about power, education, privilege, race, ethnicity, and class.

Once students are primed to question some of their basic assumptions about language, I lead them into direct teaching about prescriptivism vs. descriptivism. In short, prescriptivists believe that there is a correct way to use language, while descriptivists are solely interested in describing the various ways language is used in the world. Episode 1 of the PBS documentary *Do You Speak American?* provides illuminating perspectives from both a prescriptivist and a descriptivist (Cran & MacNeil, 2005).

Students then engage in an examination of attitudes about language in their communities by surveying their peers, parents, and teachers using the opinionnaire, which they have completed themselves on the first day of class. They begin to notice where attitudes about language are expressed in the media (e.g., In what contexts do they see people making fun of the ways other people talk? Where do they see people lamenting the downfall of the English language when another "slang" term is added to the dictionary?). Conversely, students also identify where they see people expressing pride in their language, especially in a local accent or other nonstandard form of English. Here in Massachusetts, for example, students point out the road signs that playfully remind drivers to "use yah blinkah!" or caution that there's a "wicked stahm comin'!" These learning tasks introduce students to the various and sometimes contradictory attitudes people hold about language and encourage them to examine the factors that influence their own linguistic ideologies.

We revisit linguistic ideology later in the course during our unit on dialects. Once we've talked about the various geographic and social forces that contribute to language diversity, we turn our attention to the essential questions of the course. Knowing why people speak in different dialects is interesting, but examining attitudes about linguistic variation encourages an empathetic and questioning attitude useful beyond linguistics class.

One of the simplest but most effective activities replicates Dennis Preston's 2005 study on "perceptual dialectology," or how people perceive dialects. Preston gave subjects a blank map of the U.S. and asked them to draw lines indicating where various accents were located. He then asked subjects several questions about those accents, such as which were more "correct" or "pleasant," or which were most and least similar to the subjects' own dialects.[1]

Students perform this same task, identifying different dialects, naming them, describing their attributes, and explaining which ones they think are more or less similar to their own (see eResources for assignment). By this point in the course, they usually understand the problem with labeling dialects as "correct" or "pleasant," so I ask them to form a hypothesis about how people they know might answer these questions. They test this hypothesis by recreating Preston's experiment with friends and family members. Depending on time, students might write up their findings in a formal lab report, or simply make notes of their findings and report them back to the class.

Students continue to study attitudes about language by examining how they're implicitly expressed in media, especially in TV and films. One of my favorite activities involves presenting clips from several films where dialect plays an important role in the plot or the development of a character. In *My Cousin Vinny*, a Southern

---

1 Episode 1 of *Do You Speak American?* shows Preston informally replicating this part of his study and can be a good model for students doing this on their own.

judge struggles to understand a New York lawyer's pronunciation of "two youths" because the lawyer pronounces it "two yoots" (Launer, Schiff, & Lynn, 1992). The scene between William H. Macy's car dealer and Frances McDormand's sheriff in *Fargo* portrays a notably nonconfrontational, vulgarity-free police interview of a murder suspect (Coen & Coen, 1996). Alicia Silverstone's character in *Clueless* provides a classic example of the stereotypical Southern California "Valley Girl" accent (Berg, Lawrence, Rudin, Schroeder, & Heckerling, 1995). My students recognize the class differences represented in the bar scene in *Good Will Hunting*, where working-class Will confronts a snooty Harvard student in a Cambridge pub (Bender & Van Sant, 1997). An investigation of Key and Peele's sketch "Substitute Teacher," in which a self-identified inner-city Black teacher substitutes in a mostly White, suburban classroom, examines the ways the creators and the audience perceive African American Vernacular English and naming traditions (Atencio, Key, & Peele, 2012). Students might also suggest their own ideas for clips to add to their study.

I present these clips not as accurate or factual representations of a dialect or the people who speak it, but to examine the attitudes the filmmakers express or exploit in the portrayal of those dialects. I ask students to describe how the audience is meant to perceive the characters: the judge in *My Cousin Vinny* is genteel if a bit of a hayseed, while Joe Pesci's character is unsophisticated and aggressive. The teenage girls in *Clueless* are ditzy. Both characters in *Fargo* are courteous and deferential. Then I ask which characteristics of speech create this effect: the slow, deliberate drawl of the Southern judge; the sound represented by <th> in "youth" changing to "yoot" when spoken by the New York lawyer; the "upspeak" and slang of the California teenagers in *Clueless*; the rounded vowels and cheerful politeness on the part of the Minnesota characters; the r-dropping of the working-class Bostonian. A careful discussion about Key and Peele's comedy and the intended audience of their sketch pushes students to question why names like Jaqueline, Blake, and Aaron are considered "normal," while traditionally African American names and pronunciations are used as a source of humor. I also use this opportunity to point out that while nonmainstream names from the African American community are often treated with scorn by outsiders, nontraditional White names are generally met with less derision.

These discussions help students consider how, to varying degrees, the filmmakers and sketch writers have emphasized linguistic features to convey a shorthand for characters, and how the stereotypes are often played for laughs. We question whether these portrayals in popular media might influence people's attitudes about dialects and the people who speak them. Students arrive at the conclusion that our perceptions of dialects—unsophisticated or posh, educated or ignorant, polite or vulgar—have nothing to do with the grammar or sound system. They readily identify these perceptions as stereotypes and, crucially, recognize language as an essential part of identity.

These activities ask students to confront and interrogate their own linguistic ideologies and to acknowledge the factors that have influenced these ideologies.[2]

---

2 See eResources for additional activities including "Bilingualism Mind Map," "Etymology Paper," and "Language Autobiography."

Students examine the forces that shape their views of themselves, their language, and other people, and the ways they see these ideologies playing out in their society. A student who has developed the ability to look beyond stereotypes and find interest, joy, and empathy in linguistic diversity is, for me, a student who has met the essential objective of a high school linguistics class.

Lesson Plan: "Word Crimes"—Examining Linguistic Prescriptivism and Attitudes about Language

Recommended Grade Level(s)

Tenth grade through twelfth grade

Context

This lesson prompts students' examination of their own attitudes about language and the social forces that teach these attitudes. This lesson works best either near the beginning of an introductory linguistics course or at the beginning of a unit on language ideology in any ELA class. This lesson could easily lead into a lesson on linguistic descriptivism and prescriptivism. Students may need a brief introduction to *parody* to access the activity.

Objectives

Students will be able to:

* identify commonly held beliefs about language, including their own;
* develop a hypothesis about why people hold certain attitudes about language.

Common Core Standards

CCSS.ELA-Literacy.SL.9–10.1

Initiate and participate effectively in a range of collaborative discussions (one-on-one, in groups, and teacher-led) with diverse partners on grades 9–10 topics, texts, and issues, building on others' ideas and expressing their own clearly and persuasively.

CCSS.ELA-Literacy.SL.9–10.1c

Propel conversations by posing and responding to questions that relate the current discussion to broader themes or larger ideas; actively incorporate others into the discussion; and clarify, verify, or challenge ideas and conclusions.

CCSS.ELA-Literacy.SL.11–12.1

Initiate and participate effectively in a range of collaborative discussions (one-on-one, in groups, and teacher-led) with diverse partners on grades 11–12 topics, texts, and issues, building on others' ideas and expressing their own clearly and persuasively.

CCSS.ELA-Literacy.SL.11–12.3

Evaluate a speaker's point of view, reasoning, and use of evidence and rhetoric, assessing the stance, premises, links among ideas, word choice, points of emphasis, and tone used.

Procedures

Step 1: Activator (15 Minutes)

Hand out an opinionnaire asking students to agree or disagree with the following statements and explain why:

- If a word is in the dictionary, it's a real word.
- The English language is deteriorating over time.
- Some accents sound nicer or more intelligent than other accents.
- Words like "ain't" or double negatives are examples of incorrect grammar.
- Words like "selfie," "Imma," and "BAE" should not be in the dictionary.
- Some languages and dialects are more complex than others.
- People who speak nonstandard dialects of English need to learn how to speak correctly.

Ask students to reflect honestly. When they are finished, engage students in a discussion about their answers. You might ask which questions they felt most strongly about, which questions they hadn't thought about before, and why they answered the way they did. Specific items can lead into a more targeted discussion with follow-up questions; for example, you might ask students what they believe is the purpose of the dictionary, or what makes a word "real."

Step 2: Text Analysis (15 Minutes)

Listen to the "Weird Al" Yankovic song "Word Crimes" (Yankovic, 2013, track 5). Guide students in a discussion on the attitudes about language reflected in the song. For example, you might ask, "What are some of the ways people use language that bother 'Weird Al'?" "What does 'Weird Al' think about people who don't use language 'correctly'?" Encourage students to identify specific lines from the song that support their answers, drawing their attention to some of the harsher language such as "moron" and "get out of the gene pool." Then, ask students if they've heard people verbalize similar attitudes about language or people who don't use language "correctly." Prompt students to provide examples if possible.

Step 3: Reflection (15 Minutes)

As a turn-and-talk or informal written reflection, ask students to discuss how prevalent the attitudes of "Weird Al" are in their world. Which statements on the opinionnaire would "Weird Al" have strong opinions about? Have they heard people voice similar ideas? Then, ask them what might contribute to these attitudes, and, as a class, make a list of the social factors that might influence ideas about language. Some examples might include schooling, standardized testing, social media, general media, peers, etc. Depending on the students' prior knowledge and the time frame, you might introduce some ideas about privilege and power here.

Step 4: Exit Ticket (5 Minutes)

Ask students to write down at least one influence that shaped a belief they have about language.

Extension Activities

1. Have students do informal surveys of their parents, siblings, and/or peers using the opinionnaire and report back some of their findings in writing or discussion.
2. Ask students to notice attitudes about language expressed in their lives—in media, in conversation, in school—and report back with their findings.
3. Use this lesson to lead into a lesson on descriptivism and prescriptivism.

References

Atencio, P. (Director), Key, K. M., & Peele, J. (Writers). (2012, October 17). Substitute teacher pt. 1 [Television Series Sketch]. In K. M. Key, J. Peele, I. Roberts, & J. Martel (Producers), *Key & Peele*. New York, NY: Comedy Central.

Bender, L. (Producer), & Van Sant, G. (Director). (1997). *Good Will Hunting* [Motion Picture]. USA: Miramax Films.

Berg, B., Lawrence, R., Rudin, S., Schroeder, A. (Producers.), & Heckerling, A. (Director). (1995). *Clueless* [Motion Picture]. USA: Paramount Pictures.

Coen, E. (Producer), & Coen, J. (Director). (1996). *Fargo* [Motion Picture]. USA: PolyGram Filmed Entertainment & Working Title Films.

Cran, W. (Writer, Director, & Producer), & MacNeil, R. (Writer). (2005). Up north. [Television series episode]. In C. Buchanan (Producer), *Do you speak American?* New York, NY: WNET.

Launer, D., Schiff, P. (Producers), & Lynn, J. (Director). (1992). *My cousin Vinny* [Motion Picture]. USA: 20th Century Fox.

Preston, D. R. & Robinson, G. C. (2005). Dialect perceptions and attitudes to variations. In M. J. Ball (Ed.), *Clinical Sociolinguistics* (pp. 133–150). Malden, MA: Blackwell.

Yankovic, A. M. (2013). Word crimes [parody]. On *Mandatory fun* [MP3 File]. Los Angeles, CA: RCA.

Chapter 2

Prescriptive and Descriptive Lenses

How a Teacher Worked with Local Linguists to Develop a Language Ideologies Unit

Andrew Bergdahl, Stoneleigh-Burnham School, Massachusetts

My name is Andrew Bergdahl. I am a teacher of high school mathematics. I coach my school's math team, and both of my degrees are in math—but they were very nearly in linguistics. In college, I fell in love with phonology and morphology, and linguistic analysis was my best class. Though none of the linguists in that course thought of themselves as mathematically minded—in fact, they held me in a sort of reverence for my major—I saw how much computation and logic was built into the study of language. I took as many linguistics classes as I could in order to enrich my understanding of math.

As a teacher, I brought phonological rule order into discussions of the order of operations. When I coached students to participate in the annual American Mathematics Competition, I slipped in problems from the North American Computational Linguistics Olympiad. Finally, in the spring of 2017, I offered linguistics as a semester course to twelve students in grades 10, 11, and 12. Like an introductory linguistics course in college, I wanted my elective to cover the breadth of fields that language touches: history, science, culture, and more. I was, however, most suited to create content around computational analysis, so in order to broaden my understanding of linguistics, I reached out to the linguistics department at the University of New Hampshire (UNH).

Going Back to University

Professors Rachel Burdin and Shelly Lieber of UNH were welcoming and enthusiastic when I visited their campus and sat in on classes. At the university level, linguistics is often referred to as a "found major," as the majority of incoming students aren't aware the field even exists. Professors Burdin and Lieber were, somewhat understandably, then, excited to hear that linguistics instruction was happening at the high school level. They were both generous with their time and recommended texts and resources that I might adapt for my class; adaptation was necessary because everything was written for college, which only highlighted the dearth of secondary-level linguistics materials. When I asked Professor Burdin which one skill or piece of knowledge she most wanted incoming college students to have when taking Introduction to Linguistics, she seemed a little sad and answered immediately, "I would like it if they knew what linguistics is."

She did then think for a moment and offered another answer: descriptivism and prescriptivism. Professors Burdin and Lieber both agreed: they would like for students to come to college knowing that grammar can be charted through a descriptive lens and formalized through a prescriptive one. They had been seeing a deficit in students' understanding that language is both a firm ruleset and a living, changing thing.

I had been excited to teach linguistics because I wanted to share with students the joy of solving a morpheme puzzle in a foreign language, or the fun of interpreting a humorously ambiguous newspaper headline. After my meeting at UNH, I started to wonder if something more important was lacking from the education that I and others were delivering to students. Certainly, many teachers are aware of language theory, but our students often are not, even upon graduation. By teaching language skills without exposing the underlying structure of language itself, are we preventing real excellence in our students' writing and reading?

Teaching Descriptivism and Prescriptivism

Surprisingly, many of my students are more prescriptivist than I am. I opened a unit on prescriptivism and descriptivism by showing examples in a variety of sources, both serious and tongue-in-cheek: PBS's documentary *Do You Speak American?* (2005), Vox's interview with an associate editor at Merriam-Webster (2017), and "Weird Al" Yankovic's song "Word Crimes" (2013), a sort of prescriptivist's anthem. I also began the semester under the assumption that, as a trained mathematician and an admitted early-onset curmudgeon, I would be more pedantic about language than the average teenager. Instead, I found myself talking to students who argued for precision in communication and expressed annoyance at the fast pace of changes in slang. This (unanticipated) prescriptivism seemed often to come from a place of pragmatism. My students were highly aware that in online chat and text-messaging—a vital part of their social lives—poor phrasing or a misused word, in the absence of tone and body language, could easily lead to misunderstanding. When I was teaching this class, use of the word *lit*—meaning 'excellent'—was already being replaced with *fire*. Students saw such change as a genuine inconvenience!

One video in particular kicked off an impassioned discussion in my class: PBS Idea Channel's episode on hyperbole, titled "LITERALLY OUR MOST AMAZING EPISODE EVER!!" (2014; see also eResources). The host poses the question that if extreme hyperbole is used at every opportunity in colloquial speech, does it become difficult to truly qualify one's opinions? My students scrambled over one another to express frustration with this very theme in their lives. Unkind things were said about friends and schoolmates who would claim that an exam had killed them or who had said a mediocre television show was "the best."

Though many of the students' complaints about (supposed) language misuse seemed grounded in practical experience, their prescriptivism still felt performative at times. Especially on written assignments and tests, they would often argue for an academic structure to language which did not necessarily reflect the way they spoke to one another. In a reflection essay on the concept of Standard American English, students described words or accents as being "correct" or "incorrect," "appropriate," "casual," or "for business." Since high school students involuntarily enroll in a system that grades them on accuracy at every turn and then marries those grades to the prospect of future success in life, is it any wonder that they would conform to an academic register? I began to reflect on how to use our time in linguistics to find my students' true voices without weakening their competence in writing for school.

Knowing the Rules, to Break Them

This is not to say that the twelve teenagers in my classroom that spring were automatons, unaware of the fluidity of language. I asked them to invent new slang to go along with a comic that lampoons fake dialects in science fiction (see eResources), and they rose to the task with creativity. In class discussion, students were able to explain how their speech was different from their parents' and how it changed when they left home. They delighted in an assignment in which they accosted their friends at lunchtime with the question *Jeet yet?* and recorded how many understood the meaning to be 'Did you eat yet?' It was as if the students needed permission to slip into descriptivism, as if thinking descriptively was an abandonment of the rules, only allowable in some contexts.

As the semester progressed, so did our familiarity with each other. The students showed flexibility and began to embrace both descriptivism and prescriptivism, not in discrete scenarios, but blending an understanding of the two. Before they included a quote or a source in their writing, I—and in time, the students—would ask, "What would a prescriptivist think of this?" and "What would a descriptivist say is happening here?" This led them to be more skeptical of what they read and watched, but with less judgment about what language was "correct" or "incorrect." Instead, the students developed a critical sense that cut both ways—neither sloppy prose nor needless pedantry escaped their attention.

One week we explored the idea of tautologies, defining them as unnecessary redundancies in speech or writing, but I spoke as little as possible about my own opinions on the topic. I found a web page (Funny Tautology Examples, n.d.) that listed a hundred or more supposed tautologies, in various categories such as popular music and common expressions. I asked students to find their favorite examples and to share with the class whether they felt tautologies were something to avoid. We discussed phrases that were disliked by everyone, such as "In my opinion, I think you are right," and others that had some value or nuance coded in their redundancy, such as "I might go, or I might not"—a phrase everyone agreed implied ambivalence. However, students soon drifted from tautology when they began to find phrases that seemed intentionally pedantic. Bon Jovi's lyric "I want to live while I'm alive" was quoted here, and students immediately recognized it as an attempt to pad the list with a phrase that, while redundant on a technical level, was clearly poetic. Now there was blood in the water, and they began scouring the curated list, looking for other places where the author had been purposefully obtuse in order to adhere to the rules of tautology.

My students had learned to be critical of prescriptivism the same way that their schooling had once taught them to embrace it. Over a semester, I watched these students find the contexts in which prescriptive grammar was king and the times when it was right to discard the rules in favor of what worked. In art, in writing, and even in mathematics, I teach that "You must know the rules in order to break them." Only in linguistics, however, have I ever seen a class come to this conclusion on their own.

What I Learned

Early in my career, I fell out of love with lecturing. I found that lecturing reinforces what I know and shows me nothing of what my students don't know. To paraphrase Tolstoy, "Students who can graph a polynomial are all alike; every student who can't, can't in their own way." My teaching is reactive now; I make students try, and discuss, and fail in front of me. Only then do I know what they need. In my linguistics class, which was a very new sort of endeavor for me, I solicited feedback in the form of reflection assignments: a variety of surveys—about how well my students understood the material, how they thought it would apply to their other classes, and what they liked best or least—were disguised as writing prompts. I was uniquely able to get away with this sort of meta-chicanery thanks to the way linguistics examines language, and itself.

Feedback from students was strongest regarding the unit on descriptivism and prescriptivism. Some directly referenced descriptivism as opening their eyes to "breaking the rules" in their own writing. They also expressed surprise over how nuanced their teachers' feelings on language were. I gave my class an assignment in which they wrote survey questions regarding language use and asked these of their teachers in every department. In class discussion, while we wrote these questions, students predicted their teachers would remain prescriptivist in the context of academic work but be more flexible outside of school. I, perhaps projecting just a little, predicted that math and science teachers would be very concerned with accuracy in speech and notation, while members of the art department would be more creative and experimental with their language.

Results of the survey came back with an unexpected finding: every one of my students' other teachers were, in fact, human beings. They had complicated feelings about language and did not define themselves only by their subject area. Students were delighted to hear their teachers speak without a prescriptivist tone; for example, a science teacher admitted that she did not care how or with what vocabulary a student described biological processes—only that she understood what they meant. Another of my colleagues, a theater teacher, responded to the survey with wit, while giving away a pedantic streak where misuse of *literally* was concerned. The students seemed to draw confidence from hearing their teachers speak frankly about language in a complex way. Their writing continued to evolve to include more colloquial language.

I expected teachers to think one way about language, and students, another. This is where I learned the most from my class. By the end of the semester, I heard from them clearly: they did not want to be assigned to one camp or the other, descriptivism or prescriptivism. They wanted the training to express themselves ably and authentically. I believe linguistics gave it to them.

Lesson Plan: Identifying Prescriptivism and Descriptivism

Recommended Grade Level(s)

Tenth grade

Context

Students have been introduced to the definitions of prescriptivism and descriptivism.

Objectives

Students will be able to:

- identify prescriptivist attitudes in common grammatical English;
- reflect on the value they place on prescriptivism and descriptivism;
- consider the cultural stigma around grammar.

Common Core Standards

CCSS.ELA-Literacy.L.9–10.1

Demonstrate command of the conventions of standard English grammar and usage when writing or speaking.

CCSS.ELA-Literacy.L.9–10.3

Apply knowledge of language to understand how language functions in different contexts, to make effective choices for meaning or style, and to comprehend more fully when reading or listening.

Procedures

Step 1: Warm-Up (5 Minutes)

Lead full-class discussion: What is prescriptivism? Why would someone have a prescriptivist stance toward grammar? How prescriptivist do you feel you are?

Step 2: Analysis of Song "Word Crimes" (25 Minutes)

As a class, listen through "Word Crimes" twice. Help students identify as many rules of grammar referenced as possible. Students will then devise a point system for ranking the importance of each rule and score themselves on how they feel about each one. Students will tally their own scores and chart them on a number line on the board.

Step 3: Full-Class Discussion (15 Minutes)

Students will then discuss the validity of the scoring system, considering the following:

- Where do you fall on the scale of prescriptivism?
- Are you surprised by your score? How accurate do you feel your score is?
- Can prescriptivism be charted on a scale in this way?

Step 4: Closing (5 Minutes)

Remind students that the song "Word Crimes" is tongue-in-cheek. Ask their opinion of the song, and discuss the importance of context when each rule is used—or ignored. Ask students to consider why someone might take grammar infractions personally, to the point of annoyance.

References

Cran, W., & MacNeil, R. (2005). Do you speak American? Retrieved from www.pbs.org/speak/

Edwards, P. (2017, March 14). *How a dictionary writer defines English* [Video File]. Retrieved from www. vox.com/videos/2017/3/14/14887560/dictionary-english-kory-stamper-lexicographer

Funny tautology examples. (n.d.). On *Penlighten*. Retrieved from https://penlighten.com/tautology-examples

Rugnetta, M. (2014, November 5). Literally our most amazing episode ever!! *PBS Idea Channel*. [Video File]. Retrieved from https://gpb.pbslearningmedia.org/resource/80f37f0a-0f9b-47ef-ae0a-7f541da3bfbf/literally-our-most-amazing-episode-ever-pbs-idea-channel/#.Wvr1aJPwY8Y

Yankovic, A. M. (2013). Word crimes [Parody]. On *Mandatory fun* [MP3 File]. Los Angeles, CA: RCA.

Chapter 3

Profiling, Prejudice, and Prestige

Language Ideologies across Contexts

Stacy Ishigaki Arevalo, Eastside College
Preparatory School, California

My high school might seem an ideal place to have conversations about language varieties and ideologies, considering that approximately two-thirds of our students speak a language other than English at home.[1] In addition, the sophomore American literature curriculum invites discussions of race, identity, and culture. Despite this rich environment for critical conversations, my students' reactions to the language in *Their Eyes Were Watching God* revealed a need for explicit conversations about language variation and ideologies. Rather than celebrating Zora Neale Hurston's vivid imagery or relishing that her use of eye dialect allowed them to read in a Southern accent, students decried her use of the vernacular, labeling it either as "uneducated" or impossible to read. My attempt to ease students into the novel with the audiobook did not address their underlying assumptions about language. These reactions were even more confusing since our previous unit (on immigration short stories) highlighted the complicated power dynamics of linguistic assimilation. Despite their reactions, I knew my students were conscious of language variation: they often spoke about pride in their ability to code-switch (i.e., to shift between dialects or languages), seeing that as an essential part of "being a good student" and interacting politely around adults.

While teaching this unit, I was mentoring a student teacher whose supervisor, Mike Metz, was researching this very topic (see Metz, this volume, pp. 69–75). Seeking his help with addressing my students' resistance to Hurston's writing, I realized I first needed to learn more myself.

In this chapter, I detail the challenges and successes of my curriculum revision with an eye toward promoting more effective student engagement with language variation.

Reflecting on My Teaching Practices

Self-reflection, already core to my teaching practice, became even more salient as I developed a language-focused curriculum. I am hyper-aware of classroom power dynamics; I strive to maintain structure while giving space for students' voices. Additionally, there is little overlap between my students' linguistic identities and my own. While my students speak many dialects of English (including African American Vernacular English and Chicanx English) as well as languages (Spanish,

---

1 An independent high school serving first-generation college-bound students in a low-income community in the San Francisco Bay area.

Tongan, Fijian, and Tagalog, among others), I only have intimate knowledge of different registers of standardized English. I, therefore, needed to examine my linguistic identity to responsibly craft this curriculum. As a native-speaking teacher of English, I would be telling students, many of them non-native English speakers, that all varieties of English are equally valuable. This led me to wonder, *Who am I to tell them which forms of language are more or less valuable?* Furthermore, in this curriculum I would be pushing them to identify and dismantle their language prejudices. Years of observation suggested that some students cling to carefully enunciated academic English as a sign of being "educated," and challenging the centrality of academic English could be problematic for a population that holds tightly to the hope that education will lead to socioeconomic advancement for themselves and their families. It seemed easy for me to say that all language varieties are equal from my position of privilege, where I am sheltered from the implications of such a claim.

Yet, after learning more about code-switching, I committed to teach language variation in my classroom. I wanted students to recognize the agency they had already been employing via code-switching and encourage their multilingual, multidialectical abilities. Terms like *language profiling* (i.e., judging people based on the variety of language they speak) connect to gatekeeping positions. Just as our school makes the path to college transparent, such terms give form and substance to language and power dynamics. There is tremendous value in naming the forces that shape our reality. I had cultivated a classroom culture in which students and I could openly discuss race, class, and gender; expanding that to include language felt right. Rather than avoiding potentially charged or awkward conversations, addressing language varieties directly might convey to students that the topic is indeed "worthy" of serious study.

A Revised Curriculum

The goals of my revised unit are both curricular and personal: students will be able to describe Hurston's craft, interpret nonstandard and phonetic spelling, and analyze the imagery and depth achieved through language variation. Students will also be able to examine their own language use and ideologies, adopt an informed orientation toward language varieties, discuss the relationship between language and power in different contexts, and acquire relevant vocabulary.

The unit begins with a survey on language attitudes coupled with explicit instruction on linguists' understanding of language: all forms of language are structured, and "there are no inherently 'good' or 'bad' dialects" (Wolfram & Schilling, 2016, p. 2). Next we define terms—*dialect, register, vernacular, eye dialect, code-switching, language prejudice, language prestige,* and *language profiling*—then use this newly acquired vocabulary to discuss the following texts:

- Jenny Rothenberg Gritz, "When Presidents Say 'Y'All': The Strange Story of Dialects in America"
- Videos of President Obama in various contexts
- Malcolm London, "Why You Talk Like That?"
- Dean Baquet's interview with Jay-Z
- Jamila Lyiscott, "3 Ways to Speak English"
- Amy Tan, "Mother Tongue"

(For more on how to teach with these resources, see the lesson plan at the end of this chapter and additional materials in eResources.)

Students take the *New York Times* survey "How Y'all, Youse, and You Guys Talk" and research a range of dialects in the U.S. using PBS's *Do You Speak American?*.

Each year I vary the texts. This year, one student asked, "Hey, did you hear that Jay-Z talked about 'talking White' in an interview?"—yet another reminder that students are aware of the landscape of language variation and code-switching. They collect anecdotes and experiences to form attitudes toward language.

To close the unit, on an ungraded exit slip, I ask students to respond to someone insisting that they "speak *proper* English." Most students respond that they would explain that "proper" is a relative term: every variety is considered "proper" in some context. To show me the extent to which they were convinced by these lessons, they identify ways their language varieties give power in different contexts. Most report feeling validated that code-switching is valuable, adding that they now have a response when others accuse them of "talking White."

A few key aspects especially help to shape students' attitudes. It is powerful to distinguish between dialect and register. For example, to illustrate that African American Vernacular English can be spoken in a formal register, I ask them to imagine a preacher in a Black church, or I play a clip of Dr. Cornel West. Students' examination of all the ways they code-switch among peers and adults highlights the agency they exercise regularly. Jamila Lyiscott artfully conveys this in "3 Ways to Speak English"—and the image of a Black woman teaching a majority White audience is striking and worthy of class conversation. Students embrace "Mother Tongue": Tan's reflection on her mother's language varieties and the resulting challenges deeply moves them. We focus on Tan's criticisms of "broken" and "limited" English, two terms that are personally familiar to many students.

After this introduction to *Their Eyes Were Watching God*, students' reactions to Hurston's language change dramatically. They are excited to see that Hurston moves from a formal register of academic English to a rich blend of African American Vernacular English and Southern American English on the very first page. They note how shifts in language underscore the mood of the scene and power dynamics between characters. There is a palpable sense of curiosity and celebration, rather than frustration or rejection. One student even noted hints of the Gullah/Geechee dialect and researched Hurston's background to confirm that she indeed worked in this region.

This unit directly addresses language variation and gives students the vocabulary to engage in such inquiry. Their own ways of speaking serve as examples for serious study; their code-switching abilities are celebrated in their own right, not merely called upon to conform to the standards of academic English. Devoting lessons to exploring and celebrating language variation anchors the curriculum in the actual contexts in which students communicate.

Language Variation, Language Ideologies, and Teacher Training

Despite taking a language policy and practice course in my teacher preparation program, I felt unprepared to teach language variation and ideologies to students. The course focused on educational policy and strategies for teaching content-area vocabulary to English language learners (ELLs). While important, the course felt sterile. My section leader, an experienced teacher, shared anecdotes and sample lessons but was constrained by time and the program's obligation to meet state requirements for teachers of ELLs. By the end of the quarter, I could recite my legal obligations and knew to "catch students up" so they could learn the content. But the course neither required me to examine my own biases nor nurtured within me a sincere appreciation for students' language varieties. We were taught how to capitalize on students' assets for our purposes rather than understand the myriad ways they were already using language or develop strategies to engage with content from the richness of their own language varieties.

As a beginning teacher, I realized that classrooms include students whose language expression is more fluid and wide-ranging than indicated by official ELL status. I had less of a need for specific strategies for ELLs and more of a need for a broader understanding of language variation. Just as our school explicitly taught about college admissions, in my classroom I could explicitly address language variation. My early years in the classroom came with some significant shifts in my teacher talk. Instead of giving feedback like "fix your grammar" or "check for errors," I first adopted the term "clean writing," but even this term assigns value to academic English: if academic English is "clean," what about other varieties? I now use phrases like "proofread so your writing meets the standards of academic English," which implies that each variety of a language has its own conventions.

Teacher preparation programs can do more to spark critical reflection and further integrate linguistic research and classroom fieldwork. Just as many programs require self-reflection about racial identity and attitudes in the discussion of equity, pre-service teachers need to explore their linguistic identities and attitudes. A linguistic ideologies survey would serve as a launching point from which to deconstruct ideas about language prejudice and prestige and actively address these biases in one's thinking and teaching. It is essential for teachers of all subjects, not just English language arts, to uphold this orientation toward language variation across the curriculum.

Conclusion

For curricula focused on language variation and ideologies to be sincere, appreciation of students' language varieties must exist separately from any attempt to leverage language skills for classroom use. Students' language varieties are not obstacles to overcome but assets with inherent value—as Jamila Lyiscott declares, "This is a linguistic celebration!" Only through observation, relationships, and examining my own biases did I learn to celebrate my students' language varieties, to embrace them as evidence of complex decision-making necessary for interacting within their worlds of friends, home, and school.

Lesson Plan: Even Presidents Code-Switch: Exploring Language Variation

Recommended Grade Level(s)

Ninth grade to twelfth grade

Context

This lesson introduces language variation before students read *Their Eyes Were Watching God*. Students come to class having already surveyed others—preferably representing a range of ages and races/ethnicities—about attitudes toward language. Subsequent lessons include discussion of Amy Tan's "Mother Tongue" and application to the novel. See eResources for additional materials.

Objectives

Students will be able to:

- define key terms;
- recognize code-switching and contrast language styles;
- apply new terms to the content and delivery of a text.

Common Core Standards

CCSS.ELA-Literacy.RL.9–10.2

Determine a theme or central idea of a text and analyze in detail its development over the course of the text, including how it emerges and is shaped and refined by specific details; provide an objective summary of the text.

CCSS.ELA-Literacy.L.9–10.6

Acquire and use accurately general academic and domain-specific words and phrases, sufficient for reading, writing, speaking, and listening at the college- and career-readiness level; demonstrate independence in gathering vocabulary knowledge when considering a word or phrase important to comprehension or expression.

Procedures

Step 1: Complete Survey and Discuss Responses (5 Minutes)

Survey available in eResources.

Step 2: Read "When Presidents Say 'Y'all'" (10 Minutes)

Step 3: Videos of President Obama in Various Contexts (10 Minutes)

Show the Ben's Chili Bowl clip. For contrast, show Obama greeting Team USA Basketball players then delivering the Nobel lecture.

- What is the setting? Who is the audience?
- What details do you notice about his speech? What differences stand out?
- What details do you notice in his body language and dress? How do these reflect the context?
- According to the article, why might a president specifically code-switch like this?

Step 4: Define Terms (10 Minutes)

Present definitions with relevant examples (potential examples in parentheses): *dialect* (Appalachian English, California English), *register* (African American Vernacular English [AAVE] on a hip-hop track or in church), *code-switching, language profiling, language prejudice* (e.g., assuming speakers of the Valley Girl dialect are less intelligent), and *language prestige* (e.g., assuming speakers with British accents are more intelligent). See eResources for teacher notes on these terms.

Step 5: "3 Ways to Speak English" (15 Minutes)

- As you watch, look for examples of these terms.
- Discuss:
  What is the setting?
  Who is the audience?
  How does Lyiscott address these terms?
  What is her message?
  What are some misconceptions about language and intelligence?
  Why is context important?
- Write: Using today's terms, write a sentence summarizing Lyiscott's message.

References

Baquet, D. (2017, December 3). Jay-Z discusses rap, marriage and being a black man in Trump's America. *T magazine*. Retrieved from www.nytimes.com/interactive/2017/11/29/t-magazine/jay-z-dean-baquet-interview.html

Cran, W., & MacNeil, R. (2005). *Do you speak American?* Retrieved from www.pbs.org/speak/

Gritz, J. R. (2013, February). When presidents say "y'all": The strange story of dialects in America. *TheAtlantic.com*. Retrieved from www.theatlantic.com/national/archive/2013/02/when-presidents-say-yall-the-strange-story-of-dialects-in-america/272974/

Katz, J., & Andrews, W. (2013, December 21). How y'all, youse and you guys talk. Retrieved from www.nytimes.com/interactive/2014/upshot/dialect-quiz-map.html

London, Malcolm. (2012). Why you talk like that? On *Louder than a bomb 2012*. Chicago, IL. Retrieved from https://beta.prx.org/stories/75941

Lyiscott, J. (2014, February). 3 ways to speak English [Video file]. Retrieved from www.ted.com/talks/jamila_lyiscott_3_ways_to_speak_english

Tan, A. (2008). Mother tongue. In C. Miller (Ed.), *Strange bedfellows: Surprising text pairs and lessons for reading and writing across genres* (pp. 179–184). Portsmouth, NH: Heinemann.

Wolfram, W., & Schilling, N. (2016). *American English: Dialects and variation*. Chichester: Wiley-Blackwell.

Chapter 4

"Working With" Instead of "Pushing Against"

Meeting Testing Standards while Teaching Language Ideologies

Mike Williams, Joseph Wheeler High School, Georgia, and Dundalk High School, Maryland

During my first year of teaching, the administration and teachers were frustrated: They felt that the N-word was being used too frequently and casually in the halls. Their solution was to hold an assembly to denounce it. The event organizers invited a professor of psychology from a nearby university; he argued that the use of the N-word is manifestly dehumanizing, explaining that its use, and pejoratives like it, have provided the pretext for the most horrifying abuses in history. After his address, students, teachers, and administrators of diverse racial backgrounds conducted a panel discussion on the topic. Among the selected panelists, there was remarkable agreement with the speaker: many described how the word has hurt them in the past, or how they've been disgusted when close family members have used it.

Only one Black student spoke in favor of using the N-word in certain settings between friends. He expressed skepticism that the N-word he uses and hears in hip-hop is the same one that White supremacists use. He was allowed very little time to speak, received the only rebuttal that came from the university professor that day, and was not permitted to respond to that rebuttal. The assembly closed with more statements and personal accounts of how the word had been used as a weapon to demean and degrade, but, beyond that one student, no one pushed the discussion further. For a few days after, conversation about the N-word flourished, but students did not stop saying it. They simply were not buying the arguments.

And neither was I. For school leaders to participate in a complex language debate in this way was, in my view, fraught with all sorts of contradictions. The desire to improve school culture by encouraging the speech equivalent of tucking one's shirt into a pair of khakis is obvious and predictable. School's codes of signification align closely to middle-class, hegemonic values—the perpetuation of these codes, it is argued, is a matter of preparing them for participation in college and career settings. As a young, Black teacher, I saw the culture clashes that these "mainstream" codes produced between my less affluent students of color and their whiter, wealthier teachers and administrators. There seemed to be little I could do to overturn an entrenched cultural dynamic from my position as a rookie teacher.

But teaching students that a word—any word—has only a single definition regardless of context is problematic: it contradicts clearly stated objectives in Common Core standards, and it also undermines the very skills students need to master in order to be successful on words-in-context and tone questions on the SAT and other standardized tests. In other words, while school leaders want hallways to look and sound as sterile as any corporate workspace, they also always *need* test scores to improve. And exploring contextual language use is a key way to increase those scores. For example, this is a sample vocabulary question from the 2017 SAT released by College Board:

(25) As used in line 20, "rule" most nearly means

A) mark.
B) control.
C) declare.
D) restrain.

Studying for a standardized test is no longer about memorizing a list of words and simply filling in the "correct" out-of-context definition for a word like *morose* or *stalwart*. Common Core-aligned standardized tests require a deep understanding of how language functions, specifically that words often have multiple definitions and that their meaning is contingent on the context in which they are used. Students need to be able to read a passage carefully and consider the author's main idea, tone, and purpose—all skills they regularly use, perhaps unsystematically, when navigating their encounters with taboo words in their day-to-day lives. How can we teach students that these skills are poisonous during an assembly but necessary during a test?

While I may not have been able to convince my peers about words and the importance of recognizing their contextual meanings, I had a captive audience in my classroom: I thought my students might benefit from a deeper dive into the issues introduced at the assembly. So I began developing a lesson on the use of the N-word—one I thought could win at least hesitant administrative approval, improve student knowledge and skill, teach interesting and challenging literature, and, finally, encourage a more democratic exploration into the power dynamics of pejorative usage.

A couple of days after the assembly, I made my first attempt at introducing the topic of the N-word to my class. The lesson, if I can even call it that, was just an open discussion with a bunch of prepared questions. Even though my students seemed to enjoy the open format and the opportunity to speak honestly about the subject, I'm fairly sure I didn't even consider standards or have an assessment in mind. Students quickly began to rehash old arguments, and the lesson fizzled with all of the educational value of a Michael Scott conference-room meeting.

We never had another N-word assembly at my school, but as the years went by, it seemed like the entire country was having nightly semiotic seminars in the news and through social media on topics of varying degrees of seriousness: the true meaning of the word *thug*; whether hoodies and sagging pants are responsible for the death of a Black teen; how to protest police brutality in a way Dr. King would approve; the meaning of the Confederate battle flag; the meaning of the American flag; and whether or not using the phrase *All Lives Matter* is racist. New orthodoxies (and their corresponding memes) formed along all points of the political spectrum, and I was watching my diverse-in-every-way students bring in various ideas to class: from Fox News talking points to concepts that used to be the jargon of the social sciences like "cultural appropriation" and "intersectionality."

And although I continued to improve upon my initial lesson of the N-word, it became clear quickly that in order for me to teach the semantics of taboo racial language effectively, I needed to center the discussions around a text complex and thoughtful enough to dislodge my students from the trap of merely exchanging slogans with one another. For this challenge, I chose William Faulkner's short story "Dry September."

Faulkner's story is familiar enough to my eleventh-graders who read *To Kill a Mockingbird* in ninth grade: a Black man is falsely accused of raping a White woman in a racist town, and a White male hero attempts but fails to save the Black man's life, risking his own life and social standing in the process. Although "Dry September" is a familiar story, it's also more complicated than ones they've read before. Faulkner's White male hero, Hawkshaw, appears to be overtly racist and sexist at least by modern standards—he says the term "good nigger" when describing the accused, Will Mayes, and attempts to discredit the alleged victim, Minnie Cooper, on the basis that she's forty and unmarried. Additionally, in a mob scene in the story, Hawkshaw's negotiations with the mob are merely attempts to get them to make an exception on this occasion and exchange one form of supremacy for another. He doesn't try to undermine the logic of White male dominance, and his effort to negotiate with these evils is completely ineffective.

Often in the literature we teach, we see heroes give powerful, high-minded speeches about justice and our ability to overcome impossible odds. Heroes in these stories certainly do not use dehumanizing language for any reason under any circumstances. However, we see Faulkner's *hero* conform to the political realities of his society.

My students, even the most socially conscious, are usually able to empathize with Hawkshaw on some level, despite his deep, seemingly unforgivable flaws. He risks his own life and reputation to defend an innocent Black man, and perhaps he thinks the use of racist, sexist language allows him to retain his status as a trusted member of the group. "What could he have done or said differently?" my students often ask me after they've argued with each other for a time and fully appreciated the total despair of the situation. I always reply honestly, "I don't know. Maybe nothing. I look forward to reading what you write." They groan.

I share this lesson with every group of new students I receive, and I add something new to it each year as the world around us changes. Recently in response to the growing power of #MeToo and LGBTQ movements, I introduced an activity called "Boys and Girls" in order to demonstrate how seemingly innocuous gendered terms can be used destructively when we ignore the relationship between the speaker and listener (see lesson plan). When students can articulate why calling someone *girl* or *boy* can be demeaning or uplifting based on context, they can begin to recognize how even non-taboo standard words can function as destructively as they've been told the N-word does. This activity exposes a crack in the (supposed) certitudes of standard language ideology; it helps students make standard and non-standard language choices thoughtfully and evaluate the choices that other writers and speakers make. Although these sorts of lessons on language can be a bit unsettling for many, encouraging the N-word to be debated and discussed in a safe classroom environment is engaging and interesting preparation for standardized tests. And, more importantly, it provides students with tools to navigate the complicated social and ethical issues we all continue to face.

Lesson Plan: Is It Ever Alright to Say *It*? The N-Word in Context

Recommended Grade Level(s)

Eleventh grade and twelfth grade

Context

Students will enter the lesson immediately after reading William Faulkner's short story "Dry September." This lesson precedes the culminating assessment for this mini-unit, in which students compose an argumentative essay that evaluates the heroism of the White male protagonist Hawkshaw. Before this lesson, students should be able to organize an argumentative essay and form a thesis.

Students will note Hawkshaw's use of the N-word while he defends Will Mayes, a Black man living in Jim Crow Mississippi, from vague accusations of sexual misconduct with Miss Minnie Cooper, a White woman. Hawkshaw's eventual failure to stop the lynch mob, his use of the term "good nigger," and his sexist remarks used to discredit Minnie make him a complex character who challenges students to make precise claims and careful arguments concerning his behavior while weighing the complexities of power, language, and ethical engagement in a different cultural context.

Objectives

Students will be able to:

*   discuss the ethics of controversial uses of language in literature;
*   plan a careful, precise claim about literature that includes an analysis of a character's problematic use of language;
*   evaluate the use of pejoratives in contemporary and historical contexts.

Common Core Standards

CCSS.ELA-Literacy.L.11–12.3

Apply knowledge of language to understand how language functions in different contexts to comprehend more fully when reading or listening.

CCSS.ELA-Literacy.RL.11–12.4

Determine the meaning of words and phrases as they are used in the text; analyze the impact of specific word choices on meaning and tone.

CCSS.ELA-Literacy.SL.11–12.1A

Come to discussions prepared, having read and researched material under study; explicitly draw on that preparation by referring to evidence from texts and other research on the topic or issue to stimulate a thoughtful, well-reasoned exchange of ideas.

CCSS.ELA-Literacy.W.11–12.1.A

Introduce precise, knowledgeable claim(s).

Procedures

Step 1: Philosophical Chairs, Part 1 (7–10 Minutes)

Arrange the seats in a U shape. Label the three respective seating sections "agree," "disagree," and "undecided." As students enter, ask them to find a seat on the side of the room that applies to their position on the following statement: "Hawkshaw the barber behaves heroically in defense of Will Mayes."

Allow as many students as possible to support their position during this period of time. Listeners should take notes on the arguments of their classmates, evaluating their effectiveness and adjusting their positions. Allow undecided students to ask follow-up questions. If his use of racist and sexist language does not come up during the first seven minutes, prompt students to reflect on how these elements of his speech affect their opinions of him. Invite undecided students to summarize and record responses on the board, so you can revisit initial beliefs as new information is presented.

Ask students to keep their notes handy and add to them throughout the class.

Step 2: Boys and Girls (3–5 Minutes)

As pre-reading diagnosis for Step 3, ask students to write a short sentence addressing or referring to someone as "boy" or "girl" in a non-offensive way. (Examples: "This is my boy Mike." "Mike, this is my girl Bianca.") Ask students to label the speaker and listener after they've written it. Next, ask students to imagine a scenario in which the same sentence could be construed as offensive by changing the speaker or the context for the exchange. It's possible that some sentences will not work (e.g., What if Mike is an older man and the speaker's servant? What if Bianca is gender nonconforming and prefers nonbinary pronouns?)

Ask students to share examples to the class. It's possible that not every student will be able to do this successfully, but enough will be able to in order to begin to answer the following question: "What makes a word offensive?"

Step 3: Read "In Defense of a Loaded Word" (10–12 Minutes)

Students will read Coates' essay, "In Defense of a Loaded Word" (2013), and annotate it, making note of his arguments and adjusting their positions on their "philosophical chairs" notes as they conduct the reading. I suggest silent, individual reading because understanding will be assessed during the discussion.

Step 4: Philosophical Chairs, Part 2 (20–22 Minutes)

The class will end the same way it began. Following the procedures from Step 1, students will have more information and a language with which to discuss the issues surrounding usage of controversial words. Provide students with two minutes to review each of the claims below before beginning. Prompt them to refer back to the texts when making arguments, if necessary.

1.   It is unethical for Hawkshaw to refer to Minnie Cooper's age and marital status to defend Will Mayes.
2.   It is unethical for Hawkshaw to refer to Will Mayes as a "good nigger" while defending him.
3.   Hawkshaw behaves heroically in the face of extreme danger.

Step 5: Claim Writing/Exit Ticket (3 Minutes)

Students will hand in a claim statement that clearly explains their positions on the issues described and that demonstrates a clear understanding of the issues of language use discussed in the article and throughout the discussion. If these issues are avoided in the claim, provide students with additional support as needed.

References

Coates, T. (2013, November 23). In defense of a loaded word. *New York Times.* Retrieved from www.nytimes.com/2013/11/24/opinion/sunday/coates-in-defense-of-a-loaded-word.html

College Board. (2016). SAT Practice Test #8 Reading Test. Retrieved from https://collegereadiness.collegeboard.org/pdf/sat-practice-test-8.pdf

Faulkner, W. (1995). Dry September. In *The collected stories of William Faulker.* New York, NY: Penguin.

Chapter 5

"Mr. D, Is This, Like, a Real Word?"

Stories of a Linguist in a High School English Classroom

John A. Damaso, Brophy College Preparatory, Arizona

After more than a decade teaching English at Brophy College Preparatory, an all-boys Jesuit Catholic high school in Phoenix, AZ, I've begun to think that the digression—the student-goaded teacher tangent—might be the greatest boon for learning about language variation and ideology. Certainly, this volume illustrates specific ways teachers can build units for students that investigate the linguistic vs. literary view of language, but perhaps the ripest moments occur when student curiosity leads to genuine questions: *Is slang real language? Why do people say we shouldn't end a sentence with a preposition? When does a word become an accepted word? Why don't we write like we talk? Is "Spanglish" a thing?* In these moments, when I choose to engage, scrap the lesson plan, and model my commitment to a nuanced understanding of language's inherent mutability, students often follow. Through digressions, a prepared teacher can capitalize on students' puerile desire to get the teacher off task. When the tangent becomes the most significant learning of the day, the tangent is the lesson.

There is a hunger among students to discuss linguistic prescriptivism, language standardization, and language variation. But doing so in an English class may seem countercultural, and students may shy away. I recently ran a Language and Society elective description in our course catalog; the course would include language attitudes, historical language change, language in context, slang, and lexicography. Only three students signed up, so we cancelled it. The flexible parts of language, the beautiful parts, the wild parts, those often get hidden from adolescent view by the cultural insistence on Standard English. Schooling traditionally teaches students that language is something to wrangle, to master, to wield over others, to use as a wedge, to mark status or educational prestige. Perhaps the student body balked at Language and Society because it didn't fit neatly into their trained understanding of what a language arts class could be. Classroom digressions allow me, a sociolinguist by training and an English teacher by profession, to provide a nonjudgmental space for students to process the realities of language change amid the compulsion and necessity to learn Standard English.

The easiest entry point to these discussions occurs at the lexical level of isolated words. When I screen *The History of English in Ten Minutes*, students are astonished by the many words borrowed into English over the centuries: *cannibal, canoe, yoga, zombie, voodoo, mafia*. When I pause the video and ask them if *zombie*, borrowed in 1871, "should be an English word," students enthusiastically say, yes, of course it should. Borrowed words that precede my students seem to garner immediate acceptability. When, a month later, social media introduces words like *woke* ("suddenly and keenly aware of social injustices"), they ask me, "Is *woke* a word?" I refer back to *zombie*. "If we use it and two or more people generally agree to its meaning," I tell them, "then linguists consider that a word." Recently, the word *clout* has reentered the adolescent lexicon (likely via hip-hop through social media). When I drop the word knowingly into class discussion, students exchange glances, as speakers often do when someone without in-group membership breaches lexical boundaries. In these moments, I'll stop class and have an improvised discussion with students about meaning-making rights and how linguistic choices can solidify social choices. Students can relate because they have parents who might jump at the opportunity to correct their children's language. "Never end a sentence with a preposition," they might say. Much to students' delight, I share with them the witticism often (but perhaps apocryphally) attributed to Winston Churchill: "That is the kind of arrant pedantry up with which I will not put." From here we can discuss why standard grammar is taught and how applying standards of writing to speech allows for overcorrection (e.g., "Don't say 'with Juan and *me*,' say, 'with Juan and *I*'") as well as, well, pedantry. The simple existence of loanwords in English creates moments for teachers to honor linguistic diversity in front of students, many of whom have rich language traditions in their families that may not always be honored in our classrooms.

To begin a class period of Honors English 2 last year during our unit on tragedy, I posted a PollEverywhere question and encouraged students to answer with a single emoji. This poll and subsequent discussion of emoji meaning unexpectedly led to an impromptu exercise asking students in ten minutes to author an emoji-only summary of *Antigone*. Unsurprisingly, students crafted their summaries of Sophocles' play in diverse ways and often used the same emojis to mean different things. I seized the opportunity to discuss language choice and language variation. I then displayed the emoji for *expressionless face* and asked for all students to define its meaning. There was little agreement and a great deal of productive debate on meaning-making. Why does the Unicode Society, for example, get to decide which particular image represents 'expressionless face'?

At this moment, I introduced with demonstrative flourish the *52 Flashcards for Emoji Literacy* I got from Domino's Pizza (Damaso, 2016). This was an unplanned moment, but my classroom shelves are littered with linguistics knickknacks that make for productive impromptu debates: slang dictionaries of all sorts (*The Future Dictionary of America*), writing games (*The Writer's Toolbox*), artifacts from travel (*Speak Italian: The Fine Art of the Gesture*, an Argentine slang dictionary called *¡Che Boludo!*). Each card in the *Emoji Literacy* deck displays an emoji or set of emojis and a corresponding meaning. Immediately, students debated not only the definitions of the emojis but also the appropriate order in which to place them. I took this opportunity to talk diction and syntax as well as idiolects (the language habits particular to an individual).

I have another deck of cards called Vintage Slang Flashcards (1900–1965). The deck includes terms like *dingus, the bee's knees, melvin*—an assortment of sixty cards containing slang from generations past. When new slang enters the classroom (cf. Connie Eble 1996), or when existing words like *tight, lit, fam, squad* explode with polysemy (the many possible meanings of a word), I'll often grab the deck and deal everyone a card. Students chuckle at the antiquated slang of their grandparents and great-grandparents. They'll read definitions and illustrative sentences and wonder at the origins of *spizzerinctum* or *finger popper*. One student might say, "Nobody talks like this," to which I might respond, "What makes *your* slang so hella tight?" As you might expect, the teenage boys shake their heads in disapproval, all the while planning to ask their parents about these terms and have conversations at home that border on linguistic fieldwork. Some students, linguistic ethnographers in the making, report back on their findings from the dinner table. What begins as a tangent ends with a student developing sociolinguistic skills.

Classroom study of literature often creates opportunities for these fundamental digressions. If students read *Adventures of Huckleberry Finn*, they learn that Mark Twain was an American Henry Higgins before his time. In the novel's "Explanatory," Twain warns his readers not to misconstrue the several dialects of Southern English he's reconstructed for his characters. Twain's pride in his linguistic precision helps underscore for students that language variation deserves celebration, not derision. He writes:

> In this book a number of dialects are used, to wit: the Missouri negro dialect; the extremest form of the backwoods South-Western dialect; the ordinary "Pike-County" dialect; and four modified varieties of this last. The shadings have not been done in a hap-hazard fashion, or by guess-work; but painstakingly, and with the trustworthy guidance and support of personal familiarity with these several forms of speech.
>
> I make this explanation for the reason that without it many readers would suppose that all these characters were trying to talk alike and not succeeding.
>
> (Twain, 2009, p. 4)

We turn Twain's imploring of the reader into a close reading and diction analysis. Students draw out words like "painstakingly," "trustworthy guidance," and "personal familiarity" to confirm that language variation in literature is done (as here by Twain) with care by authors who value the characters and want readers to as well. By representing spoken dialects in fictional dialogue, authors give readers pride in various forms of English. In fact, just using the word *Englishes* with students can create worthy digressions into language diaspora, linguistic diversity, and language and power. I recall a moment when contextualizing *A Streetcar Named Desire*, set in New Orleans, that a student asked what creole meant. We began to discuss the linguistic phenomena of pidgins and creoles. "Is it broken English? Is it a combination of languages? What does it have to do with Cajun food?" I asked one student if he knew how to differentiate a pidgin from a creole language. He didn't, but I was able to quickly teach that one is a simplified language of circumstance and contact (pidgin) and the other is a complete language learned natively by children (creole). That same student returned the next day with research he had done on Supreme Court Justice Clarence Thomas, whose first language was the Afro-English creole Gullah. I then directed this student and his classmates to George Mason University's *Speech Accent Archive* (2018), which allows users to hear English speakers from across the globe (including New Orleans) recite the same English paragraph. My students continued to use this resource when they encountered other characters in regional American literature.

Here in Phoenix, nearly a quarter of households may speak Spanish, and many of my students do as well, so the topic of language contact surfaces frequently.

When my students read Arizona Poet Laureate Alberto Rios' memoir *Capirotada* about his youth in Nogales, Arizona, they often approach the blend "Spanglish" as if it were a dirty word. My student Sergio, for example, was astonished, during our annual Poetry Out Loud contest, that he could choose to memorize a poem called "Spanglish" by Tato Laviera. He asked me with uncertain eyes and a look expecting to be told *no*, "Is that even a poem?" A week later, I asked him privately about his question, and he said he had wondered, "Is this a mistake?" when he saw the poem in the approved anthology. I pressed him further about his hesitation. He said, "I didn't want to be considered a SJW [Social Justice Warrior] or a kind of cultural person." To help Sergio understand that poems are "language concentrate" (like frozen orange juice, I told him), full of dense meaning, beauty and worth, I reminded him of his classmate Rex's similar question when I screened *Def Poetry Jam*, a spoken-word series from HBO hosted by Mos Def: "Mr. D, is slam poetry even poetry?" Both Sergio and Rex had a panicked glee in their eyes when asking their respective questions. "Yes, 'Spanglish' is valid, slam poetry is valid, *especially* since they vary from the standard." This moment afforded me the opportunity to ask my students why they think language changes, why certain registers of language fit certain moments, and how standard forms are often prioritized over nonstandard ones.

When students read *The Great Gatsby*, they note the title character's frequent use of "Old Sport" as a moniker for Nick Carraway, the narrator. One day I asked them to jot down the twenty-first-century equivalent of this term of endearment. Inevitably, several words emerged: *homie, dude, man, fam*. One group of students argued over variant spellings of *bro*: <bro>, <brah>, <bruh>, <bruv>. In that moment, a pop-up creative writing lesson was born. I asked students to pick any dialogue-heavy scene from the novel, known for Fitzgerald's Jazz Age stylistic precision, and to recreate it by "updating the look and feel" of the scene. Not only did student writers update the language exchanged by Daisy and Jay or Tom and Myrtle, they updated Nick's narrative voice, as well as the cultural trappings that define the day (see lesson plan). When students become practitioners through these types of exercises, they can see and understand the value in language change.

To date, I can recall digressive, pop-up lessons on the Northern Cities Vowel Shift (the gradual change of vowel sounds in Great Lakes regional dialects); African American Vernacular English (sometimes derisively called "Ebonics"); prejudicial, racial, and "Otherizing" language during the 2008 presidential election (Barack Obama as "uppity" or "articulate"); the relationship between linguistic diversity and biological diversity; endangered languages; and, of course, the history of English. Classroom tangents often create energetic trajectories of learning that can be countercultural in nature, affirming of diversity, and celebratory of the realization that language ought not always be pinned down.

Lesson Plan: Daisy and Jordan Snapchatting on the Couch: Updating the Language of *The Great Gatsby*

Recommended Grade Level(s)

Eleventh grade

Context

This lesson plan asks students to understand literature written in another era and to update it in terms of diction and syntax. Students should review narrative techniques of description and dialogue before this lesson and have done a "close reading" of a passage from the novel.

Objectives

Students will be able to:

- examine a scene in a novel that possesses linguistic markers tied to the era;
- contrast diction of the early twentieth century to that of the early twenty-first century;
- compose an adapted scene of fiction;
- experiment with word choice that reflects a contemporary ethos and aesthetic.

Common Core Standards

CCSS.ELA-Literacy.W.11–12.3.D

Use precise words and phrases, telling details, and sensory language to convey a vivid picture of the experiences, events, setting, and/or characters.

CCSS.ELA-Literacy.L.11–12.1.A

Apply the understanding that usage is a matter of convention, can change over time, and is sometimes contested.

CCSS.ELA-Literacy.L.11–12.5

Demonstrate understanding of figurative language, word relationships, and nuances in word meanings.

CCSS.ELA-Literacy.RL.11–12.5

Analyze how an author's choices concerning how to structure specific parts of a text (e.g., the choice of where to begin or end a story, the choice to provide a comedic or tragic resolution) contribute to its overall structure and meaning as well as its aesthetic impact.

Procedures

Step 1: Warm-up (5–10 Minutes)

Ask students, "When you read *The Great Gatsby*, how do you know when it takes place? How do you know the socioeconomic class of the characters?" Responses will vary and can be written down and/or shared in discussion. Students may note the narrative style, the dialogue, the setting.

Step 2: Scene Selection (10 Minutes)

Tell students to look through the novel, pick a passage of 100–250 words for adaptation, and rewrite or paste the passage at the top of the document including chapter and page number.

Step 3: Scene Adaptation (30 Minutes)

Ask students to rewrite the passage/scene in the vocabulary, tone, voice, and aesthetic of today. For example, what would Jordan and Daisy lounging on the sofa in the opening scene look like today, and how would they converse? Tweeting rumors to @SmackHigh, Insta-ing, Snapchatting, Tumblring, watching TMZ, hosting a Reddit AMA, etc. Students can change the diction, syntax, names, places, activities, and backstories to reflect the varying ways thinking, speaking, and narrating has changed over time.

Step 4 (Optional): Sharing (15 Minutes)

Students read their adaptations to each other in small groups of three to four. Listeners try to recall the specifics of the original Fitzgerald text that the student writer has updated. Listeners might suggest other ways the student writer could update the prose.

References

Bracken, J. (2007). *¡Che Boludo! A gringo's guide to understanding the Argentines*. San Carlos de Bariloche: Continents.

Cat Callan, J. (2007). *The writer's toolbox*. San Francisco, CA: Chronicle Books.

Damaso, J. (2016). Emoji literacy, face with tears of joy, Domino's, and Urban Dictionary. Retrieved from http://www.johndamaso.com/new-blog/2016/1/28/emoji-literacy-dominos-and-urban-dictionary

Eble, C. (1996). *Slang and sociability: In-group language among college students*. Chapel Hill, NC: University of North Carolina Press.

Knock Knock. (2007). *Vintage slang flashcards*. Los Angeles, CA: Who's There Inc.

Munari, B. (2005). *Speak Italian: The fine art of the gesture*. San Francisco, CA: Chronicle Books.

Open University. (2011, June 22). The history of English in ten minutes [Podcast]. Retrieved from www.open.edu/openlearn/languages/english-language/the-history-english-ten-minutes

Safran Foer, J., Krauss, N., & Eggers, D. (2004). *The future dictionary of America*. London: Hamish Hamilton.

Speech Accent Archive. (2018). George Mason University. Retrieved from http://accent.gmu.edu/

Twain, M. (2009). *Adventures of Huckleberry Finn*. Mary Reichardt (Ed.). San Francisco, CA: Ignatius Press.

Chapter 6

Linguistics in an English Language Arts Class

Elevating Language Awareness

Beth Keyser, Superior High School, Montana

Teaching language awareness taps into students' linguistic intuitions, surfacing their unconscious knowledge as native English speakers. Further, such instruction encourages students to solve problems, to respect themselves and each other as language users, and to be prepared for the demands of reading complex literature and writing grammatically in Standard American English.

Students love to learn about themselves as language users language is both universal and personal. One way I help students identify who they are as English speakers and juxtapose that with Standard English is by discussing dialect variation. Students love to hear, for example, that soft drinks have different names throughout the country. One student laughed that his mother made him say "soda-pop" because mom, from Illinois, calls it *soda*, and dad, from Montana, calls it *pop*. One student said that "I seen" (as in "I seen something") is really a shortened way to say "I have seen"—an excellent example of students' linguistic intuition. By learning about language varieties, students who have been corrected feel vindicated, and all students begin to distinguish between the demands of Standard English and those of personal dialects.

In learning about language variation, students also become researchers. They listen to variation in their own communities, discovering that some Montana dialects treat *our* and *are* as homophones. Rather than labeling this as incorrect, I explain that pronunciations have many variants. Other regional examples in Montana include that a creek is pronounced like the word *crick*. To many of my students, a creak is the noise a squeaky floorboard makes. Through these applications and subsequent conversations, students understand that different isn't necessarily wrong and that language changes across geographical areas.

Students learn that language not only changes geographically but over time as well. When my students claim *ain't* isn't a word, I discuss its etymology, which leads to the history of words in English and the history of English more broadly. Students are impressed that Old English sounds so different from Early Modern English.

In addition, I relate dialect variation to speaking and writing. I talk about the difference between a writing voice and a speaking voice, a colloquial voice and a formal one. Students readily understand that they speak more formally when in front of an official than they do in front of peers. With this awareness they can begin to accept that both standard grammatical conventions and their home dialect are valuable.

By utilizing students' linguistic intuitions, I teach important problem-solving skills that can be used in reading, writing, and beyond—particularly grammar from a linguistic perspective. Most students see a sentence merely as a string of words, and many enter my class having trouble identifying a complete sentence. Students need to know how words form phrases, phrases form clauses, and both form sentences. After all, how can one write well without knowing what a complete sentence is?

I set up lessons inductively. Students have a rare opportunity to become problem-solvers in an English Language Arts (ELA) class. Instead of telling them what differentiates parts of speech, what words work together in phrases, and what makes a sentence complete, they grapple, moving through discussions based on their intuitive knowledge, which helps them retain the material.

I begin by giving them a list of nonsense words from Kristen Denham's website: *dorbling, bonkled, groobies, frandled, slank*, along with *the* and *a* (2014). I then ask students to put those words in an order they think makes a sentence. They are astounded that they can differentiate between a grammatical and ungrammatical sentence with gibberish; they also learn that word placement in a sentence plays a significant role in determining its part of speech. This exercise brings to consciousness their innate ability to identify parts of speech, giving them confidence in learning grammar (see also Lobeck, this volume, pp. 77–79).

Rather than memorizing definitions (*a noun is a person, place, or thing*), I focus on the roles that suffixes and syntactic identifiers (e.g., word order and modification) play in English. For example, determiners (such as *a, an, the*, and *those*) identify the following element as a noun, as in *The _____ came in.* I give students a list of nouns, adjectives, verbs, and adverbs and ask them to select the ones that can occupy the blank position. They have no problem determining that *cat* can fill the blank but *pretty, quickly,* or *eat* cannot. I call these tests *syntactic frame identifiers.*

Suffixes can also mark parts of speech. For example, nouns take suffixes like the plural *-s* and possessive *-s*. They also take numerous other endings like *-ity* (as in *solidity*) and *-ness* (as in *wretchedness*). These suffixes can be used to identify the roots they are attached to and help students see that *-ity* and *-ness* make nouns out of adjectives. To teach this inductively, I ask students to figure out which suffixes attach to verbs to make nouns. They come up with pairs like *adopt/adoption* and *rotate/rotation*, identifying the suffix *-ion* as a possible marker for a noun. This activity also allows us to consider the difference between words such as *lion* (which doesn't contain the *-ion* suffix) and *action* (which does). We form small groups in which the students create lists of words and identify them as a particular part of speech using the tests we have introduced thus far.

These lessons can be translated to vocabulary instruction, too. Reluctant readers in junior high and high school can be intimidated by long words, so I present them with an opportunity to break these words down. I give them words they can easily analyze like *modernization* and then provide them with more difficult words like *conceptualization*. They work in groups to identify the suffixes and then identify the root word (see lesson plan). They can then apply this method to many new words in novels or science textbooks.

In a broader unit on grammar, I teach the rest of the open-class lexical categories in the same way I teach nouns.[1] For verbs, I teach the suffix test. Students switch verbs from present and past tense, whether regular or irregular. For adjectives, the syntactic test asks students to analyze the clause *I am very _____.*

---

1 Open-class lexical categories include nouns, verbs, adjectives, and adverbs. Closed-class lexical categories include prepositions, conjunctions, articles, and pronouns. For a discussion of how to teach concise writing using open and closed classes, see Crovitz and Devereaux (2017).

If the blank can be filled with a word and the resulting clause makes sense, then that word is most likely an adjective. For example, *I am very pretty* works, but **I am very cat* does not. Students figure out which endings are associated with adjectives, and again those endings become further suffix tests for adjectives. If a word has an *-ous* ending, for example, it is most likely an adjective. Like with adjectives, students figure out the suffixes for adverbs, then test them. The syntactic test for adverbs is that they usually have freedom to move around the sentence. For instance: *Quickly he ran down the sidewalk. He quickly ran down the sidewalk. He ran down the sidewalk quickly*.

After students learn the different properties of the parts of speech, I teach them basic function words like conjunctions, prepositions, and pronouns. (There is no point in teaching prepositional phrases if students can't identify prepositions.) Once they know all of this, I teach syntax trees, which help them see how phrases and clauses are dependent on one another. I start by creating a key: sentence (S), noun phrase (NP), verb phrase (VP), prepositional phrase (PNP), noun (N), verb (V), determiner (DET).[2]

I begin with a basic (NP) and then introduce (PNP). In Figure 6.1, NP *the car* shows the dependency that *the* (DET) and *car* (N) have to one another. They are sister nodes of the same mother (NP). In the PNP *in the park*, the NP *the park* is the object of P *in* (see Figure 6.2). The dependency is the same as in the NP. P and NP are sisters of PNP.

I use analogies to explain this dependency. For instance, I suggest that certain words are attracted to other words like magnets are to certain metals. I then describe how other words are repelled by certain words or phrases like two magnets with the same poles. Students are allowed time to figure out which words work in PNPs and which don't. They discover that nouns and adjectives occur in PNPs but verbs don't because nouns attract adjectives but not verbs. In other words, if there is an adjective in a PNP, there must be a noun. I then introduce a VP *jumped over the fence* (Figure 6.3).[3] Students identify the NP, the PNP, and the V. I show them how to tree this VP.

I then provide students with a subject, *the cow*. Since it is an NP, the students recognize it right away. I show them how to tree the whole sentence (see Figure 6.4).

We then discuss the dependency relationship between the subject NP and the predicate VP at the top of the tree—the two necessary parts of a complete sentence (independent clause).

I methodically build more complicated sentences with the class. For example, in the sentence *Grandma drank coffee in the morning*, the phrase *in the morning* is a prepositional phrase that functions adverbially—i.e., it modifies the verb *drank*, telling readers when the coffee was drunk. Remembering that most adverbs (like *quickly*) can be moved around a sentence, students can easily see the adverbial behavior of the phrase *in the morning* by moving it around (for example, to the front of the sentence: *In the morning Grandma drank coffee*). I call such sentence adverbials *swinging monkeys* because they can swing around to different places in a sentence.

---

2 For a fuller discussion of linguistic terminology for different lexical categories (similar to the traditional parts of speech), as well as further examples of how to construct syntax trees, see Curzan and Adams (2012, chapters 5 and 6).

3 In traditional grammar, "jumped over the fence" would be labeled as a *predicate*; however, in linguistics it is labeled as a *verb phrase* to emphasize that the verb is the head (the main word) of the phrase.

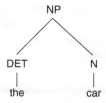

Figure 6.1 Noun phrase tree

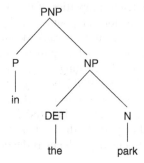

Figure 6.2 Prepositional phrase tree

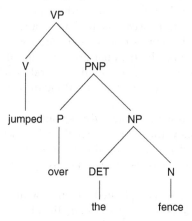

Figure 6.3 Verb phrase tree

After students understand what makes up a sentence, we discuss other contexts where they can extend this knowledge. For example, after studying syntax trees, students understand that in formal writing they typically cannot use fragments. Reading each other's essays, they make conscious decisions about where sentences begin and end, and they are able to write more complex sentences that conform to Standard English.

Beyond their own writing, students can also consciously analyze sentence structure as it relates to meaning. One example comes from *The Adventures of Tom Sawyer*, a popular book for seventh-grade reading: "He had discovered a great law

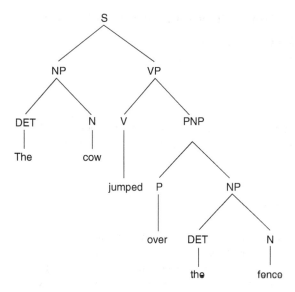

Figure 6.4 Sentence tree

of human action, without knowing it—namely, that in order to make a man or a boy covet a thing, it is only necessary to make the thing difficult to attain" (Twain, 2008, p. 13). Because students understand that sentences are made up of words, phrases, and clauses, they are better prepared to understand such a sentence. In this particular example, students see that "without knowing it" is a *swinging monkey*. It can be moved to the beginning of the sentence as well as the end. This knowledge helps them figure out the main idea. Students see that language is malleable, and clear writing is contingent on phrase, clause, sentence, and passage construction.

Integrating linguistics into the ELA classroom doesn't have to be done alone. There are countless resources to help teachers begin their journey. Reaching out to willing linguists has been an essential part of my education. In my case, I reached out to my father, Samuel Jay Keyser. But there are also publicly accessible resources, such as Kristen Denham's website at Western Washington University, which offers many lesson plans. Dr. Richard Larson, at Stony Brook University, is currently heading up the creation of an Advanced Placement Linguistics class. And Suzi Loosen, a teacher in Wisconsin, has created a Facebook page called High School Teachers Incorporating Linguistics.

Teaching linguistically enables students to accept without judgment that dialect variation is both personal and universal, while simultaneously recognizing the realities of learning to write and speak in Standard American English. Teaching grammar linguistically allows students to break words into meaningful units and to visualize sentences as a series of phrases and clauses that relate to one another— thereby gaining a greater understanding of how language works in their worlds and in the world of literature. Through such instruction, students become problem- solvers who engage authentically with the mysteries of language. Rather than being afraid and overwhelmed by language, they learn, as I did, to delight in its complexity and fluidity.

Lesson Plan: Morphology—Application in Literature

Recommended Grade Level(s)

Ninth grade

Context

Before teaching this lesson, students should first learn about suffix identifiers (such as the suffix -ous changing a noun to an adjective: danger—dangerous).

Objectives

Students will be able to:

*   apply their knowledge of breaking down words to their root forms to decode and deduce the meaning of unfamiliar words in literature;
*   apply context-clue strategies to deduce the meaning of words;
*   use the dictionary only when necessary to deduce the definition of an unfamiliar word.

Common Core Standards

CCSS.ELA-Literacy.L.9–10.4

Determine or clarify the meaning of unknown and multiple-meaning words and phrases based on grades 9–10 reading and content, choosing flexibly from a range of strategies.

Procedures

Step 1: Think Aloud (10 Minutes)

Think aloud using the lessons learned from morphology suffix identifiers, modeling how to break down polysyllabic words to their root meaning. Potential words include modernization, unbelievable, or replacement.

Step 2: Silent Reading (10 Minutes)

Ask students to read several pages of Jack London's Into the Wild silently and write words they find difficult to understand or decode on Post-it notes then attach them to the page.

Step 3: Sharing Words (5 Minutes)

After silent reading, the students choose one or two words they identified during their reading and write them on the board.

Step 4: Practicing Word Parts, Whole Class (20 Minutes)

The teacher and students talk about each word individually and break the words down until the students recognize the meaning of the word. If there are words that cannot be broken down, students go back to the sentence in the text and try to figure out the meaning through context clues. If that strategy fails, students look the word up in a dictionary.

Step 5: Practicing Word Parts, Individually (10 Minutes)

Students practice independently with the remaining words they've chosen from their silent reading, analyzing the word into parts until the word is recognizable, looking for context clues, or looking the word up in the dictionary. They continue this task for homework.

References

Crovitz, D., & Devereaux, M. D. (2017). *Grammar to get things done: A practical guide for teachers anchored in real-world usage.* London, New York, NY and Urbana, IL: Routledge and NCTE.

Curzan, A., & Adams, M. (2012). *How English works: A linguistic introduction* (3rd ed.). Boston, MA: Pearson.

Denham, K. (2014). *Exploring language: Daily language investigations for English language learners.* Retrieved from www.explorelanguage.org

Twain, M. (2008) *The adventures of Tom Sawyer.* New York, NY: Signet Classics.

Chapter 7

Using Music to Bridge Language Diversity

Jillian Ratti, McMinn County High School, Tennessee

Introduction

My students mostly look alike, and they generally celebrate the same religious holidays. They all live in the same county in East Tennessee, the county where I grew up, and many have roots that go back generations. Despite these connections, the overwhelming linguistic challenge I face in my classroom is diversity. The similarities in race and religion can easily obscure major differences that are more salient to our classroom experience: suburban vs. rural; middle class vs. working class; with Internet vs. without.

These differences are complicated further: some of my students have a criminal background, some are homeless, others are in foster care. I also have students who come from stable two-parent families, where parents are doctors, professors, or lawyers. And while the majority of my students are White, I also teach students outside of the majority—students of other races, ethnicities, and religions—who must confront their own difference every day. Seemingly as a result of this diversity of race, ethnicity, religion, class, and lived experience, a recognizable tribalism has developed. Students see their "kin" as those with whom they share a key identity feature, whether that be race, class, or lived experience. As a result, each "tribe" shares a general set of preferences toward clothing, music, and language.[1] Some of the tribes operate in alliance with the educational system, others in conflict. The consequence is that one sophomore English classroom of thirty students can contain a bewilderingly diverse array of attitudes toward schooling in general and the English language in particular. No lesson can assume the students have the same starting point.

Across many of the tribes is a shared belief of their own inferiority (I use the word *belief* deliberately). Many of my students believe fully that they aren't particularly smart, aren't good at school, and have no way to succeed in the world. These beliefs seem to originate in their tribal identity and extend to the tribe's other members (i.e., *We rednecks don't care about writing essays*). Some others have more self-confidence but believe that the deck is so stacked against them or their tribe that there's little point in trying. In fact, in many cases it seems their tribal identities have been formed directly in opposition to an educational system that has told them implicitly and explicitly that they—their language, their culture, and their interests—are wrong. These conditions result in a classroom where a sizable portion

---

1 In this context I define *tribe* as "a group of persons having a common character, occupation, or interest."

of the student body approaches the teacher as the antagonist, resulting in apathy and rebellion as the primary expressions of student voice.

This self-perceived inferiority can result in a kind of double-bind for the teacher when it comes to teaching language variation. Appalachian English, the home language variety of some of my students, is often viewed as a degraded form of communication, even by those who speak it. Therefore, attempts to elevate it reduce the teacher's credibility (i.e., *If you think this is a good way to talk, you must not be much of a teacher*). At the same time, a lack of respect for the home language, or a too-intense focus on teaching Standard English, results in students feeling disrespected and alienated by the educational system.

Under these conditions, I've found that it's generally best to address language variation embedded in other content. My typical approach could be described as "make a comment when it's relevant." We discuss code-switching when we write job applications; we discuss language change over time when we study Shakespeare; we discuss the word *ain't* when we focus on academic language in our essays.

I have also identified one technique that has proven surprisingly effective at integrating language variation into classroom instruction: using popular music. Even in accelerated courses, music can build a strong bridge between the students' real-world experiences and the world of academia. For students struggling with self-confidence, using accessible texts to teach academic skills can be a game-changer. When I used Sir Mix-a-Lot's song "Baby Got Back" to introduce rhetorical analysis to my Advanced Placement Language students a few years ago, one of them actually responded, "I didn't know learning could be fun."

As teachers, we may see the relevance of Toni Morrison, Frank McCourt, or Sandra Cisneros to our students' experiences, but some students are so skeptical of academia that they approach every text in English class the same way: like a plate of brussels sprouts—probably good for you, everyone says so, but a chore to be suffered through. Music is enticing and delicious, and the more provocative the song choice, the greater their appetite.

The Tournament of Songs

I've had great success over the past few years with my Tournament of Songs. Every March I have the students nominate popular songs for a March Madness-style tournament. The unit is intended to teach literary analysis and argumentative writing, but a by-product has been the elevation of nonstandard English as a mode of discourse worthy of serious analysis. Whether it's the metaphors of Iggy Azalea, the vivid imagery of Luke Bryan, or the inspirational themes of Nickelback, popular music allows students to hear their own language being taken seriously in the classroom. The tournament has been my most successful unit in terms of student growth in writing, especially for my lowest-achieving students, and I attribute that to the potent combination of explicitly modeling academic language while simultaneously showing respect to language variation.

Objectives and Background

The goal of the tournament is to identify the "best song" as determined by student votes. Votes must be written in academic language and based on literary analysis.

As the tournament progresses, the process of voting evolves from writing sentences to writing paragraphs, eventually building to a multi-paragraph response. During the nomination phase, it's helpful to discuss what makes a song *good* and establish some criteria for judgment. I try to avoid prescribing standards to judge the songs. Instead, I teach that almost any position can be argued—as long as students provide sufficient evidence and explanation.

Tournament Procedure

In the week before the tournament, students nominate songs for consideration and then vote for their favorites. When the top songs emerge, I review lyrics to exclude any that I don't feel comfortable discussing in the classroom. Deciding where to draw the line can be difficult: the norms of one's community should factor in. I have found, however, that including as many songs as possible that do address mature themes not often discussed in school (i.e., *drugs, sex, and rock 'n' roll*) sub-stantially increases student investment in the project. I have also found it important to balance the representation of the tribes' music. At my school, that means I must include country, hip-hop, rock, pop, and alternative music. Eight songs are chosen for the tournament. I arrange the bracket so that in the early rounds two songs of similar genres will be paired, ensuring that one of them will reach the semifinals. Otherwise, all the country songs could be eliminated in the opening round, leaving my country-lovers disappointed and indifferent in the later rounds.

The tournament proceeds in three phases: the opening round, the semifinals, and the finals. In the opening-round matches, we focus on identifying literary devices in the lyrics, using those devices to guide our evaluation of the songs. At first, I model the entire process for students to follow, showing my annotations and explaining my observations. I draw students' attention to features they are unlikely to notice on their own: extended metaphors or motifs, unusually clever or complex rhyming, diction contributing to mood, overreliance on cliché, language revealing the speaker's tone or values, etc. Powerful learning can result from the teacher pointing out unnoticed artistry in a well-known text.

As I decrease my involvement in later matches, I still encourage the students to share their observations and their evaluations with each other. Through all the rounds, students must support their claims with evidence from the text, phrased and punctuated in an academic style. Votes in the first round are phrased as complete sentences. Students may vote multiple times by writing additional sentences that each make a distinct claim. Votes that do not meet all the requirements are not counted.

In the semifinal round, students are required to write full paragraphs with multiple pieces of evidence supporting their claim. In the final round, students are encouraged to write multiple paragraphs and address counterarguments. Paragraphs are graded on a four-point proficiency scale with the score deter-mining the number of votes, thereby providing an authentic incentive for more developed writing.

Outcomes

In terms of writing, the conditions of the tournament (quick feedback, instruc-tional scaffolding, escalating requirements, and student investment) build the skills of argumentation and elaboration almost painlessly. Students learn how to embed and punctuate brief quotations illustrating their claims. It's also the only way I've found to teach capitalization and punctuation of titles so that it actually sticks. By the end of the unit, my lower-level students see a substantial increase in both confidence and skills with analytical writing.

There is a similar payoff in reading skills. Students come to see familiar songs in new ways, realizing the depth of artistry displayed by some of their favorites. In other cases, they see that a song has practically no depth at all. The literary analysis this unit produces is far beyond anything I've accomplished in a traditional poetry unit. By working closely with the text of the songs' lyrics, students develop a much deeper understanding of literary concepts like simile, paradox, rhyme, allusion, narratives, and patterns of imagery. At the same time, language that might typically be criticized in a classroom setting has instead been upheld and celebrated.

Many former students have told me the song tournament was their favorite part of the course, one they remember fondly even years later. I suspect that the magic of the unit comes from the juxtaposition of academic English with the informal and nonstandard language found in the songs. Demonstrating how academic language can be used to discuss anything, including slightly racy song lyrics, gives students an avenue into scholarship. Furthermore, the music of each tribe has been seen, studied, and affirmed. Showing respect to students in this way disarms them, allowing them finally to see the teacher as a collaborator rather than an enemy. During the song tournament, school becomes a place where the students' music, their language, and ultimately their culture are all taken seriously and evaluated on their own merits. Linguistic diversity then becomes a source of richness, not a problem to be solved.

Lesson Plan: The Tournament of Songs—Match I

Recommended Grade Level(s)

Ninth grade and tenth grade

Context

Students need a basic familiarity with common literary terms, incorporating quotations into sentences, and providing evidence to support claims. Prior to this lesson, the class will choose eight songs for the tournament, which are set in a single-elimination tournament bracket. Criteria for choosing the best song will also have been discussed.

Objectives

Students will be able to:

*   analyze literary elements in popular songs;
*   defend the merit of one song over another;
*   employ academic language to support a claim.

Common Core Standards

CCSS.ELA-Literacy.L.9–10.3

Apply knowledge of language to understand how language functions in different contexts, to make effective choices for meaning or style, and to comprehend more fully when reading or listening.

CCSS.ELA-Literacy.RL.9–10.4

Determine the meaning of words and phrases as they are used in the text, including fig-urative and connotative meanings; analyze the cumulative impact of specific word choices on meaning and tone (e.g., how the language evokes a sense of time and place; how it sets a formal or informal tone).

CCSS.ELA-Literacy.W.9–10.1

Write arguments to support claims in an analysis of substantive topics or texts, using valid reasoning and relevant and sufficient evidence.

CCSS.ELA-Literacy.L.9–10.2

Demonstrate command of the conventions of standard English capitalization, punctuation, and spelling when writing.

Procedures

Step 1: Introduce the Tournament (2 Minutes)

Show and describe a March Madness basketball tournament bracket. Explain that teams are paired up over a series of games to determine which team is the best. Tell the students that we are going to pair up songs to choose the best song of the year, according to us.

Step 2: Distribute and Explain Materials (5 Minutes)

Direct students' attention to the resource materials on the cover of the packet, the lyrics and worksheets inside, the vote boxes, and the semifinal match sheet on the back (see eResources).

Step 3: The First Listen (10 Minutes)

Play the first song. While the song plays, students should be reading the lyrics in their packet and annotating the literary features they notice. Annotate along with them and share your annotations for this match. If you have a document camera, consider annotating while the song plays, allowing the students to see your work. Repeat for the second song.

Step 4: Complete the Analysis Protocol (10 Minutes)

Instruct students to answer the analysis questions on the worksheet for each song (see eResources). Consider dividing the class so half of them focus on each song, then have representatives from each group share their findings. Discuss.

Step 5: Discussion: Preparing to Vote (5–10 Minutes)

Guide students toward various possible rationales for their votes. Ask questions like which song has the more original figurative language, which contains interesting or surprising rhymes, which has a stronger message, or which creates the more compelling mood. As students share their views, encourage them to support their claims with references to the text.

Step 6: Voting (5–10 Minutes)

Students must choose one song to vote for. All votes must contain evidence (usually a quotation from the song) to support their claim. Votes must be phrased as a complete sentence including the title of the chosen song. Remind students about appropriate punctuation of titles and quotations. Students may vote multiple times by making multiple claims of their song's merit, and all votes that meet the criteria will be counted.

Follow-up (The Following Day)

Before beginning the next match, display several examples of votes that counted and votes that didn't. Work with students to repair faulty votes. Encourage students to craft multiple or more sophisticated votes as the tournament progresses.

Chapter 8

Power, Society, and Identity
Language and Life in a Ninth-Grade English Classroom

Holly Hoover, Kennesaw Mountain High School, Georgia

The thought of teaching language ideologies can be intimidating. As teachers, we often feel that we have to be 100 percent confident in our teaching and relate to our students. Teaching language ideologies may make us question both our confidence and relatability—yes, that is intimidating.

I work at a school with approximately 2,200 students (52 percent White, 26 percent Black, 13 percent Hispanic, and 9 percent from other ethnic backgrounds); 28 percent of the students are on free or reduced lunch in a Georgia county some might deem "wealthy." Although the school's majority identifies as "White," my classrooms are far more diverse. Since I am the only English teacher certified to teach English language learners (ELLs), my classes are some of the most ethnically and racially diverse in the school. But while my students' experiences span numerous countries and cultures, my personal background, that of a 5'4", young, Caucasian girl, kept me wondering if I had what it took to bring a strong conversation about language diversity to the classroom. I quickly realized that my own language had never made me feel like an outsider. But I also knew my students' experiences were different.

In this chapter I share the challenges I have faced, from wrestling with my perspectives of language ideologies, to language-themed lessons and activities that focus on canonical texts, to the open-mindedness that teachers need in order to push the boundaries of "standard English" and "standard teaching" while maintaining the classroom standards. Essentially, this chapter is the journey of one teacher trying to integrate language ideologies into her classroom.

Me? Teach Language Ideologies?

Teaching language ideologies has been a process. For example, I used to think that Standard English was the *only* way that people should speak. I would be that annoying teacher or friend who corrected people after they "misspoke." Me, young and White, correcting students whose language of home varied from the language of school—needless to say, students didn't react very well to my corrections. I had a one-track mind when it came to speaking English, and, whew, was I wrong.

My first discussions of cultural identity with my ninth-graders were challenging because I thought that I didn't connect with them. Who was I to talk about society's "correct" way of speaking? In a class of freshmen where more than one-quarter of the class were on free or reduced lunch and the majority of my classes did not look like me, I, for the first time, felt like the outsider. I was honest with them about my challenges in relating to them, especially those who were ELLs from other countries. But instead of fighting with the idea of "not connecting," I was honest with them about my fears.

So my classes started talking about real-world experiences—from racial tension to feminism to social-media representations—and how those related to culture, language, and identity. They were pretty quiet at first, nervous to be the first person to talk about these "taboo" topics. But students *do* want to talk about these issues. They *do* care about their culture, language, and identity. And I have learned that if you show that you care about who they really, truly are deep down, students will literally move heaven and earth for you.

Those first lessons may have taught me more than they taught my students. I learned that students equate language with experiences—they thought the more "standard" one speaks, the fewer challenges that person has experienced. Some students said, "You don't understand my dialect or who I am—I speak a certain way with my friends, and you would cringe if you heard it." I was honest with them: I told them that, growing up, I was taught that there was a "right" way to talk, but I had since learned that this attitude was wrong. The students appreciated my honesty and were then more prone to be honest with me. This shared sense of trust ultimately enriched our discussions of culture via their own personal experiences, and we explored these topics most effectively through the lenses of "language and power," "language and society," and "language and identity" (Devereaux, 2015).

Language Ideologies and *Romeo and Juliet*

Now, imagine discussions about cultures, dialect, power, and identity as the beginning of a unit on *Romeo and Juliet* by William Shakespeare—certainly not a traditional pairing.

I begin our *Romeo and Juliet* unit with the essay "Ovuh Dyuh" by Joanne Kilgour Dowdy (2002). Dowdy's essay shows students how certain language choices make some feel empowered and others disempowered. Dowdy had to make a choice of whether to side with her society's language expectation or her own. The idea of language and power strikingly hits home with students because they often feel as if they lack power (or even a voice). The essay begins important discussions about language variation, helping students see how different dialects enact different versions of power in different societies and in their own lives.

When discussing language ideologies in *Romeo and Juliet*, we often refer back to Dowdy's essay. The different levels of society in the play and how the characters' language symbolizes their power (or lack thereof) reflect Dowdy's world; the connections between these texts frame our exploration of the topics of language and society. A key theme of my Language and Society unit is that we cannot fully separate the two topics, and I often relate this idea to students by discussing the language choices we make and how these choices affect our lives (and those of our parents, friends, etc.). We refer back to Dowdy, discussing how she wrestled with which language variety to use and for what purpose. Sometimes students do not even notice that they are actively code-switching—that is, shifting the way they use language throughout their day depending on who they are speaking with at a particular moment.

After describing and identifying examples of real-life code-switching, we look closely at language and society in the play. For example, in Act I, Scene 5, when Romeo, Benvolio, and Mercutio enter with masks, Tybalt immediately recognizes their language and wants to fight Romeo. Beyond this, Shakespeare also uses language to identify characters' social classes: when a person from a lower class (e.g., the Nurse) is speaking, Shakespeare uses prose; for the upper class (e.g., the Friar), he uses verse. Identifying these examples in the play allows students to consider different character perspectives in relation to class, society, power, and identity, all of which relate to the theme of language variation (see lesson plan).

We also talk about how language can be nonverbal, such as when Sampson in *Romeo and Juliet* bites his thumb (Act I, Scene 1). As a class, we brainstorm about how we view nonverbal cues in the present day. Many times my students bring up television shows such as *The Office*, where the camera pans to an actor staring at the audience to show their sarcasm without verbalizing. Students enjoy relating real-world concepts, shows, and ideas to the text.

As we move through the ideas of language, power, and society in *Romeo and Juliet*, students often connect larger issues to the questions we are posing. For example, one student noted that many dismiss Shakespeare's language because it is hard to understand, which raises important questions: Does lack of understanding impact the level and type of power in our social relations? Do we dismiss each other completely when we have difficulty understanding one another's language and, as a consequence, disempower others (and ourselves)? When looking at different levels of society, we are really looking at different levels of power and the effects of those power differentials on people.

As you can see, language, power, society, and identity are not separate issues that can easily fit into some specific formula. Instead, they are messy concepts demonstrated through verbal and nonverbal cues in *Romeo and Juliet* and many other texts that we teach in the English language arts classroom—difficult to categorize but impossible to miss. It is important for me as a teacher to show different types of examples of language ideologies at play so that students can see how these concepts occur daily in our lives and how they are a part of a much larger focus: changing the idea that there is one "correct" way to speak.

Conclusion: More Linguistics in Teacher Training, Please!

Thinking on how my own beliefs about language varieties and ideologies have changed, I realize my new lenses have been bolstered by the linguistic training that I received in my undergraduate and graduate education. Although the linguistic classes helped me, I think linguists could do even more for teachers like me by focusing on how to connect real-life dealings with classroom pedagogy.

As much as university schooling prepares you for teaching, there is absolutely nothing like getting out there in the classroom. The important thing to remember is that teaching is about taking risks—students do not want mediocre book teaching. I can say that my linguistics professors, both in my graduate and undergraduate courses, didn't give me mediocre book teaching. I took an Introduction to Linguistics course in my undergraduate degree where we discussed the power of words (and their power in society), but I do not recall discussing the connection between our language and identity. In this undergrad class, I do wish we had had more application directed toward teaching, but it wasn't a pedagogy course.

It wasn't until a few years later that I realized what teachers need in order to openly and confidently discuss language ideologies: We have to figure out what those ideologies mean to us first. What is our language story? What are our beliefs about language, and where did those beliefs originate? What are others' language stories? What can I learn from listening to others? After this exploration, there must be a focus on the *how* in the classroom: How do I teach this stuff? I got this instruction in my graduate linguistics course, which was pedagogy-focused. We really spoke about application of language ideologies. My professor made us not only learn the material but also develop lessons (finding lessons, analyzing lessons, creating lessons, etc.).

What I do wish my master's class had taught me, in addition to the language ideologies, was how to negotiate the space of being "politically correct" with every word that I chose. However, in this reflection, I realize that I, like my students, am caught in the bubble of what is "correct" or "good" English. Until we change as a society and start taking risks, we will forever be in the loop of wondering if we are "correct" or not. We have to start by being vulnerable with our students. We need to show them the barriers that society has placed on them (and the barriers they place on each other, for that matter) and how to break through them. By giving them freedom in their speech and writing, we are giving them the gift of acceptance and growth. I have learned that teaching language ideologies is not easy, but it sure is worth it because our students need to see us being vulnerable in order to grow.

Lesson Plan: Party Perspective[1]

Recommended Grade Level(s)

Primarily used in ninth grade but can be adapted to fit any story in sixth grade through twelfth grade.

Context

This "party perspective" activity can really be done any time after Act I, but I usually complete it toward the end of *Romeo and Juliet* so that students fully know the different characters. This lesson works with many different units of study because it allows students to think about characters' different perspectives and how those perspectives relate to social class, identity, and language choices. Before completing this lesson plan, students should understand that language ideologies exist and are present in literature.

Objectives

Students will be able to:

*   analyze the party scene found in Act I through the eyes of a different character;
*   analyze the motives of the author's language, societal, or identity choices;
*   construct a group project from the perspective of one of the characters while focusing on language—i.e., whether it gives that character power, identity, or a place in society.

Common Core Standards

CCSS.ELA-Literacy.RL.9–10.3

Analyze how complex characters (e.g., those with multiple or conflicting motivations) develop over the course of a text, interact with other characters, and advance the plot or develop the theme.

CCSS.ELA-Literacy.W.9–10.9

Draw evidence from literary or informational texts to support analysis, reflection, and research.

Procedures

Step 1: Preparation (15 Minutes)

Put the students into groups and have them analyze a moment from the party scene from a different perspective. For example, write the script from a bystander who sees Romeo and his men come in with masks or write it from the perspective of Juliet who views

Romeo from the first moment. Other examples include the serving man who sees Tybalt's desire to fight against Romeo, or even the nurse who views Romeo kissing Juliet's hand. This rewrite should demonstrate the class, society, power, and identity of the character who is retelling the story (Act I, Scene 5).

Step 2: Application (20 Minutes)

Give each student a large piece of butcher paper and allow them to create the scene from the eyes of another character. Students should write the scenario on the back of the paper and create an image on the front from the perspective of the character. What is that character seeing in that scene? What's the focus, and how does the written scene reflect that focus? Students should remember to show a different class, society, power, or identity. For example, if they were to visualize from the nurse's perspective, it could be Romeo kissing Juliet's hand and her thoughts being similar to "What is happening? This is such a bad idea! I must go tell her and break this up." The nurse does not see herself as a lesser being because of her social status, but rather a caretaker of Juliet.

Step 3: Review (15 Minutes)

Have each group share their scenes with the class. The students should share with the class why they chose the specific character's point of view. After, have a class discussion about their favorite and why. Have the students be specific.

Examples:
- Serving man: a minor character, involved with higher and lower classes;
- Romeo or Juliet: major characters;
- Lady Capulet: a higher-class, minor character.

References

Devereaux, M. (2015). *Teaching about dialect variations and language in secondary English classrooms: Power, prestige, and prejudice.* London and New York, NY: Routledge.

Dowdy, J. K. (2002). Ovuh dyuh. In L. Delpit & J. K. Dowdy (Eds.), *The skin we speak: Thoughts on language and culture in the classroom* (pp. 3–14). New York, NY: The New Press.

Shakespeare, W. (1993). *Romeo and Juliet.* New York: Dover Publications.

Chapter 9

Language Awareness in Education
A Linguist's Response to Teachers

Walt Wolfram, NC State University, North Carolina

Introduction

Though it may be an ideal goal, it is far beyond linguists to solve problems of language inequality and linguistic discrimination in the U.S. Linguistics is a highly specialized, somewhat esoteric discipline housed almost exclusively in institutions of higher education, with a highly technical, often-opaque jargon and obscure public reputation. The linguists who care about language, society, and education need a synergistic relationship with primary practitioners who stand at the intersection of language use in everyday venues of social and educational life. This is the reason why I excitedly devoured the essays of the classroom teachers who have experimented with and incorporated dimensions of linguistics and language awareness into their secondary education curricula. These essays constitute a rich set of perspectives on the utility and integration of linguistic understanding and the relevance of language ideology and language variation in education. The inclusion of lesson plans and activities for each chapter also provides substantive models for other educators and practitioners.

Taken together, these chapters raise critical questions: What notions about language structure and language variation are essential for students, and what is the potential impact on students and instructors when engaging with these topics? Though different chapters focus on diverse curricular themes, a core of underlying interests and methods emerge. As a linguist dedicated to the application of linguistic principles in K–12, I am interested not only in the content selected and the educational approaches utilized but also in the background experiences and personalities of those willing to take on this kind of challenge. These essays have led me, as the coauthor of a set of curricular materials on language awareness for middle school currently endorsed by the Department of Instruction in the State of North Carolina (Reaser & Wolfram, 2007), to reflect further on the utility of our own materials.[1] What inspired these educators to engage in these activities, and how can we entice more teachers to follow suit? How do we make these kinds of activities more routine rather than the exception? What are the challenges confronted by both linguists and educators in expanding the utility of such materials? In the first section, I consider some of the common issues of language variation and ideologies addressed in these essays as well as the disparate topical concerns. In the following section, I consider the background experiences

---

1 See eResources for links to this curriculum and other teacher resources.

and teaching profiles of the educators that have inspired them to take the unique educational risks involved in this enterprise. Finally, I conclude with a section on the challenges that confront the linguist–practitioner interface that might lead to the adoption of language-awareness activities and to more engagement of educators in these practices.

Issues and Applications: Commonality and Diversity

As I read the different essays and classroom activities, I was struck by both the commonality and the diversity in the themes and applications. All of the essays focus in some way on language ideology and variation while connecting those themes with a highly diverse range of topics. Amy L. Plackowski summarizes the central questions that drive student inquiry: "What attitudes and beliefs do you have about language? How did those attitudes develop? and How do those attitudes and beliefs influence your worldview?" (p. 3). Perhaps the most common underlying theme in the essays is the conflict between "prescriptivism" and "descriptivism" at the ideological core of language variation. As John Damaso observes, "There is a hunger among students to discuss linguistic prescriptivism, language standardization, and language variation" (p. 32). At the same time, he concedes that "doing so in an English class may seem countercultural, and students may shy away" (p. 32). Challenging extant norms such as "correct" and "incorrect" in a way that seems both counterintuitive and countercultural is an intriguing discussion for secondary (and university) students that is bound to engage them in meaningful discussion and reflection. It also offers an opportunity to understand the linguistic notion of structural well-formedness, or "grammaticality," as independent of social valuation, as highlighted in the chapter by Beth Keyser (pp. 39–46). Linguists study language by observing and recording the language structures and uses of speakers apart from their social valuation—the descriptivist approach. The descriptivist approach is often set up in opposition to the prescriptivist approach, in which some forms of language are judged as "correct" or "proper" and others as "incorrect" and "improper" based on tradition and social valuation. The notion that language patterning is found in ALL language varieties regardless of social valuation is, in fact, one of the most meaningful and enduring lessons learned by students in a dialect awareness curriculum that we have taught in one form or another for over two decades (Reaser, 2006; Reaser, Adger, Wolfram, & Christian, 2017).

The so-called descriptivist–prescriptivist debate is, of course, a preliminary, fundamental issue in Linguistics 101 that surely deserves to be considered by inquiring secondary students as well, and it is further relevant to issues of linguistic equality and social justice. The descriptive–prescriptive positions have often been set up as a simple "good guy–bad guy" dichotomy in the study of language, but a cautionary caveat is necessary here—for both linguists and educators. If we are honest, we have to admit that a "prescriptivist instinct" resides within all of us, and the prescriptive-descriptive distinction is not a binary division. Linguist Deborah Cameron (1995) suggests that the interesting questions about prescriptivism are not the issue of descriptivism versus prescriptivism but "who prescribes for whom, what they prescribe, and for what purposes" (p. 11). Anne Curzan (2014) identifies four strands of prescriptivism:

1. Standardizing prescriptivism, in which rules and judgments aim to promote and enforce a uniform, socially ratified variety of proper English (e.g., The use of *were* versus *was* in *They were here*).
2. Stylistic prescriptivism, in which rules aim to differentiate the "finer" points of style in the standardized variety (e.g., The use of *I hope* instead of the sentence adverbial *Hopefully* in *Hopefully, Elliot will figure it out*).
3. Restorative prescriptivism, in which rules aim at restoring relatively obsolete or older forms to "purify" language (e.g., the use of *shall* vs. *will* or, more currently, the use of *said* as opposed to the newer form *was like* for introducing quotations, as in *She was like, "This is ridiculous!"*).
4. Politically responsive prescriptivism, in which rules are chosen to promote inclusive and/or egalitarian language use (e.g., the avoidance of the masculine pronoun *he* or *his* to refer to groups comprised of both men and women, as in *Every student should bring his book*).

Linguists might be opposed to strands of prescriptivism that reinforce and reproduce social inequalities in language, but, at the same time, take an active role in politically responsive prescriptivism under the of rubric of "language reform" to foster linguistic equality. By nuancing the discussion of prescriptivism, teachers and students can examine deeper questions regarding underlying language ideologies and the purposes of language prescriptivism in society, including the kind of prescriptivism actually embraced by sociolinguists. Accordingly, we can also fulfill Andrew Bergdahl's goal of giving knowledge and freedom rather than being assigned to "one camp or the other, descriptivism or prescriptivism" (p. 14).

Most essays touch on fundamental issues about language structure and variability, but the diversity of themes and applications in the representative curricular materials is striking. It ranges from using music in Jillian Ratti's essay to the discussion of "cultures, dialect, power, and identity" (p. 55) in studying *Romeo and Juliet* by William Shakespeare in Holly Hoover's essay. In between are direct discussions of language ideology, sensitive felicity conditions on the use of the N-word by Mike Williams, language crimes by Plackowski, and other applications that would unquestionably be appealing and appropriate for secondary students, though a couple might seem somewhat risky for a standard course of study. It is also noteworthy how the essays seamlessly align with the required grade-level standards, an observation that we noted in the construction of our dialect awareness curriculum (Reaser & Wolfram, 2007). Such a connection is essential in these activities, as it underscores the potential for language instruction to fit naturally with existent core standards. We don't need to change the course of study; we just need to demonstrate how seamlessly language variation and ideology align with current standards.

Several of the essays apply language variation to literature routinely read by students. In fact, many of these books employ literary dialect, ranging from Mark Twain's *Adventures of Huckleberry Finn* to Zora Neale Hurston's *Their Eyes Were Watching God*, providing a natural and essential intersection of dialect and literature. In fact, it is hard to imagine discussing canonical literature utilizing literary dialect without a meaningful discussion of language variation. It is an easy and accessible bridge between linguistics and literature. In an analogous way, Plackowski's essay demonstrates how dialects are central to the presentation of regional, social, and ethnic characters in film. Language variation indeed has a broad scope of application over time and space. Furthermore, it is highly relevant to discussions of word choice, stance, code-shifting, and social negotiation as pointed out in essays by John Damaso, Stacy Arevalo, and others. Furthermore, the essays demonstrate that language variation and language ideology are relevant for a wide spectrum of student demographics, from Arevalo's class, where two-thirds of the students speak a language other than English, to Ratti's class, where "students mostly look alike ... celebrate the same religious holidays" and "all live in the same county in East Tennessee"—where she also grew up (p. 47). Notwithstanding the generational continuity and many background similarities of her community, Ratti concludes that "the overwhelming linguistic challenge I face in my classroom is diversity" (p. 47).

Another constant is the robust reflection by students as they grapple with traditional notions and current events. Bergdahl notes,

> In my linguistics class, which was a very new sort of endeavor for me, I solicited feedback in the form of reflection assignments: a variety of surveys—about how well my students understood the material, how they thought it would apply to their other classes, and what they liked best or least—were disguised as writing prompts. I was uniquely able to get away with this sort of meta-chicanery thanks to the way linguistics examines language, and itself.
>
> (p. 14)

The essays point to a level of discussion that is both productive and encouraging for instructors trying to engage students in issues and critical thinking. And that's a good thing.

The Engaged Practitioner

What kinds of educators get involved in language awareness and language ideology? Why would a teacher already overladen with instructional and administrative demands in the standard course of study take on the responsibility of language-awareness education? This is not easy work, as noted by Hoover's straightforward assertion that the "thought of teaching language ideologies can be intimidating" (p. 54). The discussion of teachers' language-awareness experiences uncovers several traits of those who have chosen to engage in this instruction. It takes considerable self-reflexivity, openness, and vulnerability to confront language ideologies that have been socialized into all of us, including educators, since we started uttering our first words within the earshot of adults. It takes a teacher who can confront their own language socialization and the accumulation of language biases. Arevalo's essay notes that "Self-reflection, already core to my teaching practice, became even more salient as I developed a language-focused curriculum" (p. 18). Certainly, all of the educators' essays reveal directly or indirectly a reflexive spirit needed to confront reified language beliefs that are often unexamined because they are so implicit and dominant that they qualify as "commonsense and obvious facts." As Norman Fairclough notes in *Language and Power* (1989, p. 2), "The exercise of power, in modern society, is increasingly achieved through ideology," and consent is much more effective than coercion in the exercise of power. By the time we get to secondary education, we have been thoroughly socialized and schooled into the unquestioned inevitability of language standards and norms. It takes a critical eye and reflexivity to question assumed truth, a trait exhibited by all of the authors in one form or another.

The essays also indicate prior exposure to linguistics in undergraduate or graduate education that, in many cases, planted the seed for reflection on language ideology and language variation. This exposure might have been through formal or informal education, ranging from a formal course in linguistics to personal exposure in natural conversation where language beliefs and practices may have been discussed, including the home of Beth Keyser, the daughter of an eminent generative linguist. Exposure to some of the principles of language structure and issues of language variation sets the stage for subsequent reflection and proactive initiative. As I have been telling students in introductory linguistics classes for a half-century now, it is not the facts in this class that make a difference, it is the perspective on language that should be transformative. Without being too self-congratulatory, glimpses of this effect are revealed in these reflections.

I hope I am not reading too much into the essays, but I also see a significant measure of social and educational activism that inspires teachers to reflect, explore, innovate, and apply in their classrooms in ways that go beyond the obligation to follow the required curriculum. An educator willing to consider how issues of language variation might be taught under the rubric of a standard course of study is probably a dynamic educator to begin with. We would like to see this spirit evidenced throughout secondary education, but it often takes a back seat to the extraordinary instructional and administrative demands already placed on teachers. To be honest, the most common practical objection we've faced in the adoption of our language awareness curriculum has been that teachers are currently so overburdened with current obligations that they just can't take the time or additional effort to learn something new to teach. This is not intended to be judgmental but to acknowledge the demands on educators' time and effort—and to recognize those exceptional educators willing to step beyond that line of responsibility in a proactive way.

The Challenge

I wish I could conclude that the essays offered here represent a routine response to the challenge of language variation and ideology. Unfortunately, these kinds of responses are the exception. A decade after introducing a curriculum endorsed by the Department of Public Instruction (Reaser & Wolfram, 2007) in social studies, our struggle remains wide-scale adoption. We have conducted webinars, done various workshops, and spent weeks in the summer introducing and training educators about the curriculum, but it remains underutilized by classroom teachers, notwithstanding research supporting its utility in language awareness education (Reaser, 2006).

How do we enlist more educators in similar kinds of engagement? As noted earlier, the teachers typically had been exposed to some linguistic notions as a part of their own education, stressing the need for education about language structure and variation in the process of their preparation. I'm not advocating a required course in linguistics for all educators, but background exposure can plant a seed that can be germinated later within an aligned, appropriate field of educational application. At our university, for example, all English majors in secondary education take a required course in Language and Writing that devotes up to a third of the course to issues in language variation and ideology that directly have an impact on English education (Reaser, personal communication). In fact, this course has inspired a number of educators to continue pursuing these topics as they assume their instructional role in the classroom.

We can further use such initiatives as a way of making the educational process more relevant to beliefs about life and language, and a highly engaging activity for students. For example, end-of-year student comments about the eighth-grade social studies curriculum in one of our schools noted that students' favorite and most meaningful unit of the year was the one on dialects, suggesting the potential for a transformative educational experience. In the process, we can also share the inspiring accounts of teachers who have successfully navigated the challenge and made a difference in student understanding about the role of language beliefs in our worldviews and the reality of language variation in everyday life—like those who thankfully shared their essays here and inspired me.

References

Cameron, D. (1995). *Verbal hygiene*. London and New York, NY: Routledge.

Cameron, D., Fraser, E., Harvey, P., Rampton, M. B. H., & Richardson, K. (1992). *Researching language: Issues of power and method*. London and New York, NY: Routledge.

Curzan, A. (2014). *Fixing English: Prescriptivism and language history*. Cambridge: Cambridge University Press.

Fairclough, N. (1989). *Language and power*. London and New York, NY: Routledge.

Reaser, J. (2006). The effect of language awareness on adolescent's knowledge and attitudes (unpublished doctoral dissertation). Durham, NC: Duke University.

Reaser, J., Adger, C., Wolfram, W., & Christian, D. (2017). *Dialects at school: Educating linguistically diverse students*. London and New York, NY: Routledge.

Reaser, J., & Wolfram, W. (2007). *Voices of North Carolina: Language and life from the Atlantic to the Appalachians* [Teachers Manual and Student Workbook]. Raleigh, NC: North Carolina Language and Life Project.

Wolfram, W., & Schilling, N. (2016). *American English: Dialects and variation* (3rd ed.). Hoboken, NJ: John Wiley & Sons.

Part 2

Linguists' Perspectives

Principles to Navigate the Challenges of Teaching English Language Variation

A Guide for Nonlinguists

Mike Metz, University of Missouri, Missouri

The field of linguistics is daunting. The content of linguistics covers an impressive range: from the study of sound patterns in Bantu languages, to explorations of the distinction between the modal adverbs *possibly* and *conceivably* in British English. Even within the narrower field of English language variation, the abundance of technical language—e.g., *syllable-initial consonant deletion, cluster reduction*—can leave an adept English teacher feeling lost. When I began studying linguistics, I was overwhelmed.

Fortunately, for teachers who want to teach how language works in the world from a linguistic perspective, a doctoral degree in the field is not necessary. As the chapters in Part 1 of this book make clear, many teachers are weaving linguistic knowledge into their teaching without needing to delve into the levels of nuance that linguists find fascinating. In this chapter, I provide five key principles for thinking about linguistic variation in ways that foster inquiry and encourage teachers to learn gradually alongside, and from, their students.

We teachers can't possibly know all there is to know about the language varieties that our students bring into the classroom, but we can draw students' attention to the interesting linguistic differences we observe. We can model a stance for our students that views those differences as puzzles to explore rather than problems to fix. And we can give them resources, tools, and time to explore the differences in language all around us. When we open language use as a site of inquiry, as opposed to a set of rules to be mastered, students become engaged in language-learning. And we, their teachers, get to learn with them.

As a teacher educator, I know that teaching is more than developing a set of lesson plans or following a how-to manual. Teaching is about making imperfect decisions in complex situations. It is about dealing with new and novel contingencies day after day and figuring out how to adapt one's expertise to fit classrooms of consistently unique students. In my own fifteen years of classroom teaching, what I found most valuable to my classroom practice were guiding principles that helped me make effective choices in the moment (e.g., when a student asked a question I had never thought of, or presented an example I'd never considered). The five principles below are intended to help guide teachers' decision-making as they navigate the challenges of teaching English language variation.

Principle 1: Adopt Description over Prescription

English teachers have earned the unfortunate reputation as guardians of the language. Some of us take this role to heart, eagerly hunting for perceived errors in our students' (and even our friends' and family's) language use. This tendency comes from a belief that there is one right way to use language and that our job as English teachers is to teach others to use that version of English. Telling people how they *should* use language is *prescription*.

Traditional grammar books are based on a prescriptive ideology, meaning they start with the assumption that there is a single English grammar based on a particular variety of English. (For a nice history of grammar instruction in U.S. schools, see Kolln & Hancock, 2005). The goal of prescriptive grammar books is to help students adopt this one version of English, without consideration of the wide range of English grammars operating in the world around us.

As the other authors in this volume clarify, from a linguistic perspective, there is no one right way to use language. All dialects and varieties of English are linguistically equal. Thus, prescriptive approaches are more about social conformity than about linguistic *correctness*.

If we strive for linguistic accuracy, we've got to stop calling certain language uses correct and other language uses incorrect. Instead, we should *describe* the way people use language, striving to understand how different language uses convey nuances of meaning in important ways. The exploration of language use and the meaning of that language use makes up a *descriptive* approach to grammar. To deepen students' language knowledge, it is useful to adopt a *descriptive*, rather than *prescriptive*, approach.

An example helps to clarify. A common refrain from students in schools I've worked in is "I didn't do nothing." My fellow English teachers cringe and point out the double negative. Most say that a double negative is incorrect or even illogical. They will say, "If you *didn't* do *nothing*, then that means that you *did* do *something!*" These teachers apply a form of mathematical logic to language, arguing, "In math, two negatives make a positive." While it is true that a negative number multiplied by a negative number yields a positive number, that has nothing to do with the way language works. No one hearing "I didn't do nothing" misinterprets the meaning. Any pretend confusion is a power play intended to discredit the student, and not really about understanding.

If, instead of prescribing single negatives, we seek to describe the use of double negatives, we find that double negatives are often used as an *intensifier*. Likewise, in math, a negative number *added* to a negative number yields a *more negative* number. By describing how double negatives *are* used, instead of simply prescribing how negatives *should* be used, we get to teach students the term *intensifier*. We also validate students' language and help them understand that there are many correct ways to speak and write. At the same time, we need to teach students that double negatives are socially stigmatized and that people may make discriminatory judgments about them if they use double negatives (a point I discuss more in Principle #4). Even so, this kind of discussion is much more accurate than telling students, falsely, that double negatives are incorrect.

Working to describe how language actually works makes grammar and language study much more interesting for students—and also for teachers. This effort to describe involves exploration and discovery. It positions students as experts in their own language use, as valuable contributors to classroom language-learning. Their perspectives move language-teaching beyond traditional rule memorization and error correction into exciting and generative classroom learning activities.

Principle 2: Take a Repertoire Approach

Language is infinite. There is no limit to its use. To take advantage of this linguistic flexibility, the more language tools that students possess, the better. Why, then, would we teach students about only a small sliver of the linguistic possibilities available to them?

When linguists talk about the structures of language, they often distinguish *languages*, *dialects*, and *registers* from one another. (These are contested terms with fuzzy borders, but they can be useful to think about.) Different *languages* tend to be unintelligible to different users; a Mandarin speaker will not understand Spanish. Different *dialects* within a single language are usually mutually understood, although there may be different grammatical structures, and words may carry different meanings or connotations. The dialect labeled African American English uses grammatical forms not found in the dialect labeled Standardized English and vice versa.[1] Different *registers* within a dialect tend to follow the same grammatical rules but often draw on different vocabulary. Levels of formality are considered registers, as are the linguistic forms associated with certain jobs—legalese or teacherese, for instance.

Few people would argue with the goal of helping students understand and produce as many of these linguistic forms as possible. Knowing multiple languages, several dialects in each language, and a range of registers within each dialect gives a person extreme linguistic flexibility and power.

And yet schools traditionally focus on one tiny sliver of this linguistic landscape. They focus on one language (English), one dialect within that language (Standardized English), and one register within that dialect (formal, academic English). Formal Standardized English is the only language variety that is taught in most schools. If we can agree that more language knowledge is better, then shouldn't we expand what varieties of language are taught?

Taking a repertoire approach means valuing all language and helping students incorporate as much language as possible into their linguistic toolkits. When we seek to expand students' linguistic repertoires, a descriptive approach makes sense. All the language that students bring into the classroom becomes a resource for expanding their collective language knowledge. Instead of *prescribing* a limited set of linguistic forms, we *describe* the expanse of linguistic forms we encounter, tapping into students' curiosity about language.

Principle 3: Embrace an Inquiry Stance toward Language

I'm a city kid. Throughout my life I have acquired and am familiar with a wide range of urban-affiliated dialects and registers. When I recently moved to mid-Missouri, I encountered Southern-influenced, rural, and mid-American dialect features that were new to me. One that particularly stuck out was when students from Southern states said, "I might could do that."

A prescriptive approach requires correcting the student and telling them "might could" is wrong. It is possible to say "I might do that," or "I could do that," but you can't put "might" and "could" together. You've got to pick one.

---

1 I use the term *Standardized English* rather than *Standard English* to emphasize that standardization is a process enacted on language rather than an inherent property of a particular dialect of English.

Instead, a descriptive approach leads to an inquiry stance. Instead of correcting the student, inquiry leads one to wonder how "might could" is being used and what, precisely, it means, which then leads to a greater understanding of language. This exploration starts by drawing students' attention to this use of "might could" and noting that it is a *marked* feature for me, meaning that the particular use stands out in some way that makes some listeners aware of the language. Using the term *marked*, as opposed to *incorrect* or *inappropriate*, removes the value judgment and simply signals that this is an unfamiliar or notable use of language. I also note that it is marked *for me*, because markedness is dependent on the listener and context. What sticks out as unusual to one person in one context may go completely unnoticed to another person or in another context.

We then discuss if the feature is marked for anyone else, and perhaps discover where this use of language is common and where it is uncommon. From there we can explore what the language use means to different students and consider in what contexts it is or isn't used, looking for patterns in usage. This classroom-based exploration can be followed by broader research into the particular language feature—e.g., sending a small group of students to investigate the feature and to report back their findings.

There is a wealth of useful resources for learning about the many features of American Englishes. I recommend the online resources attached to Wolfram and Schilling's *American English: Dialects and Variation* (3rd ed., 2016).[2] According to Wolfram and Schilling (and a range of other sources), the previous example of "might could" is an example of a double modal—words that express a degree of probability or obligation such as *should, could, might, can, must, shall*, etc. In Standardized English, single modals are used with another verb (e.g., "I *should* stay after school"). In many Southern varieties of English, modals can be used in pairs (e.g., "I *might should* stay after school"). In contrast to the double negative, which is an intensifier, the double modal is a *softener*. In this case it softens the possibility of an event or action. A range of certainty from more certain to less certain might be: "I *definitely should* stay after school."; "I *should* stay after school."; "I *might should* stay after school." While the first two examples in this range follow the commonly accepted rules of Standardized English—a modal adverb combined with a modal verb, and a single modal verb, respectively—the third example, with the double modal verbs (*might* and *should*), is marked by some listeners as unusual. An important point here is that double modal verbs follow clear grammatical patterns and serve a useful and clear purpose, allowing an additional degree of gradation in this sequence.

By embracing an inquiry approach to unfamiliar language forms, those forms become opportunities to learn rather than instances of correction. In this case, students might actually be motivated to learn what modal verbs are. In a traditional classroom, students who use such language forms might be corrected, shamed, or stigmatized; in a classroom that embraces an inquiry stance, students who use such language forms contribute new knowledge to the classroom learning community. The more linguistic diversity that exists in a classroom, the greater the opportunities for everyone to learn. Involving students in this type of language investigation helps build their understanding of how language works and takes the pressure off teachers to be the definitive holders of all language knowledge.

2 See www.americanenglishwiley.com/appendix.html

Principle 4: Talk Explicitly about Language, Identity, Power, and Prejudice

While valuing all forms of language is the linguistically and pedagogically correct thing to do, we can't pretend that students won't be judged by their ability to demonstrate proficiency in Standardized English. While most forms of discrimination are frowned upon in our society, linguistic discrimination remains an accepted, even promoted, form of prejudice. Comments that tie linguistic forms to speaker characteristics—"She sounds like a criminal" or "He talks like he was raised in a barn"—are accepted forms of stereotyping.

Teachers have a choice about how they approach this linguistic discrimination. Many accommodate the prejudice. We hear this accommodation in phrases like, "You can't talk that way at a job interview." In fact, on a prominent website for job seekers there is a page dedicated to "Sloppy Speech Habits" (Diresta, n.d.). A tip on the page suggests, "The interviewer may question your education when you use incorrect grammar or slang." The examples provided are all language features found in Southern or African American English. Phrased more explicitly the page is saying, "When you use features of Southern or African American English, the interviewer is likely to discriminate against you." And this is considered perfectly acceptable by many teachers. Rather than teaching interviewers to check their linguistic prejudice, we routinely teach students to accommodate that prejudice.

The linguistic prejudice found in American society exists around the world. Rosina Lippi-Green (2012) describes this phenomenon succinctly calling it "The Principle of Linguistic Subordination." As she explains, the speech of a socially subordinate group will be interpreted as linguistically inadequate by comparison with that of the socially dominant group. In other words, there is nothing inherently better or worse about any particular language variety; it is the association of the language with powerful or stigmatized social groups that creates a linguistic hierarchy. In the U.S., the language features associated with ethnic or racial minorities and with people of lower social classes are stigmatized. This stigmatization isn't caused by the language itself but by the association between these groups and their language. This is linguistic prejudice. And it is perpetuated in schools every day through the teaching of some language forms as "correct" or "proper" in contrast with other equally legitimate forms that are branded "incorrect" or "improper."

No single English teacher can undo the principle of linguistic subordination, nor can any English teacher undo the impact of societal beliefs about language use on their students. Thus, it would be an injustice to send students out into the world believing that all language varieties are *socially* equal. At the same time, we cannot ignore the injustice of current language attitudes and the negative impact they have on already stigmatized social groups. So, what do we do?

We teach students about language and power.

We can teach students that all language varieties are *linguistically* equal *and* that they exist in a *social* hierarchy. We can talk explicitly with students about the principle of linguistic subordination and explore how social prejudice leads to language prejudice. We can use a descriptive approach to show them the grammatical patterns of all language *and* make them aware that certain features carry loaded social meanings. We can talk explicitly about the connections between language and identity, including the role of race and class.

As students learn more about language as a tool for social identity and social power, they gain the ability to critique the way narrow prescriptive views of language perpetuate linguistic and social prejudice. At the same time, students gain the ability to make informed choices about how they use language for a range of purposes in varying social contexts.

Traditional approaches to teaching Standardized English in school focus on a simple view of "appropriate" language without questioning who establishes the norms for what is appropriate. By learning *more* about language, not less, and by exploring the dynamics of power and identity alongside explorations of linguistic features and forms, language study becomes a fascinating topic integrated into considerations of society at large.

Principle 5: Teach Students to Hear Language Differently

Much traditional language instruction focuses on the *production* of language. Teachers spend a great deal of time helping students speak and write according to the rules of Standardized English. Here, too, a descriptive approach leads to a shift in perspective. Rather than focusing on the production of language, a descriptive approach trains students (and teachers) to *receive* and *interpret* language differently.

Many English teachers have become skilled at finding and correcting "errors." They hear language through a prescriptive filter. Often, they create students who become adept at finding and correcting "errors." The traditional English classroom thus becomes a place where language is *produced* according to prescriptive norms and also where students are taught to *receive* language according to prescriptive norms.

In contrast, a descriptive approach to language, and the broader understanding of language that comes with it, helps students receive and interpret language differently. Once students have an understanding of the social implications of language use, they can become aware of how they assign social meaning to different types of language they *hear* and *read*. Teachers can help students question the assumptions they use to ascribe identity traits to language users.

I often use audio clips from movies to drive this point home. I play a short clip of a character speaking and then ask students to describe the character. They provide rich descriptions of these characters from very short sound bites. They quickly identify characteristics like gender, age, and race/ethnicity. And they also include personality traits such as kindness, intelligence, morality, etc. We then unpack how students came to these understandings of the characters. What surfaces are a range of societal stereotypes about which kinds of people use which kinds of language.

Our discussions explore how filmmakers use these available stereotypes as shortcuts for character development. We identify tropes like the deep-voiced effeminate British accent for the evil genius in American movies. Or the use of Middle Eastern or Indian accents to signal "foreignness" or "otherness." We examine what a Southern accent signals in a female movie character (innocence, sweetness) versus in a male character (ignorance, lack of intelligence). By making the linguistic stereotypes visible to students, we begin exploring the processes by which these stereotypes are created and perpetuated. We also begin a process of naming and describing linguistic features.

It is a small step to transfer these ideas to literature. Authors use many of the same shortcuts for characterization that are found in film. We often start by exploring the language of characters in young adult literature and move to more canonical literature. As students begin to perceive language differently, they are prepared to dive more deeply into the descriptive study of language.

Conclusion

As I've studied teachers trying out these ideas with their students, I've documented pitfalls and successes (Metz, 2018a, 2018b). The investment students demonstrate in learning about language is both intimidating and exciting. There is more to learn than one teacher (or linguist) can ever know. At the same time, I know that whenever I talk with teachers or students about English language variation I have a solid foundation, based in linguistic facts, to work from. By drawing on these five principles in any unique situation, I know I'm making thoughtful, intentional choices that help grow student knowledge about language. And growing students' language knowledge and students' linguistic repertoires is the ultimate goal.

References

Diresta, D. (n.d.). Six sloppy speech habits. Retrieved from www.monster.com/career-advice/article/six-sloppy-speech-habits

Kolln, M., & Hancock, C. (2005). The story of English grammar in United States schools. *English Teaching: Practice and Critique*, 4(3), 11–31.

Lippi-Green, R. (2012). *English with an accent: Language, ideology and discrimination in the United States* (2nd ed.). London and New York, NY: Routledge.

Metz, M. (2018a). Challenges of confronting dominant language ideologies in the high school English classroom. *Research in the Teaching of English*, *52*(4), 455–477.

—— (2018b). Pedagogical content knowledge for teaching Critical Language Awareness: The importance of valuing student knowledge. *Urban Education*, 1–29. https://doi.org/10.1177/0042085918756714

Wolfram, W., & Schilling, N. (2016). *American English: Dialects and variation* (3rd ed.). Hoboken, NJ: Wiley-Blackwell.

Chapter 11

Teaching Linguistic Diversity as the Rule Rather than the Exception

Anne Lobeck, Western Washington University, Washington

Introduction

Wolfram and Schilling (2016) note that disparaging someone's language (for example, as "bad grammar" or "broken English") is socially acceptable in public discourse. Language is central to our identity, yet it is commonplace in U.S. society to devalue language varieties not considered "Standard American English" (SAE), and, in so doing, to devalue the speakers of those varieties.

A similar institutional devaluing of language difference emerges in schools and universities. Linguistic diversity often goes unrecognized in institutional diversity policies and statistics, which are typically based on students' race, ethnicity, ability, gender, etc., but not language. There is little institutional effort to celebrate students' home languages, or understand how their linguistic autobiographies contribute to identity, learning, and school experience. Students are expected to master the language of the mainstream (SAE), though much research has shown that SAE is not an actual dialect of English but rather a socially constructed variety considered acceptable by those in authority (often White, middle-class speakers, a demographic to which not all students belong). This creates inequity, placing the burden of language shift or code-switching on some students but not others. Institutional adherence to what Lippi-Green (2012) calls "Standard English Ideology" is also at odds with curricula that otherwise celebrate equity, social justice, and multiculturalism, directed at preparing students to participate in a global society.

Nevertheless, linguistic diversity is here to stay, and it is the rule rather than the exception. Students bring with them to school a vast range of different voices and modes of expression, and, through the Internet and social media, diverse voices are accessible now in ways never before possible. In the classroom, this diversity is a strength rather than a liability, providing teachers with the opportunity to develop and support a more inclusive notion of "the language of school."

In what follows, I describe a 400-level college English class I regularly teach for pre-service teachers at a regional university in the Pacific Northwest. The goals of this course are to provide students with the tools to analyze the diverse and varied structure of language that they encounter on a daily basis and to empower them to recognize, question, and challenge, in productive ways, their own and others' language attitudes and ideologies that aim to suppress this diversity. The examples and methodology I describe here target my particular student audience but could be tailored to classrooms of different levels and demographics.

Discovering Grammar

I begin class by asking students to reflect on what they have learned about grammar in school. Students typically define *grammar* as a list of dos and don'ts and offer up an extensive list of prescriptions (e.g., "Avoid passive voice"; "Use *may* rather than *can* when asking permission") and language pet peeves (e.g., interchanging *they're/there/their*; saying *Where's it at?* rather than *Where is it?*). We discuss how these prescriptions and pet peeves are arbitrary; they are not consistent among students nor among the teachers who correct them. We also discuss how such arbitrary rules are learned rather than acquired as part of natural language; as a result, prescriptive rules don't always conform to what we actually say. This leads to a discussion of language authority: *Where did these prescriptive rules come from anyway? Who are the language authorities in your life? Are you a language authority, too? Have you ever corrected someone's grammar?* Students explore their own notions of authority, based on their own experiences and perspectives. They find that what is considered grammatically correct may vary from person to person and that SAE is socially defined in terms of power and prestige rather than linguistic features.

I ask them, as a group, to come up with a definition of prescriptive grammar. After some discussion, students typically generate a definition like this:

Prescriptive grammar: grammatical rules of how you should speak and write according to some authority.

We then move on to descriptive grammar. The difference between prescriptive and descriptive grammar can be introduced in a variety of ways, but I find that analyzing a nonsense sentence works well and provides fertile ground for discussing a range of aspects of grammatical structure:

The flonkish warziles blorked six yerkons.[1]

I ask students to come to the board and label, using colored markers, the parts of speech of each word. Students label *warziles* as a noun because it follows the adjective *flonkish* and is preceded by a determiner *the*. I point out that students are relying on syntactic evidence to identify parts of speech, or syntactic categories.[2] They also note that the noun *warziles* ends in the plural suffix *-s* like other nouns; I explain that they are also using morphological evidence to identify categories.[3] Students continue to label the categories of the words in this sentence relying on their intuitive knowledge of syntax and morphology.

Students quickly grasp not only that they have quite a bit of complex knowledge of grammatical structure but also that the meaning-based definitions of parts of speech, such as "a noun is a person, place, or thing" and "a verb is an action," are

1 I use this sentence because the basic word order is subject–verb–object (which is typical of English clauses), and because each noun phrase has a different syntactic structure.
2 Syntactic evidence concerns the relationships between words, between phrases, and between clauses (e.g., how words, phrases, and clauses are ordered; how they modify or complete one another; and how they can be grouped together into larger units such as sentences).
3 Morphological evidence concerns word formation (e.g., how words combine with one another to form new words; how prefixes and suffixes attach to words and roots to change their meaning, part of speech, or communicate grammatical information such as past tense or plurality).

not particularly useful here; we don't know what a *warzile* is nor what it means to be *blorked*.

We divide this sentence up into larger units, or phrases, and discuss how we know, for example, that *the flonkish warziles* is a phrase—a noun phrase, to be more exact. Students know that *warziles* is the head noun here, another illustration of their intuitive knowledge of grammar (see also Keyser, this volume, pp. 39–46).

There are many other ways to explore this sentence. The fact that different groups of words in the sentence can be rearranged in various ways provides evidence for phrases and syntactic movement rules, all of which are part of our intuitive knowledge of language. For example, the nonsense sentence, which is in active voice, can easily be made passive by moving the object to the subject position and the subject to the end:

Six yerkons were blorked by the flonkish warziles.

Words can also change category, depending on syntactic position:

The yerkon warziles them.

Here, *warziles* is a verb, and the *-s* suffix (pronounced in some dialects of English and not in others) no longer indicates plural but rather third person, singular, present tense. Although students may not have the terminology to explain the difference between *warziles* the noun and *warziles* the verb, they nevertheless "know" this difference.

Based on our explorations we, as a group, develop a definition of descriptive grammar:

Descriptive grammar: the system of unconscious grammatical rules that allows us to produce and understand language.

Why use a nonsense sentence to introduce these concepts? (Lewis Carroll's *Jabberwocky* offers great examples to choose from!) Students come to my classes well aware of prescriptive grammar but unfamiliar with their linguistic intuitions or descriptive grammar. A nonsense sentence highlights their intuitive knowledge of language because they cannot rely on meaning-based definitions to identify categories or parts of speech. Students are surprised and rather delighted that they actually "know" a lot more about grammar than they thought and that learning about grammar isn't about arbitrary rules they must memorize. They also become aware that their knowledge of grammar in this sense is no better or worse than anyone else's, which lays the foundation for examining language attitudes and the social criteria we base them on. This approach is especially effective in the high school classroom, where students have typically had no exposure to linguistics, nor to evidence of their own intuitive knowledge of language, nor to the idea that language itself is an object of study.

This brief discussion illustrates the methodology I use to introduce grammatical concepts throughout the course. Students explore their own language to discover the patterns and organizing principles of grammar that they already (unconsciously) know. We start at the word level (i.e., syntactic category: noun, verb, etc.), move from categories to phrases, and then discuss how phrases function in the clause as subjects, predicates, complements, and modifiers. We progress from the structure of basic independent clauses to subordination and coordination, all the while using the inquiry-based tools of grammatical analysis.

An inquiry-based approach situates both instructor and students as fellow language investigators, subverting the more traditional paradigm of teacher as language authority and students as passive receivers of information. Since all students, regardless of their linguistic background, have linguistic intuitions, they can all participate and engage in the discussion, even those who consider themselves "bad at grammar." Students develop a metalanguage to describe what they learn/know, and approach language analysis as puzzle-solving rather than rule memorization.

Exploring Language Variation and Language Attitudes

The inquiry-based approach also provides a natural gateway to discussing language variation and ideology. As we progress through our exploration of the structure of English, we compare and contrast different forms of English around the country and around the globe. We discuss how some forms are stigmatized but others are not, and why. There are many different ways that language variation (and language change, which I leave aside here) come up in my class, and I illustrate this below with some examples from our analysis of the English verb system.

In discussing the morphological forms of English verbs (infinitive, past tense, present tense, present participle, past participle), we immediately encounter variation: not all of us agree on past tense and past participle forms (Table 11.1).

Table 11.1 Past tense and past participle forms

Past tense	Past participle
walked	(have) walked
sang/sung	(have) sang/sung
drank/drunk	(have) drank/drunk

But in examining these and other data, patterns emerge. For some speakers, the past tense and past participle of *sing* and *drink* have different forms (*I sang it/I have sung it; I drank it/I have drunk it*), but other speakers may use the past participle form also for the past tense (*I drunk it/I have drunk it*). Still others might use the past tense form for the past participle *(I drank it/I have drank it).*

These merged patterns, where the past tense and past participle have the same form, follow the model of regular verbs such as such as *walk* or *like*, which form past tense and past participle with the suffix *-ed* (*I walked/liked; I have walked/have liked*).

Though many of my students use or are at least familiar with the merged patterns, they are aware that certain patterns are considered nonstandard or prescriptively incorrect. But they are also aware that other examples, such as *I seen it* or *I done it*, are even more highly stigmatized, even though these forms follow the same rules as less stigmatized ones. We discuss why: in our region, *I seen it* and *I done it* (but less so *I drunk it* or *I sung it*) are associated with rural, uneducated speakers of lower socioeconomic class. The stigma against these forms is thus based on social rather than linguistic criteria.

There are endless ways to weave language variation and language attitudes into the study of the English verb system. For example, we discuss these sentences:

I lost my keys. Have you seen them anywhere? (British English *have*)
I lost my keys. Did you see them anywhere?
I BIN started my paper Ma, so quit asking me. (African American English: stressed *BIN*)
I started my paper a long time ago Ma, so quit asking me.
She was a-building a house. (Appalachian English: *a-prefixing*)
She was building a house.

We discuss how many American English speakers typically attach prestige to British English but stigmatize African American English, and how speakers in our region consider Appalachian English "quaint" or "hillbilly." Exploring the tense and aspectual systems of a range of varieties of English allows students to see for themselves that all varieties are equally expressive, complex, and rule-governed, yet we attach different social values to each, values that reflect our attitudes about speakers.

Analyzing Prescriptive Rules

Though my course focuses primarily on guiding students to discover tools of descriptive linguistic analysis, prescriptive rules also provide fertile ground for investigating grammatical structure. Analyzing prescriptive rules, many of which are writing conventions, also provides pre-service teachers with a more informed way to teach about these rules in their own classrooms. I illustrate here with the prohibition "Avoid sentence fragments." I introduce this topic after students are familiar with basic clause structure. Our working definition is given below:

A clause is a syntactic unit of a noun phrase + a verb phrase (NP + VP).

I open the discussion by asking students if they are familiar with the prohibition against sentence fragments, and they typically are, in particular from their writing classes. I then ask them to define *fragment*. Their responses usually include "a fragment is an incomplete thought/sentence" or "a fragment lacks a subject or a verb," among others. I then write the following phrase on the board:

the birds flying over the lake

Students immediately recognize that this phrase is a sentence fragment, but I then ask them to explain why, and to analyze the syntax of the phrase; does it include an NP and a VP? If so, then it is a clause, right?

[the birds]   [flying over the lake] = [the birds flying over the lake]
NP   VP   CL

They see that this phrase also includes both a subject and a verb and is arguably a "complete thought" as well; it can be a perfectly natural answer to a question, providing (only) the "new" or relevant information (rather than including/restating old information).

Q What do you see out there?
A The birds flying over the lake.

Q What did you see out there?
A *I see* the birds flying over the lake.

Students, therefore, not only become aware of their unexplanatory definition of "fragment" but also of the difference between written and oral discourse, where in the latter fragments are the norm.

We then discuss how we can repair this fragment by adding *are*, or, more specifically, by making the participial clause into a tensed, *independent* clause (a clause not contained inside a larger clause or phrase).

[The birds *are* flying over the lake]
CL

We can also repair the fragment by embedding it within a larger clause

[I saw [the birds flying over the lake]]
CL   CL

Here, *the birds flying over the lake* is a subordinate clause (a clause contained inside a larger clause or phrase, also called a dependent clause).[4]

We can now develop a more precise syntactic definition of *fragment*:

A fragment is anything that is not an independent clause.

We then investigate how writers use fragments as a rhetorical device. Consider, for example, the following excerpt from *Mockingjay*, by Susan Collins (2014):

Haymitch doesn't protest when I walk out. <u>Down the hall</u>. <u>Through the bee-hive of compartments</u>. <u>Find a warm pipe to hide behind in a laundry room</u>. It takes a long time before I get to the bottom of why I'm so upset. When I do, it's almost too mortifying to admit. All those months of taking it for granted that Peeta thought I was wonderful are over. Finally, he can see me for who I really am. <u>Violent</u>. <u>Distrustful</u>. <u>Manipulative</u>. <u>Deadly</u>.

(p. 232)

I ask students to analyze the syntax of the underlined fragments in this excerpt (prepositional phrases, verb phrase, and adjective phrases) and to consider their stylistic effect. What happens if we repair the fragments? How does that change the

---

4 Teachers will want to keep in mind that labels such as *subordinate clause* can be used differently in different grammar books. Some grammars, for example, may use the terms *subordinate clause* and *dependent clause* interchangeably; others may define a *subordinate clause* as only one type of dependent clause that begins with a subordinating conjunction (such as *because*). These differences in terminology should not be a problem as long as the teacher uses consistent labels and definitions with students.

meaning and tone of the text? Are fragments really something to be avoided, or are they stylistically appropriate here?

Exploring prescriptive rules deepens students' awareness of often arbitrary rules they have perhaps accepted but not always understood. Most of my students know they should avoid passive voice in their writing, but not all of them know what it is; most are aware of prohibitions such as "don't start a sentence with *because*," though again they have no idea why phrases beginning with this particular word should be avoided. Perhaps ironically, analyzing prescriptive rules expands students' knowledge of descriptive grammar and, at the same time, empowers them to make their own informed stylistic choices in their own writing and speech.

Language Ideologies and Discrimination

To supplement our class discussions, students write weekly discussion board posts on a series of readings that address language variation and language ideology in K-12 education. Though not all of my students are pre-service teachers, they find these readings relevant and valuable, and their online discussions are lively and candid. Topics students read about and discuss include (see full citations in the References):

*   The origins of prescriptive grammar: Where did prescriptive rules come from, and who developed them and why? (Millward, 1996)
*   Standard English: How is it defined and by whom? Who speaks it and who doesn't? (Students collect and analyze different definitions.)
*   The history of grammar teaching in the U.S.: How does historical knowledge of the controversies inform how and why to teach about language? (Denham, 2014)
*   What are the arguments, pro and con, for teaching code-switching and bidialectalism in schools? (O'Neil, 1972; Wheeler & Swords, 2004)
*   What positive tools can we use to challenge the discrimination in education that stems from Standard English Ideology? (Curzan, 2002; Sweetland, 2010)

These topics build on each other and provide pre-service teachers (and other students as well) with valuable knowledge and tools to support linguistic diversity in the classroom and beyond. Through these discussions, future teachers feel empowered to embrace diversity they will inevitably encounter, to question and even challenge linguistic discrimination, and to promote change.

Grammar in the Wild

The capstone experience for the course is a small-group project in which students analyze the grammatical structure of a text in a modality or genre of their choice. I choose this project over a research paper because I want to encourage students to explore diverse texts and apply the tools of grammatical analysis they have learned in class. I also ask them to reflect on how syntax influences the style, message, and voice.

Students analyze the language of journalistic writing, contemporary fiction, Twitter feeds, slam poetry, signage, text messages, songs, videos, memes, among other genres. They find that we all use language in unceasingly creative ways, breaking rules (both descriptive and prescriptive) for effect. Some topics they have investigated include linguistic discrimination reflected in Super Bowl ads; emojis as discourse particles; the syntax of swear words; code-switching in literature and music; the speech of drag queens; the grammar of apologies; the syntax of internet trolls. Students find that they can use the tools they have learned to analyze language in any representation and that in actual practice real language is diverse, creative, and expressive often because it does not conform to ideals.

Conclusion

Linguistic inquiry provides us with the tools to understand, question, and make informed choices about how and what we teach about language, and aligns with a more inclusive curriculum that embraces diversity of all kinds, including language. This approach to language instruction assumes an interactive, discussion-based pedagogical model appropriate for college undergraduates, some of whom have had exposure to linguistics, are familiar with prescriptive grammar, and are able to read about, reflect on, and even theorize about language ideologies and discrimination. Nevertheless, the basic approach I advocate here can be adapted to other educational levels. All students have linguistic intuitions, and all can participate in exploring those intuitions to gain some level of expertise in discovering descriptive grammatical rules. Students of all levels also benefit from learning about language change and variation, perhaps woven into explorations of what they are reading and writing about, in different genres and from different historical periods. Language ideologies can be investigated in various ways as well, by exploring different accents and speech patterns students are familiar with, and the attitudes about speakers associated with them. Most important, however, is to make language an object of inquiry.

References

Collins, S. (2014). *Mockingjay*. New York, NY: Scholastic Press.

Curzan, A. (2002). Teaching the politics of standard English. *Journal of English Linguistics, 30*(4), 339–352.

Denham, K. E. (2014). History of the study of grammar: and how historical knowledge of the controversies informs how and why to teach about language in the K12 classroom. White paper. Western Washington University.

Lippi-Green, R. (2012). *English with an accent* (2nd ed.). London and New York, NY: Routledge.

Lobeck, A., & Denham, K. (2014). *Navigating English grammar*. Malden, MA: Wiley-Blackwell.

Millward, C. M. (1996). *A biography of the English language* (2nd ed.). Fort Worth, TX: Holt Rinehart & Winston, Inc.

O'Neil, W. (1972). The politics of bidialectalism. In L. Kampf and P. Lauter (Eds). *The politics of literature: Dissenting essays on the teaching of English* (pp. 245–258). New York, NY: Pantheon.

Sweetland, J. (2010). Fostering teacher change: Effective professional development for sociolinguistic diversity. In K. Denham and A. Lobeck (Eds). *Linguistics at school: Language awareness in primary and secondary education* (pp. 161–174). Cambridge: Cambridge University Press.

Wheeler, R. S., & Swords, R. (2004). Codeswitching: Tools of language and culture transform the dialectally diverse classroom. *Language Arts, 81*(6), 470–480.

Wolfram, W., & N. Schilling. (2016). *American English: dialects and variation* (3rd ed.). Malden, MA: Blackwell Publishing.

Chapter 12

DARE(ing) Language Ideologies

Exploring Linguistic Diversity through Audio Data and Literature in Secondary Language Arts Courses

Kelly D. Abrams, University of Wisconsin-Madison, Wisconsin, and Trini Stickle, Western Kentucky University, Kentucky

Oral and written texts are shaped not only by the specific language contained within them but also by the ideological environments from which they emerge. In secondary language arts classrooms, these texts are often discussed without considering the language ideologies—or the social conceptualizations about language itself (e.g., views on correct usage, the stereotypes and biases arising from variations of standard use)—within and around them. In this chapter, we hope to demonstrate how language ideologies may be broached within secondary literature courses. Specifically, we present activities using excerpts from commonly taught American literature that attempt to recreate regional speech in tandem with audio clips of authentic regional speakers from the *Dictionary of American Regional English* archives (henceforth *DARE*). We show how the *DARE* interviews, publicly and easily accessible, can enhance literary study.[1] Using both types of "texts" allows for discussions, writing prompts, and research activities that raise students' awareness of language ideologies from which the literature emerged. Additionally, it offers a space for perceptions that may be part of the students' beliefs or the mainstream culture to be acknowledged and explored. Students then have the opportunity to see how ideologies may influence both their interpretations of literature and their views of individuals who share dialect features of literary characters. As students are guided through the linguistic choices ascribed to characters and are helped to see writers' choices not as neutral artifacts but as ideologically biased representations, the study of literature is both "enlightened and enlivened" (Simpson, 2003, p. xii).[2]

Toward that goal, we focus on works in which character speech is represented through *eye dialect* or *dialect respellings*. *Eye dialect* is the structuring of words, phrases, and sentences in an attempt to represent the linguistic attributes of a particular character, due to regional differences or nonstandard usages often correlated with education level, socioeconomic status, or race and ethnicity. A writer may choose only

---

1 The complete *DARE* interview archive may be accessed through the Fieldwork Recordings—Dictionary of American Regional English at https://uwdc.library.wisc.edu/collections/amerlangs/. Selective audio clips with corresponding lesson plans may also be found at www.discoveringdare.wordpress.com.

2 Ron Carter emphasizes the benefits of this approach to literature in the introduction to Paul Simpson's *Language, Ideology and Point of View*.

to recreate the pronunciation of a character's dialect through orthography: *dialect respelling*.[3] For example, the pronunciation of a character from a particular section of New York might be represented as "I'm drivin' on Toity-Toid Street" (*I'm driving on Thirty-Third Street*). A Southern character's pronunciation of the name "Bill" could be written to show divergence from the Standard English single vowel, a monophthong, to represent the use of two vowel sounds, a diphthong, through *dialect respelling* such as "Behill."

While some critics interpret *eye dialect* or *dialect respellings* as stylistic choices that help readers better understand characters or as the means to elicit humor, their use is not without controversy. Objectors such as Dennis Preston describe the negative effect of these literary tools: "[They] serve mainly to denigrate the speaker so represented by making him or her boorish, uneducated, rustic, gangsterish, and so on" (1985, p. 328). One reason for this criticism is the selective use of respellings among characters. This is particularly true when writers selectively use *eye dialect* to alter conventional spellings to represent sounds that all native speakers say, but they do so only for some characters. For instance, English speakers pronounce the verb "was" as "wuz"—whatever the speakers' dialect, socioeconomic status, or education levels. Writers who choose to respell "was" as "wuz" for some characters and not others are seen to overlay a level of linguistic difference, not present in actual speech, to indicate nonstandardness or less education. This practice can be reasonably interpreted as discriminatory. Such controversies make literature an accessible vehicle to introduce students to language ideologies that have political and moral significance in terms of stereotypes, biases, and prejudice. To engage in these explorations with students can be a risky endeavor, but the sociolinguistic evidence provides a powerful tool by which socially and emotionally charged topics can be discussed.

Our approach to language ideologies in secondary literature classes begins by providing students with linguistic terminology as they explore Standard English alongside other dialects. In particular, several lessons expose students to the different ways language may be affected by dialect. Simultaneously, these activities make the students aware of their own views of language use and users. These views include what is "acceptable" or "unacceptable" usage, ideas on who are the users of dialects (e.g., sex, age, geographic location, education level, socioeconomic class), and opinions about those users (e.g., friendly, rude). Linguists refer to this type of native speaker knowledge as "folk" linguistics. For example, one initial activity involves listening to and assessing the acceptability of the language used by speakers in a series of *DARE* audio clips that represent dialect variations across linguistic levels: lexical (word choice: *soda* vs. *pop*), phonetic (pronunciation: *Bill* vs. *Behill*), syntactic (grammar: *I go to the doctor anymore* vs. *I don't go to the doctor anymore*), and morphological (variation in word forms: *I did that* vs. *I done that*) (see Table 12.1). These terms are explicitly taught and reinforced throughout the initial assignments in order for students to have a concrete vocabulary to talk about the language characters use that is less reliant upon positive or negative social labels.

---

3 The term *eye dialect* is often reserved for changes in spelling and linguistic structure for reasons other than dialect representations in pronunciation; therefore, the term *dialect respelling* is the more precise term.

Table 12.1 Teaching levels of dialect from Discovering DARE: Familiar voices seen and heard, investigating "eye" dialects of American literature, student workbook

#	Audio	Sentence and/or audio link	Acceptable	Unacceptable	Okay, but I would NOT say	Explanation
Lexical						
1		There used to be mines, and then there was the soda plant down here.				
2		He said, "I got a poke full of good old candy to give you."				
3		There were somewhere close to two thousand people in this burg, if you can imagine.				
Phonetic						
4		The fish will come up against this leader, and then they'll follow that back and they get caught in this crib.				
5		You just had two bunks, didn't you? Or two cot beds.				
6		He didn't have a round pen; we had to rope them and hind foot them and throw them.				

Table 12.1 (Cont.)

#	Audio	Sentence and/or audio link	Acceptable	Unacceptable	Okay, but I would NOT say	Explanation
Syntactic						
7	🔊	I can't say as I know.				
8	🔊	They might could tell you where you get the whiskey.				
9	🔊	Most of the work anymore is done by power.				
Morphological						
10	🔊	The cane grow so late here.				
11	🔊	That's the only way you knowed where you was a-goin'.				
12	🔊	You didn't see nobody.				

Source: Stickle & Abrams, in progress.

Through preparatory activities and supplemental reading assignments,[4] students become more aware of the judgments we all make when hearing another person speak. They learn precise vocabulary words, enabling them to discuss linguistic aspects of dialects together as a community of novice researchers. While secondary students may find these new analytical approaches challenging, their skills strengthen with each exercise. By applying linguistic analyses to literary texts, they gain confidence in their abilities to critically evaluate and objectively present evidence in support of arguments, a skill transferable beyond the literature classroom.

To illustrate what this might look like in a classroom, we present several short literary excerpts in which students compare the written eye-dialect versions to recordings

4 For example, the chapter "Levels of dialect" (Wolfram & Schilling, 2016, pp. 114–146) and the entry for *dialect* at Encyclopedia Britannica (www.britannica.com/topic/dialect).

of authentic speakers, accessible as companion audio files in the *DARE* archive. First, students assess how print representations of talk contribute to their perception of the character(s)—specifically, how the written version of the "talk" contributes to their views of the characters' personal, physical, and social characteristics and, by extension, of those persons who share language features within society. For example, in Excerpt 1 below, the dialogue taken from Sarah Orne Jewett's short story "A Bit of Shore Life" allows students to experience and reflect on their perceptions of the characters whose speech represents a Maine dialect.[5]

Excerpt 1

[Note: Speakers are the two main characters: the narrator and a local fisherman]
  "Whose boy is he?" said I.
  "Why, Andrer's, up here to the fish-house. She's dead, and him and the boy get along together somehow or 'nother. They've both got something saved up, and Andrer's a clever fellow; took it very hard, the losing of his wife. I was telling of him the other day: 'Andrer,' says I, 'ye plenty o' smart, stirring women that would mend ye up, and cook for ye, and do well by ye.'—'No,' says he; 'I've hed my wife, and I've lost her.'—'Well, now,' says I, 'ye 've shown respect, and there's the boy a-growin' up, and if either of you was took sick, why, here ye be.'—'Yes,' says he, 'here I be, sure enough'; and he drawed a long breath, 's if he felt bad; so that's all I said."

                                                              (Jewett, 1988, p. 36)

Through small-group discussions, students discover differences across linguistic levels between the character's speech and Standard English, employing linguistic terminology in their analyses. These observations are charted along with the group members' perceptions and with possible teacher responses that engage the observations with sociolinguistic principles (see Table 12.2). Next, students listen to clips of talk from a *DARE* informant who shares demographic and dialect features with the story's fisherman.[6] Students are asked to evaluate the accuracy of the author's print representation and to comment on how their perceptions are shaped by the literary representation and, possibly, changed by actual speech data.

  Teachers may lead students through discussions of authentic speakers' versus literary characters' speech and the linguistic ideologies embedded in the representation of characters' use of language. They may complete additional linguistic feature charts based on sociolinguistic research of dialects.[7] We note that the classroom discussions could be more or less linguistically specific depending upon the course goals. Through these exercises, students begin to see and hear differences in the

---

5 "A Bit of Shore Life" was first published in the *Atlantic Monthly*, 44(262) (1879) followed by its inclusion in the 1879 short story collection *Old Friends and New*, Boston, MA: Houghton Mifflin Co. Depending upon the place of publication, the text of the short story may vary.
6 DARE ME 017. Complete interviews of *DARE* informants can be located using the state (e.g.,TN) and numeric code (e.g., 001, 035) at https://uwdc.library.wisc.edu/collections/amerlangs.
7 E.g., "Appendix: An Inventory of Distinguishing Dialect Features" (Wolfram & Schilling, 2016, pp. 367–390).

Table 12.2 Sample group activity chart with possible answers

Example from the text	Linguistic level (lexical, phonetic, syntactic, morphological)	Standard English/ Your dialect equivalent	Perception of speaker (examples, other answers possible)
stirring women	lexical	busy, active women (adj.)	a different part of the country; a local word; an older use
Possible teacher responses	How might we discover the meaning of older, archaic words? How could we research their meanings? What in a dictionary entry tells us the historical meaning? Segue to etymology.		
I've hed my wife	phonetic	"hed" instead of "had"	lower class, not educated a different part of the country where "a" in "cat" is said like an "e" in "head"
Possible teacher responses	Have you ever heard anyone say "hed" for this word, or do you, by chance, say this word like this? How do you say it when you say it fast or excited? Are there other ways to spell this word that would represent different pronunciations? Do this and other changes in spellings help the reader better understand the character? If so, how? If not, what effect do they have?		
there's the boy a-growin' up he drawed a long breath	morphological	There was the boy growing up He drew a long breath	a different part of the country; older form uneducated, lower socioeconomic status
Possible teacher responses	Can you think of any place you might have seen an "a-" before a verb? Hymns and older Christmas carols have this a- prefixing on verbs. So, it was an older way of adding a prefix to a verb. Why might a speaker be unaware of the irregular past tense forms of verbs like this one: draw > drew? Why might some speakers still use these irregular -ed forms? Children often make this mistake when they overgeneralize the -ed rule as do speakers of other languages learning English.		

representations and actual speech of individuals sharing demographic characteristics while recognizing linguistic ideologies embedded in and outside of the literature. After several such scaffolded exercises, students apply these analytic tools to the American literature they are reading that employs *eye dialect* or *dialect respelling*. They are also better equipped to contrast the linguistic ideologies in these works with those in works by authors who chose not to use these linguistic devices.

As students become skilled in discussing dialects and in excavating language ideologies present in both literature and society, they may apply these skills to more complex assignments. For instance, students may consider researching the discrete features of particular dialects or delineating the sociolinguistic perceptions of such dialects as revealed within the literature (e.g., through other characters or intra-textual commentary). They might explore societal views contemporary to the work, or presently within society, which may result in new approaches to research papers, essays, or even creative writing.

Here we illustrate a sample research prompt that compares the representation of persons from northern Florida who speak "cracker" dialect and the characters in Marjorie Kinnan Rawlings' short stories (see eResources). The term *cracker* is a label well established in English and American history and literature. While it began as a synonym for "a braggart" during Shakespeare's time, it became associated with the poor, White immigrants of Scots-Irish descent who helped settle the U.S. southeast—Alabama, Georgia, Florida—the people of Rawlings' stories. Presently, *cracker* can be a pejorative for White, poor, ignorant, often Southern persons with racist ideologies. In choosing this particular dialect, we tackle a challenging issue: the controversial evolution of a socially, emotionally, and racially charged term. While teaching this lesson will take appropriate framing and difficult conversations with students, we think it is important to understand and examine the power of words and the language ideologies they contain.

Prepared with linguistic terminology and their experiences from previous discussions, students are now able to review the sociolinguistic research on the language of these Floridians along with the social ideologies and stereotypes associated with them and the term *cracker*. As students analyze a series of Rawlings' excerpts (see Excerpt 2 below from the story "Gal Young Un"), they are reminded that the characters are created from the people who reside in north-central Florida, an area stymied by the many bodies of waters and swamps and isolated within the land hammock between the city life of Jacksonville to the north and the comforts of Tampa to the south. Rawlings' characters are poor, White farmers of the early twentieth century.

Excerpt 2

[Speaker is Matt, the female protagonist]
She reached out a large hand for the quail.

"I'd shore thank you for it. I'm a good shot on squirrel, an' turkeys when I git 'em roosted. Birds is hard without no dog to point 'em. I gits hungry fer quail ..."

Her voice trailed off as the hunters walked through the pines toward the road. She waved her hand in case they should turn around. They did not look back.

(Rawlings, 1994, p. 150)

Students then listen to actual speech data used by Floridians who live in the "cracker" dialect areas: DARE FL013, DARE FL018, DARE FL037. They are encouraged to implement their newly acquired vocabulary as they compare the levels of dialect presented in the Rawlings text with the dialect from the *DARE* northern Florida speakers. As students listen, they write out their individual observations, thoughtfully considering their implications. Next, the small groups are asked to transcribe one (or one part) of the audio clips. Doing so makes visible the spoken language, and the activity allows students to wrestle with how best to represent the audible dialect in print while discussing their observations. This makes the author's predicament become a shared experience: the small groups can now bring their observations together as a class. From the initial explorations and generation of ideas about this dialect to the frank but informed discussions of the social implications surrounding the label *cracker*, students continue to research the linguistic features of Floridians (a list of recommended resources is provided at the end of the lesson plan on the eResources site). Through candid class discussions and continued research, students witness how pejorative labels evolve. They have traced the use of *cracker* from its origin to perceptions built upon social and demographic characteristics. We expect this experience to transcend this single event to one that allows students a greater social understanding of stereotyping, bias, and prejudicial action. This lesson culminates with a paper comparing the literary representation of the dialect with the *DARE* audio data, and a linguistic description of Floridian dialects that considers the social implication of the language ideologies active within society. Through this and similar assignments that combine linguistic and literary research, students learn to effectively manage research, critical analyses, and argumentation. As students are learning how to engage empirical approaches to social topics, they are developing sophisticated ways of approaching emotionally charged social issues.

A final creative assignment capitalizes on the student's own language repertoire and language ideologies. Students are asked to explore their own language variations and to recreate a scene from a work of literature (or create an original scene) in which they become characters. Based on their own dialects, they must use *eye dialect* or *dialect respelling* to help create the characters. To prepare, they are prompted to reflect on the many different language variations they use, or even record themselves over multiple encounters to listen for such variation they may not even know exists. Such variation may be due to relationships (e.g., family, peers, teachers) or context (e.g., school, work, sports, hobbies, social media). They are also asked to describe differences in terms of the linguistic levels of language (i.e., lexical, phonetic, syntactic, morphological). Once the scene is written, students are asked to reflect on the ideologies they may be conveying about themselves and, consequently, members of society who share these linguistic features. They must address the following questions: Are positive or negative stereotypes being perpetrated? Which ones and how? Through these and other such activities, students are made aware of and given the tools to use linguistic data in their analyses of literature.

A major challenge for teachers is creating an environment in which students feel comfortable talking about their own perceptions of others' language and their own experiences with linguistic ideologies that have hurt them or others in some way. We believe both literature and audio clips provide safe mediums that allow students to discuss these difficult issues without having to use personal examples.[8]

---

8 Recent research has shown there are regional differences in how university students respond to discussions of language ideologies and race, including how willing students are to use personal examples, risky self-critique of past behavior, and personally held language ideologies (Bissonnette, Reaser, Hatcher, & Godley, 2016).

By talking about the characters' or the authors' linguistic choices and the voices of the *DARE* clips, teachers may redirect the focus to those objects and encourage open discussion.

Another challenge is the possible triggering of stereotypes or biases within students (and teachers) and possible discomfort discussing charged topics such as the "cracker" dialect presented above. We acknowledge this as a possible consequence of asking students to discuss their views of others' language use. We argue that both students' and societal views must be acknowledged so that we may begin the self-reflection needed to alter our own beliefs and behaviors, as linguistic prejudice often goes unquestioned in society. Frank discussions may encourage students to become advocates for change, and, ultimately, to begin challenging prejudicial actions that are built upon negative language ideologies that exist inside and outside classroom walls. Lastly, we argue that these activities are essential to society's embrace of people who are different in myriad ways—including speakers of non-standard dialects, speakers of other languages—and to the curbing of language ideologies that foster stereotypes, biases, and prejudices.

Acknowledgments

We thank Joan Houston Hall, and the present and past *DARE* staff. We also thank members of the *DARE* Board of Visitors for supporting the initiation of the *Discovering DARE* curricula with a generous grant.

References

Bissonnette, J. D., Reaser, J., Hatcher, J., & Godley, A. J. (2016). Regional differences in pre-service teachers' responses to critical language pedagogies. *Southern Journal of Linguistics*, *40*(1), 1–39.

Burrison, J. A. (2013). Crackers. *New Georgia Encyclopedia*. Retrieved from www.georgia encyclopedia.org/articles/arts-culture/crackers

Dialects. (2018). In *Encyclopædia Britannica* online. Retrieved from www.britannica.com/topic/dialect

Jewett, S. O. (1988). A bit of shore life. In C. G. Waugh, H. Greenberg, & J. Donovan (Eds.) *Best stories of Sarah Orne Jewett* (pp. 35–54). Augusta, ME: Lance Tapley.

Painter, N. I. (2011). *The history of White people*. New York: W. W. Norton & Co.

Preston, D. R. (1985). The Li'l Abner syndrome: Written representations of speech. *American Speech*, *60*(4), 328–336.

Rawlings, M. K. (1994). *Short stories*. Gainesville, FL: University Press of Florida.

Simpson, P. (2003). *Language, ideology and point of view*. London and New York, NY: Routledge.

Stickle, T. & Abrams, A. (in progress). *Teaching levels of dialect from Discovering DARE: Familiar voices seen and heard, investigating "eye" dialects of American literature* [Teacher Manual and Student Workbook].

Wolfram, W. & Schilling, N. (2016a). Appendix: An inventory of distinguishing dialect features. *American English: Dialects and variation* (3rd ed.) (pp. 367–390). Cambridge and Oxford: Wiley and Blackwell.

—— (2016b). Levels of dialect. *American English: Dialects and variation* (3rd ed.) (pp. 114–146). Cambridge and Oxford: Wiley and Blackwell.

Chapter 13

Bringing Critical Language Pedagogy to the Middle School Social Studies Classroom

Lessons for Standard English Learners

Jessica Hatcher and Jeffrey Reaser, NC State University, North Carolina

---

Introduction

Scholars and educational bodies have long advocated for more sociolinguistically informed classroom approaches (CCCC/NCTE, 1974; Fasold & Shuy, 1970; Labov, 1969, etc.). Critical language pedagogy (CLP) (Godley & Minnici, 2008) is one recent method for meeting this challenge. In CLP, teachers guide students by examining relationships between language and power, with the goal that students understand and interrogate the creation and maintenance of standard language ideology:

> A bias toward an abstracted, idealized, homogenous spoken language which is imposed and maintained by dominant bloc institutions and which names as its model the written language, but which is drawn primarily from the spoken language of the upper middle class.
>
> (Lippi Green, 2012, p. 67)

Drawing prominently from Freire's notions of "counterstories" (i.e., narratives that challenge common stereotypes) and "conscientization" (i.e., understanding how social and political institutions reproduce systematic oppression) (1968) as well as critical discourse analysis's tenet that texts are never neutral (Fairclough, 1995), CLP challenges students to engage with language so they might determine how it is both influenced by and reproduces implicit, unequal power dynamics in society. Through CLP, students develop tools for understanding, evaluating, and unmasking existing belief systems (i.e., common sense understandings about how language works) and for critiquing or unseating these ideologically driven discourses (Godley & Minnici, 2008; Godley & Reaser, 2018). In this chapter, we discuss our work creating and teaching a CLP-inspired unit to over 110 seventh-grade students in four social studies classes at a rural Southern school in which the majority (over two-thirds) of the students were Latinx. We hope that this chapter provides teachers with an understanding of CLP and some resources that might help revolutionize literacy instruction for all students, but especially underserved populations.

Educational Setting

We selected this school for several reasons. First, English language learners represent a growing presence in American schools (Hussar & Bailey, 2013). This school's large Latinx population, nearly half of which were classified as having limited English proficiency, offered a somewhat extreme manifestation of this national trend. Second, the school's administration openly said that the Latinx population was "a challenge." This framing, we reasoned, suggested that the school was not well prepared for this sociolinguistic diversity, and, therefore, struggled to meet the language and literacy needs of its students. Moreover, the non-Latinx students generally spoke stigmatized English varieties, especially Southern American and African American English. Thus, the vast majority of the school's students could be identified as Standard English learners (Wilkinson et al., 2011)—that is, learners who speak "language varieties which differ from standard or mainstream English" (Wilkinson et al., 2011, p. ix). Finally, the school resided in one of the more impoverished counties in its state, with a poverty rate of more than 25 percent and a per-capita income well below $20,000.[1] Collectively, these factors suggested the students at this school could benefit from sociolinguistically informed pedagogies.

While we believe all students benefit from understanding connections between language and power, we also feel that the personal empowerment through CLP can be transformative for Standard English learners; as such, we specifically designed materials with these students in mind. However, our activities are easily adaptable to different classrooms and a variety of learners, grades, and disciplines.

Design

We had little difficulty integrating CLP activities that spoke directly and indirectly to the teacher-specified essential standards for seventh-grade social studies. Because the class was completing a unit on geography, we relied heavily on map interpretation and creation exercises. The lessons mixed new activities and existing resources from the Language and Life Project (LLP) at NC State University—adapted for this particular audience. Below, we discuss the content and reasoning behind each of the three lessons. Due to space constraints, we do not describe all activities.

Teaching the Unit

Lesson I

Among the teacher's goals for the geography unit were differentiating types of maps and learning locations of states and regions within the U.S., so we began the lessons with an activity inspired by folk dialectology, a sociolinguistic methodology that examines nonlinguists' perceptions about language (Preston, 1989). Students were given a map of the U.S. and eight photographs of individuals representing a range of ethnic or social personae selected to evoke regional associations (e.g., a man wearing a cowboy hat or a woman in a ski suit). In groups, students were directed to place on the map where the person in each photo was most likely from. Then we

---

1 Descriptors are intentionally vague so as to protect the anonymity of the host school.

asked them to list adjectives describing how the person in the photograph might talk. Since the photographs exemplified regional, gender, and ethnic stereotypes, we hoped to evoke adjectives that would impel discussions about stereotypes and counter-stereotypes.

Although some students resisted stereotyping the people, some comments revealed less democratic views of diversity. For example, at least one student in each class remarked that an Asian-presenting person "needs to go in China, but that's not on the map." Though disheartening, such comments created opportunities for critical engagement. We probed the assumptions underlying the students' ideas and then tactfully led them to construct counter-stereotypes. In this case, we asked students to probe why they assumed the person was from China, which led to a re-envisioning of American multiculturalism absent from the initial responses. These alternative ways of interpreting the world help expose and undermine implicit assumptions about ideological orientations. This CLP approach of eliciting and then probing students' existing knowledge, assumptions, and stereotypes is important in a variety of classrooms.

Following this introductory activity, we investigated where and why geographic and dialect regions of the U.S. converge. For example, by studying different types of maps, students noticed that the Appalachian dialect region of the U.S. aligned with the Appalachian Mountains. To further analyze the relationship between language and place, students examined vocabulary from Appalachian English and Outer Banks Brogue (adapted from Filson, 2011). Using word lists, maps, and two vignettes from LLP documentaries on Appalachian English and Outer Banks Brogue, the students discussed how local geography generates local vocabulary; for example, the Outer Banks Brogue has many water-related words, like *slickcam*, which indicates 'smooth water.' As with the previous activity, this exercise could be adapted for other regions or purposes (e.g., local ecology, economy, or climate).

To investigate the relationship between language shift and geography, students compared maps of the historical distribution of American Indian languages with a current map depicting Cherokee as the sole remaining American Indian language in North Carolina, spoken in a small area of the Appalachian Mountains. While the full history is more complex, students correctly deduced that the rugged mountains provided some buffer from European colonialists not afforded by other regions of the state, like the flat Coastal Plain. This realization led into a discussion of the U.S. government's exertion of power over indigenous peoples, including the eradi-cation of ancestral languages. The discussion was extended via a short vignette from the LLP's Emmy-winning documentary, *First Language: The Race to Save Cherokee* (Hutcheson & Cullinan, 2014). We were explicit in noting that European colonists engendered social control in part through language policy that defined what could be spoken and consequences for nonconformers. Though we lacked the time to explore questions of language policy and authority more deeply, this activity could be expanded: the topic leads organically into discussions of school and national language policy, including the English Only movement.

To conclude this lesson, students engaged with an activity from Reaser, Adger, Wolfram, and Christian's (2017) *Dialects at School: Educating Linguistically Diverse Students* which uses voices from the publicly available International Dialects of English Archive. This activity, like our opening one, asked students to evaluate voices as a means of reexamining assumptions underlying societal stereotypes and personal biases. Further, it tied together the various threads of the lesson and prompted CLP-type conclusions about language stereotypes, language and culture, and language and power. Students in all classes were quick to conclude that it was unfair to judge people based on the way they speak; some students even noted that to do so would be "racist." To illustrate how such judgments could violate civil rights, we discussed linguistic profiling, which is when in the context of securing housing, employment, or services, people make judgments about others' traits over the phone (e.g., race, nationality, sex, etc.) and then use that judgment as the basis for discrimination (Baugh, 2003). To offer two illustrations of this process and its consequences, we showed a brief public-service announcement from the National Fair Housing Alliance (Ad Council, 2003) and a selection from *Do You Speak American?* (MacNeil/Lehrer Productions, 2005) in which linguist John Baugh discusses his research on linguistic profiling. We concluded the class by stressing that although it is common, judgments about people's abilities based on how they speak are just as inappropriate as judgments based on people's sex, gender, ethnicity, or social class.

The lesson proved successful in that it encouraged students to consider the intersection between language and geography while also invoking central CLP-inspired interrogation of otherwise invisible discourses through which inequality is perpetuated. We hoped that beginning with the potentially uncomfortable discussion of language, power, and discrimination would prime students to think critically about language throughout our brief instructional unit.

Lesson 2

The second lesson occurred two weeks after the first. This time, the classroom teacher asked us to connect our lesson to an essential standard: using maps and technology to make conclusions about societal issues related to the environment, social class, and economy. Since language is integral to many social issues, this standard offered numerous ways to connect geography to language variation while further interrogating issues of language, power, and discrimination.

To accomplish our lesson's objectives, we first needed to build students' tools for analyzing dialects. We used students' linguistic expertise to build fluency with linguistic terminology and analysis techniques. For example, to demonstrate the vocabulary level of dialect (i.e., pronunciation, grammar, word choice, and discourse practices), we presented images in order to elicit students' linguistic structures, such as their words for a sugary, carbonated beverage (e.g., *soda, coke, pop, soda pop, soft drink*, etc.). Students were also able to offer examples of pronunciation differences, including *water/wooder, oil/ol,* and *roof/ruff.* To develop language-pattern analysis skills, we adapted two dialect exploration activities from Reaser and Wolfram (2007). Students uncovered the rules governing a pronunciation and grammatical feature found in varieties represented at the school: the short-i and short-e merger, where the vowels in words like *pin/pen* are pronounced the same, and habitual *be*, such as "the students be talking in class," which indicates a reoccurring ("often") rather than punctual ("now") action. To tie the activity to geography, we used heatmaps, which represent regional distributions of linguistic features via a graduated color scheme (see Katz, 2016). During the habitual *be* exercise, which investigates a feature common in African American English, three African

Critical Language Pedagogy 97

American students participated for the first time during our lesson, a powerful reminder about the importance of culturally relevant teaching (Ladson-Billings, 1995). By employing examples from students' linguistic experiences and identities and demonstrating that their language has rules, we were able to validate student voices, a crucial aspect of CLP.

These activities transfer easily to other types of teaching contexts; in fact, we regularly teach them to English Language Arts (ELA) classes of all levels. Activities about language patterns can further be extended in ELA classrooms by tying them to analyses of dialect in literature. For example, many literary characters are shaped in part by their dialects. One activity we have had success with involves investigating whether an author's use of dialect is true to or deviates from previously explored language patterns. In some cases, the author may be inaccurate or use eye dialect, which involves intentional "misspellings" that capture standard pronunciations, as in <wuz> for *was*. In investigating these portrayals, students sort out authentic dialect from eye dialect and then hypothesize about the intended effects of the portrayals (see Dean, 2008 for an extended example of this approach; see also Abrams & Stickle, this volume, pp. 84–92). This activity is useful when examining literary portrayals of any regional or cultural group.

The final activity for the second lesson incorporated language variation into an existing class project in which students created maps of their school to demonstrate their understanding of cartography. To integrate language, we instructed students to add a layer to their maps that connected location and formalness of speech. For example, students might label the principal's office as the place that required the most formal language and the lunchroom as the place with the least formal. This activity drew students' attention to how usage shifts for place, purpose, or audience. Following CLP, this exercise again privileged students' prior knowledge of local language variation; however, if we had more time, students could investigate this topic empirically, which might also lead to questions about language authority and linguistic privilege in the school, as it did in the germinal linguistic-ethnography study *Jocks and Burnouts: Social Categories and Identity* (Eckert, 1989).

Lesson 3

When we returned for our third lesson, the class had begun a unit on European exploration. We targeted an essential standard exploring how culture can unite and divide societies. It seemed straightforward to investigate how language, a fundamental aspect of culture, both divides and unites. We decided to contextualize current issues by examining the long history of language's use as a tool for division in the U.S. First, we had students examine European settlement maps, which documented substantial language diversity during colonial times. We then asked students to consider why English became the dominant language in the U.S. Some students hypothesized that English was the easiest language to learn or that, for various reasons, English was better than other languages. After pushing students to apply what they had previously learned about language and power—as from the discussion of Cherokee in lesson one—they began to reach critical conclusions about language and power. With prompting, students started to connect the language's primacy with land, battles, and political power. This history could surface in the ELA classroom through canonical texts such as *The Narrative Life of Frederick*

Douglass or *The House on Mango Street* or twenty-first-century texts like *When My Name Was Keoko.*

To further explore the interconnectedness of language, power, and history, we examined the historical case study of German in the U.S. German was spoken widely—and, in some cases, taught in school—from Philadelphia through Minnesota during the period of American colonization and expansion. While there were some early fears—most notably by Benjamin Franklin—that the language would overtake English, there was little anti-German linguistic sentiment until World Wars I and II. During this period, propaganda branded the speaking of German as un-American, leading some states to enact legislation restricting its use. We offered students historical examples of renamings designed to mask German heritage, including *frankfurter* becoming "liberty sausage," *dachshunds* becoming "liberty pups," and *German Street* in Cincinnati, OH, being renamed "English Street." Students deftly explained why German was vilified and, given the distance from their own lives, lampooned the triviality of the rebrandings that arose from social hysteria. We followed up with a more modern example: In 2003, U.S. representative Robert Ney ordered that congressional cafeterias change "french fries" to "freedom fries" in protest of France's denouncement of the U.S. war in Iraq.

We hoped that these "distant" examples might prime counterstories to "Spanish as threat" discourses (Carter, 2014) prevalent in the school and community. Because CLP requires confronting institutional and ideological frameworks that perpetuate inequality, we turned to a discussion of current English-only policies, but, as previously, we contextualized it in history. We shared with the students the following quotation from President Teddy Roosevelt: "We have room for but one language in this country, and that is the English language, for we intend to see that the crucible turns our people out as Americans, of American nationality, and not as dwellers in a polyglot boarding house" (Roosevelt, 1926, p. 554). Using a series of probing questions, this quotation fostered a lively but rich discussion of language and power. Even students who had previously been reluctant to participate offered opinions. Some students, mostly bilingual speakers of English and Spanish, argued that having one national language was racist and that speaking different languages was valuable. Others expressed that having a single language promoted harmony and clear communication among people from different backgrounds.

After a productive conversation, we revealed that the U.S. has no official language, which surprised many students. Collectively, we examined some of the language diversity in the U.S. via maps from slate.com that documented the most commonly spoken language in each state other than English and Spanish.[2] Students expressed amazement that languages like French, Tagalog, and Korean were spoken by large populations. After viewing these maps, some students repositioned their stances to be more accommodating of language diversity. For example, one student maintained that the U.S. needed a national language but that other languages should be encouraged rather than eradicated. This activity demonstrated how discussions of linguistic diversity in schools promote cultural awareness and tolerance.

To encourage students to think about bilingualism in the U.S., we ended with an LLP video in which students and scholars of Hispanic linguistics spoke about

---

2 Maps available from www.slate.com/articles/arts/culturebox/2014/05/language_map_what_s_the_most_popular_language_in_your_state.html

the challenge of maintaining Spanish in a majority English-speaking context. Following the video, we examined a well-established pattern whereby heritage languages are lost within two or three generations. We then engaged students in a discussion of what would be lost should Spanish disappear in the United States. As we had hoped, the students recalled sentiments expressed by Cherokee-speaking children in *First Language* and voiced that Spanish was an important part of their identity and family relationships.

Conclusion

At the end of the lesson, we asked students to consider whether their thoughts or attitudes about language, or specific languages, like Spanish, had changed. Their responses revealed that our unit pushed them to consider connections between language, power, and identity more carefully. It was clear that they now understood that the way language is treated can unfairly harm cultural groups. At the same time, it was also clear that the three lessons were not enough to raise critical consciousness to the level of action. The responses of Standard English learners offered encouragement that, if not empowered, they at least felt validated by learning more about language variation. As such, we remain steadfast in our belief that CLP and sociolinguistic content can contribute to transformative educational experiences for the most vulnerable student populations, and that this work can and must be done across grade levels and educational contexts.

References

Ad Council. (2003). Accents: Fair housing PSA. Retrieved from www.youtube.com/watch?v=84k2iM30vbY

Baugh, J. (2003). Linguistic profiling. In S. Makoni, G. Smitherman, A. Blake, & A. K. Spears (Eds.), *Black linguistics: Language, society, and politics in Africa and the Americas* (pp. 155–168). London and New York, NY: Routledge.

Carter, P. M. (2014). National narratives, institutional ideologies, and local talk: The discursive production of Spanish in a "new" U.S. Latino community. *Language in Society, 43*(2), 209–240.

CCCC (Conference on College Composition and Communication)/NCTE(National Council of Teachers of English). (1974). Resolution on students' right to their own language. Retrieved from www.ncte.org/positions/statements/righttoownlanguage

Dean, D. (2008). *Bringing grammar to life*. Newark, DE: International Reading Association.

Eckert, P. (1989). *Jocks and burnouts: Social categories and identity in the high school*. New York, NY: Teachers College Press.

Fairclough, N. (1995). *Critical discourse analysis*. London: Longman.

Fasold, R. W., & Shuy, R. W. (1970). *Teaching standard English in the inner city*. Washington, DC: Center for Applied Linguistics.

Filson, N. (2011). *Introducing language exploration: Linguistic applications in the classroom* [Curriculum]. Raleigh, NC: Language and Life Project. Retrieved from https://linguistics.chass.ncsu.edu/thinkanddo/filsoncurriculum.php

Freire, P. (1968). *Pedagogy of the oppressed*. New York, NY: Continuum.

Godley, A. J., & Minnici, A. (2008). Critical language pedagogy in an urban high school English class. *Urban Education, 43*(3), 319–346.

Godley, A. J., & Reaser, J. (2018). *Critical language pedagogy: Interrogating language, dialects and power in teacher education*. New York, NY: Peter Lang.

Hussar, W. J., & Bailey, T. M. (2013). *Projections of Education Statistics to 2022 (NCES 2014-051)*. U.S. Department of Education, National Center for Education Statistics. Washington, DC: U.S. Government Printing Office.

Hutcheson, N., & Cullinan, D. (Producers). (2014). *First language: The race to save Cherokee* [Video]. Raleigh, NC: Language and Life Project.

Katz, J. (2016). *Speaking American: How y'all, youse, and you guys talk—A visual guide*. New York, NY: Houghton Mifflin Harcourt.

Labov, W. (1969). The logic of nonstandard English. In J. Alatis (Ed.), *Georgetown monograph series on language and linguistics* (pp. 1–44). Washington, DC: Georgetown University Press.

Ladson-Billings, G. (1995). Toward a theory of culturally relevant pedagogy. *American Educational Research Journal, 32*(3), 465–491.

Lippi-Green, R. (2012). *English with an accent: Language, ideology, and discrimination in the United States* (2nd ed.). London and New York, NY: Routledge.

MacNeil/Lehrer Productions. (2005). *Do you speak American?* [Video]. Arlington, VA: Author.

Preston, D. R. (1989). *Perceptual dialectology: Nonlinguists' views of areal linguistics*. Providence, RI: Foris.

Reaser, J., Adger, C. T., Wolfram, W., & Christian D. (2017). *Dialects at school: Educating linguistically diverse students*. New York, NY: Routledge.

Reaser, J., & Wolfram, W. (2007). *Voices of North Carolina: From the Atlantic to Appalachia* [Curriculum]. Raleigh, NC: Language and Life Project. Retrieved from https://linguistics.chass.ncsu.edu/thinkanddo/vonc.php

Roosevelt, T. (1926). *Works*, vol. XXIV (memorial ed.). New York, NY: Charles Scribner's Sons.

Wilkinson, C., Miciak, J., Alexander, C., Reyes, P., Brown, J., & Giani, M. (2011). *Recommended educational practices for standard English learners*. Austin, TX: Education Research Center, University of Texas at Austin.

Chapter 14

Grammar in the Spanish/English Bilingual Classroom

Three Methods for Teaching Academic Language

Mary Hudgens Henderson, Winona State University, Minnesota

Introduction

The purpose of this chapter is to present practical strategies for teaching academic registers of language in a classroom where students are expected to recognize and produce a standardized variety of Spanish and of English.[1] This approach is relevant for teachers in many contexts, whether all students or only a few are becoming bilingual. As educators, we must be aware of the variation in grammar that native-speaking and heritage students often bring to the classroom, and we must use the grammar that students already know to help them acquire the school-based variety of Spanish (or English) that is usually considered necessary for academic success.

From lack of familiarity with academic registers of Spanish,[2] emerging bilingual students may struggle with Spanish literacy as well as English literacy, and students are often erroneously labeled as "semilingual." While the myth of semilingualism has been debunked (MacSwan, 2000), the belief persists that many bilingual students lack development in both of their languages. Students are often caught between a rock and a hard place by those who view their English as not "complete" and their Spanish as "wrong" (Leeman, 2012). In reality, emerging bilingual students have strong proficiency in their own oral Spanish variety and need supportive educators who can help them *add on* the written school-based dialect (such as Standardized Spanish or Standardized English) to their linguistic repertoire.

The goal is not to replace the grammar that students already have with our own opinions of "correct" grammar, but instead to expand the repertoire in their native and second languages. English language learners learn academic registers of English for school purposes, and they also need informal English for social purposes. Learning about grammar variation in their home language can help students distinguish variation in a second language (such as English). Students are already experts

---

1 Standardized Spanish or Standardized English are dialects of Spanish or English that have undergone a process of standardization (Milroy & Milroy, 1999). Different regions (such as North America, Australia, or Spain) may have different conceptions of what the standard dialect is. For example, the use of the pronoun *le* for direct objects (called *leísmo*) is acceptable in formal contexts in Spain, but less so in Paraguay (Choi, 1998).

2 Academic registers of a language, such as Spanish or English, are the types of language patterns found in different topic areas. For example, the language of science is its own academic register, as is the language of social studies, literature studies, math, etc. Academic registers include vocabulary, sentence patterns, and discourse strategies. These academic registers are often lumped together under the term "Academic Language."

in their home variety of Spanish; now we are teaching them features of Academic Spanish with the goal to switch between the two Spanish varieties as the situation requires.

Our Spanish-speaking students speak many different kinds of Spanish, such as Mexican Spanish, Iberian Spanish, Honduran Spanish, Salvadoran Spanish, and/or what is often called "Spanglish." Many Spanish-speaking students who are enrolled in English as a Second Language (ESL) classes or bilingual education programs do not speak a standardized variety of Spanish, but instead language varieties that are often stigmatized by educated Spanish speakers. For example, a teacher may hear students say "Quiero comer *lonche* [I want to eat lunch]" instead of "Quiero almorzar," or "¿Ya *comistes*? [Did you eat already?]" instead of "¿Ya comiste?," or "He *escribido* el ensayo [I have written the essay]" instead of "He escrito el ensayo." Such grammatical forms are common in many oral Spanish varieties and often appear in students' writing. To support the development of bilingualism (in Spanish and English) and bidialectalism (in Standard Spanish and the home variety of Spanish), we must give students the opportunity to distinguish formal and informal features of their languages.

This chapter presents three teaching methods (linguistic inquiry, contrastive analysis, and switching) that build students' language repertoires to include the school-based dialect. These methods teach students to become aware of grammatical differences, to identify patterns hidden within language, and to practice switching to contextually appropriate varieties.

Method 1: Linguistic Inquiry

The first step in building students' grammar repertoires is to raise their awareness of grammar differences between Academic Spanish and the Spanish they know from home through a method called *linguistic inquiry*. Linguistic inquiry consists of asking a question about language, collecting data to help answer the question, and interpreting the results. Many students internalize "prescriptive" opinions (attitudes regarding what is right or wrong) about the language they use. With linguistic inquiry, the goal is not to label one way of speaking as "right" and another "wrong" but to identify and describe language differences through a neutral, scientific process. In using linguistic inquiry, students' attention is drawn to grammar differences in an explicit way while encouraging the study of language from an objective, scientific standpoint.

One way of incorporating linguistic inquiry into the classroom is to conduct grammar surveys. Simply put, the purpose of a grammar survey is to find out how many students in the class recognize or use a particular grammar feature. Students interview each other and then compare results to discover how salient a particular grammar feature is in their speech and/or writing. This type of survey is an excellent way to preview the formal study of a particular grammatical feature found in academic language.

Table 14.1 presents a grammar survey on the verbal -*s* ending on simple past-tense verbs in Spanish (for example, *fuistes* versus *fuiste* [you went/you were]). This survey can be used for many different grammar features and can be tailored depending on how much grammatical terminology students already know (such as *verbs*, *adjectives*, and *participles*). One way to conduct this survey is to instruct

Table 14.1 Example of a grammar preferences survey

Pregunta a cada persona en el salón : "¿Qué verbo dirías en las siguientes oraciones?"		
Oración	*Columna A*	*Columna B*
1	**¿Fuistes** a la fiesta de Marcos?	**¿Fuiste** a la fiesta de Marcos?
2	¿Ya **comistes?**	¿Ya **comiste?**
3	**¿Salistes** de la casa?	**¿Saliste** de la casa?
4	**¿Hicistes** la tarea anoche?	**¿Hiciste** la tarea anoche?
5	¿Qué **dijistes?**	¿Qué **dijiste?**
Etc.		
TOTAL		

students to sit down with one other person in the room and ask them their verb preference for each of the sentences. The asker puts a check mark in the column of the verb that the participant prefers. This same procedure is then repeated with everyone else in the room. At the end, students should have a rich data set to analyze: the verb preferences of all their classmates.

Once students have the data, the next step is to analyze and interpret it. For each sentence pair, they calculate how many classmates preferred the verb in Column A versus the verb in Column B. The class can then calculate averages and percentages or create a bar graph together. There is no need to collect names of classmates who use these features; the purpose is to find out *how many* students use one feature over another as opposed to *who* uses which feature. Then students analyze the data, asking questions like: What patterns emerge from the data? Do most students prefer verbal *-s* or not? Are there certain verbs that are more popular for verbal *-s* than others? Using linguistic inquiry, students become consciously aware of a grammar difference they may not have noticed before, and they develop a better sense of how widespread the grammar feature is in their classroom.

To find grammar features for these surveys, it is helpful to look at the students' writing. What features appear frequently? The language that students bring to the classroom should be the starting point for linguistic inquiry.

Linguistic inquiry can be done in English, too. Students can conduct grammar surveys with common English grammar differences, such as informal contractions *gonna* ('going to') and *wanna* ('want to'), or other features they notice. Interviewing native English-speaking peers is also an excellent way to raise awareness of grammar differences in students' second language.

Grammar surveys also help students discover grammatical rules that may not be apparent at first glance. Students can self-interview to check their language intuitions and then discuss why they would say one form over another. Table 14.2 gives an example of this type of grammar survey with the English verb *to be going to*. After completing this survey, students discuss why certain sentences with *gonna* sound felicitous and others do not. With guidance, students may discern from their data that *gonna* is used in a futuristic sense (e.g., "I'm gonna study"), but not in a movement sense (e.g., "I'm going to the store"). Students may notice clues to this pattern, such as *gonna* being followed by a verb.

Table 14.2 Example of a grammar rule discovery survey

Read each sentence and decide if it makes sense or not.		
	Makes Sense	*Does Not Make Sense*
1. I'm **gonna** study.		
2. I'm **gonna** the store.		
3. I'm **gonna** bake the cookies now.		
4. I'm **gonna** the movie theater.		
5. I'm **gonna** go to the movie theater.		
6. I'm **gonna** my house.		
(Etc.)		

Grammar surveys can be used beyond the classroom. Students can investigate how people in their social circles speak by interviewing their family or other members of their community. By reporting results back to the class, students become aware of how grammar differences extend to different locations with different social groups.

Method 2: Contrastive Analysis

With linguistic inquiry, students become aware that differences in grammar exist and that certain social groups may use certain grammar features more than others. The second step in building students' grammar repertoires—called *contrastive analysis*—teaches them to recognize patterns in the grammars of Standardized Spanish and the language variety under investigation. This step specifically compares and contrasts written Standardized Spanish and oral informal Spanish, and it emphasizes that supposedly "incorrect" grammar actually follows recognizable patterns or rules. Students come to recognize that all grammar is rule-governed, and therefore no grammar, even "informal" grammar, is sloppy or lazy.

Contrastive analysis exercises, such as the one in Table 14.3, are explicit comparisons of two grammatical features with the purpose of comparing and contrasting those features and identifying a pattern in each language variety presented (Fogel & Ehri, 2000; Rickford & Rickford, 2007; Wheeler & Swords, 2004). Students examine the grammar exhibited in each column (preferably taken from a real-life context), and they generate a grammatical rule for each variety.

Contrastive analysis can follow the work already done with linguistic inquiry. For example, once results from a grammar survey have been calculated (such as how many students use verbal -*s* versus how many students do not use verbal -*s*), the next step is to identify the grammatical pattern in each column. Students can be asked: What do the verbs in Column A have in common? What do the verbs in Column B have in common? For the present perfect subjunctive in Table 14.3, students will conclude that in informal Spanish, different conjugations of *haiga* are used, while in Standardized Spanish, different conjugations of *haya* are used.

It is important to note that we are not identifying one pattern as "correct" and the other as "incorrect." If students attempt to label one pattern as incorrect, redirect this

Table 14.3 Contrastive analysis chart for haiga vs. haya

	Español informal	Español estandarizado
1	Yo no creo que el agua se **haiga** congelado.	Yo no creo que el agua se **haya** congelado.
2	Nos importa que el líquido **haiga** sido teñido.	Nos importa que el líquido **haya** sido teñido.
3	Es importante que los estudiantes **haigan** echado el agua por el embudo.	Es importante que los estudiantes **hayan** echado el agua por el embudo.
4	Necesitamos una levadura que no **haiga** sido agregado al peróxido de hidrógeno.	Necesitamos una levadura que no **haya** sido agregado al peróxido de hidrógeno.
5	Antes de comenzar el experimento, es necesario que todos **haigan** puesto los lentes de seguridad.	Antes de comenzar el experimento, es necesario que todos **hayan** puesto los lentes de seguridad.
	Regla: En el español informal, se usa _____ para el presente perfecto subjuntivo.	*Regla: En el español estandarizado, se usa _____ para el presente perfecto subjuntivo.*

discussion toward identifying patterns in grammar in a neutral, scientific manner. After all, this study of language is a form of the scientific method: collecting data and drawing conclusions based on the evidence (such as "Two-thirds of the students in this class use verbs with -*s*," or "for some speakers, -*s* appears on the *tú* conjugation of verbs"). Follow up this scientific study of grammar patterns with a class dialogue on why some patterns are preferred over others in certain contexts. Encourage students to think critically about why one grammar pattern may be considered correct and others incorrect: Who makes this decision, and who benefits from having their own grammar considered "correct"? (see Godley & Minnici, 2008, and Hatcher & Reaser, this volume, pp. 93–100, for other examples of a critical language pedagogy approach).

Table 14.4 is a contrastive analysis chart of common calques from English to Spanish, compared with the Standardized Spanish form.[3] In this particular chart, these Spanish verbs that were calqued from English verbs (*to park, to type, to check, to pump, to sort*) have something in common: an ending of -*ear*. Other calqued verbs may have only the -*ar* ending (such as *checar* 'to check,' *ponchar* 'to perforate,' *rentar* 'to rent,' etc.). It is important that the contrastive analysis chart have a clear pattern for students to recognize. Avoid mixing grammatical patterns that are not clearly related; the point is to elucidate the grammar patterns, not complicate them.

Especially when it comes to "Spanglish," some students may have very strong opinions on what they consider to be "correct" or "incorrect." For some people, switching between two languages or using calques is a sign of linguistic laziness or low language proficiency. To the contrary, research has established that Spanglish speakers rarely switch due to lack of vocabulary or grammatical knowledge but instead employ code-switching, loanwords, and calques for communicative

---

3 A calque is a literal translation from one language to another.

Table 14.4 Contrastive analysis chart for calques vs. Standardized Spanish forms

	Calcos del inglés	Español estandarizado
1	Voy a **parquear** el carro.	Voy a **estacionar** el carro.
2	Necesito **taipear** el ensayo.	Necesito **escribir a máquina** el ensayo.
3	Debemos **chequear** los resultados.	Debemos **comprobar** los resultados.
4	Queremos **pompear** la gasolina antes de irnos.	Queremos **echar** la gasolina antes de irnos.
5	Hay que **sortear** los participantes en grupos diferentes.	Hay que **clasificar** los participantes en grupos diferentes.
	Regla: En el español informal, algunos verbos aparecen con la terminación -ear y son traducciones literales del inglés.	*Regla: En el español estandarizado, los verbos aparecen con las terminaciones -ar, -er, -ir.*

purposes (Rothman & Rell, 2005; Zentella, 1997).[4] Sharing these patterns and discussing the communicative purposes often used between Spanglish speakers can produce an empowering moment for students who have been told all their lives that they speak incorrectly.

Common grammar features that can be used for contrastive analysis include verbal *-s* on preterit *tú* verbs (*comistes*), *haiga/haya*, pluralizing impersonal *haber* (*habían* vs *había muchas personas* [there were many people]), regularization of participles (*escribido/escrito*, *rompido/roto*, etc.), and other features particular to each teacher's individual classroom. Remember to acknowledge all these grammar patterns as valid: the teacher is not replacing students' grammar, but *adding on* to it. Students should not be asked to stop using specific features. They need to maintain their current grammar for communication between friends, at home, and within the community. The goal here is to use what students already know to expand, not to limit, the language they use every day.

Method 3: Switching from One Variety to Another

Through linguistic inquiry and contrastive analysis, students have consciously noticed grammar differences and identified patterns or rules embedded in the grammar. The third step in building students' linguistic repertoires is giving them practice in using different grammar patterns according to the needs of the situation. This next step, *switching*, teaches students to switch their grammar use according to the needs of particular contexts.

There are many ways to give students opportunities to switch between the two language varieties or grammar features under focus in a lesson. First, the teacher may implement translation tasks, in which students translate the grammar from one variety to another. (To avoid stigmatizing a variety, always ask students to translate from the informal to the formal *and* vice versa; translating in both directions

4 Code-switching is the practice of switching between one language or dialect and another. Loanwords are words that have been borrowed into another language.

is necessary.) Second, students could use both varieties (Standardized Spanish and Spanglish, for example) in fiction writing in which the narration appears in Standardized Spanish but the characters speak in Spanglish. Third, students may attempt to communicate the same message to a variety of audiences who have different expectations in terms of language. For example, students could protest the shortness of the lunch hour first to fellow students, then to the principal or school board, switching the language features to fit the expectations of the audience. They can brainstorm contexts where one grammar feature would be acceptable over another (e.g., "How would you congratulate a close friend versus someone you hardly know?"). Students will discover that many of these unspoken rules are culturally bound, and what is expected in mainstream American culture is different in many Latinx cultures.

Concluding Remarks

This chapter has presented three methods that teachers can use in their classrooms to build students' awareness, recognition, and production of academic registers of Spanish or English. Many students are experts in Spanish varieties that happen to be stigmatized, and they require instruction that validates their linguistic knowledge and builds their linguistic repertoires. This growing awareness of language variation helps students understand why they use one feature in one context but not another, and why the language of peers is different from the language of an academic textbook. Therefore, knowing a language is more than knowing grammar terminology; it is about being able to use the different language features to maximize the communicative effect on an audience. To help students move beyond the notion of correct/incorrect grammar, educators can use the language that students bring to the classroom as a resource to study and to compare with the school-based dialect.

As educators, we must not reproduce the denigration that often occurs toward speakers whose language varieties have not gone through the process of standardization (see Milroy & Milroy, 1999). It is important to acknowledge that the Spanish (or Spanglish) that students speak is grammatically valid, not corrupt or damaged. ELA teachers, bilingual classroom teachers, and teacher trainers can incorporate Spanish-language variation into the teaching of academic registers to help students become academically literate in Spanish and English. This approach, building students' linguistic repertoires in both languages, can teach students to become bilingual and biliterate without having to abandon the speech patterns of their home communities.

References

Choi, J. K. (1998). Languages in contact: A morphosyntactic analysis of Paraguayan Spanish from a historical and sociolinguistic perspective (doctoral dissertation). Georgetown University, Washington, DC.

Fogel, H., & Ehri, L. C. (2000). Teaching elementary students who speak Black English vernacular to write in standard English: Effects of dialect transformation practice. *Contemporary Educational Psychology*, 25(2), 212–235.

Godley, A. J. & Minnici, A. (2008). Critical language pedagogy in an urban high school English class. *Urban Education*, *43*(3), 319–346.

Leeman, J. (2012). Investigating language ideologies in Spanish as a heritage language. In S. M. Beaudrie & M. Fairclough (Eds.), *Spanish as a heritage language in the United States: The state of the field* (pp. 43–59). Washington, DC: Georgetown University Press.

MacSwan, J. (2000). The threshold hypothesis, semilingualism, and other contributions to a deficit view of linguistic minorities. *Hispanic Journal of Behavioral Sciences*, *22*(1), 3–45.

Milroy, J. and Milroy, L. (1999). *Authority in language: Investigating standard English* (3rd ed.). London and New York, NY: Routledge.

Rickford, A. E. & Rickford, J. R. (2007). Variation, versatility and contrastive analysis in the classroom. In R. Bayley and C. Lucas (Eds.), *Sociolinguistic variation* (pp. 276–296). Cambridge: Cambridge University Press.

Rothman, J. and Rell, A. B. (2005). A linguistic analysis of Spanglish: Relating language to identity. *Linguistics and the Human Sciences*, *1*(3): 515–536.

Wheeler, R. S., & Swords, R. (2004). Codeswitching: Tools of language and culture transform the dialectally diverse classroom. *Language Arts*, *81*, 470–480.

Zentella, A. C. (1997). *Growing up bilingual: Puerto Rican children in New York*. Malden, MA: Blackwell Publishers.

Chapter 15

Attitude Change Is Not Enough

Changing Teacher Practice to Disrupt Dialect Prejudice in the Classroom

Rebecca Wheeler, Christopher Newport University, Virginia

In our English classrooms, we do not typically welcome vernacular varieties of English. Instead, we correct students' language, urging "proper" and "good" English, urging that they cease such "sloppy" and "uneducated" ways. We demand minority-dialect students abandon the language of the home, as we red-pen papers, making circles and arrows and notes in the margins, signaling divergence from the Standard English norm. In doing so, we enact dominant language ideology, the belief that "Standard [American] English [(SAE)] is the only legitimate dialect of English" and consider "other dialects such as African American English as incorrect" (Godley, Carpenter, & Werner, 2007, p. 104; Godley & Minnici, 2008). In this fashion, our traditional English approach to vernacular dialects embodies dialect prejudice, discrimination against a person based on how they talk (Alim, 2005; Delpit 1995; Godley, Carpenter, & Werner, 2007; Godley & Minnici, 2008; Lippi-Green, 2012; Sweetland, 2006; Sweetland & Wheeler, 2014).

For over half a century, linguists and cultural theorists have warned that our traditional English instruction directly and seriously harms students who speak vernacular dialects such as African American Vernacular English (Fasold & Shuy, 1970; Labov, 1969, 1972a, 1972b; Wolfram, 1969).

Changing Attitudes: Enhancing Dialect and Critical Language Awareness

In response, some schools now offer programs in multicultural awareness to introduce and affirm students' cultural diversity (Banks & Banks, 2010). Teachers learn that dialect is a "variety of the language associated with a regionally or socially defined group" (Reaser, Adger, Wolfram, & Christian, 2017, p. 7). Aware of the centrality of language to culture, linguists have developed locally based dialect-awareness programs. Indeed, one such landmark program through the North Carolina Language and Life Project is now an official part of the statewide eighth-grade social studies curriculum (Reaser & Wolfram, 2007; see also in this volume Wolfram, pp. 61–66, and Hatcher & Reaser, pp. 93–100).

Through such programs, teachers learn that notions of "proper English" are far from neutral, innocent, and benign. They learn classroom consequences of dominant language ideology, discovering that students who speak a non-mainstream dialect suffer misdiagnosis and misclassification from their earliest moments in school (Rickford & Rickford, 2009; Reaser, Adger, Wolfram, & Christian, 2017; Wheeler, Cartwright, & Swords, 2012).

The good news is that trainings in multicultural education and dialect awareness *do succeed* in changing teacher attitudes. Once alerted to the normally invisible structures of systemic prejudice (Alim, 2005), teacher attitudes improve (Sweetland, 2006).

And yet, this chapter will demonstrate that attitude change is not enough.

Improved teacher attitude toward the work of vernacular-speaking students means little if teacher *practice* remains the same. If we keep "correcting" dialect differences as errors in Standard English, then we continue enacting a discriminatory language arts to the great, lifelong disadvantage of vernacular-speaking students.

Unseating dominant language ideology requires more than unbinding negative attitudes. We must change teacher practice. This chapter offers tangible ways to do just that.

General Knowledge about Dialect Diversity: A Good Beginning

Secondary English teachers at one Virginia district eagerly participated in a three-day training on linguistically informed responses to language varieties in schools. After learning about dialect diversity and dialect prejudice, teachers explored how to use contrastive analysis and code-switching to build upon the language of the home to add the language of the school (Wheeler & Swords, 2004, 2006, 2015). My work focuses on the patterns of African American Vernacular English (AAVE) because this is the minority-dialect group most dominant in my home region, and in many regions of the U.S. Further, as we disaggregate demographic groups nationally, African American students consistently suffer in assessments of educational achievement (see also Reed Marshall & Seawood, this volume, pp. 138–146). For these and many other historic reasons, my work has long focused on helping teachers better understand the language variety spoken by many African American students.

In our training program, teachers explored lessons addressing the most frequently found AAVE patterns, discovering the equivalencies between AAVE grammar and the grammar of SAE (see Figures 15.1 and 15.2).

After the in-depth training concluded, participants returned to their classrooms prepared with new awareness of dialect diversity, with knowledge of common vernacular structures, and with new understanding that all dialects are structured and linguistically equal. Teachers were relieved to find ways to respect the language of the home, and, consequently, to respect their students. Sobered by the dialect prejudice they had lived, teachers were committed to reversing dialect prejudice in their classrooms.

But Attitude Change and General Dialect Knowledge Are Not Enough

Then student papers came in.

A secondary-school teacher, a participant in our intensive linguistic awareness workshop, had assigned her class the essay topic "Explain why your house is a special place." As she sat down to comment, dominant language ideology roared back in (see Figure 15.3).

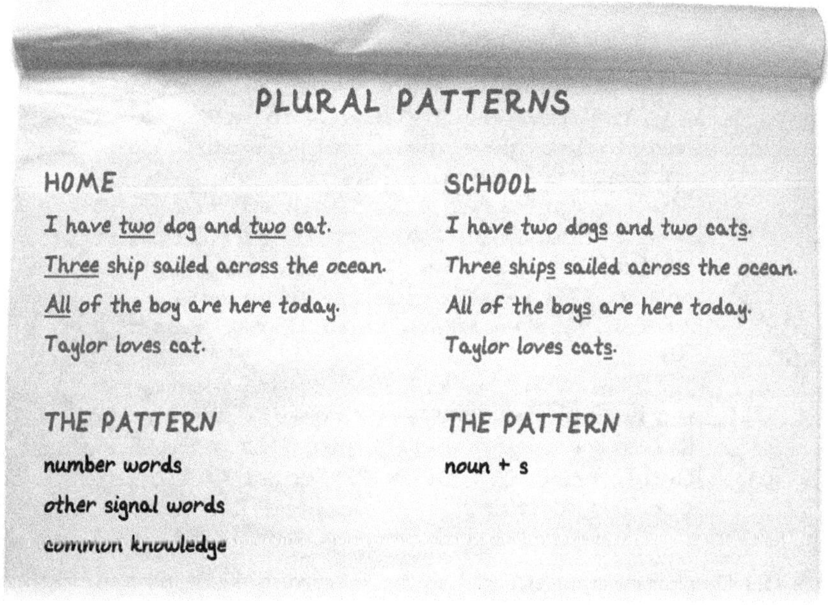

PLURAL PATTERNS

HOME

I have <u>two</u> dog and <u>two</u> cat.

<u>Three</u> ship sailed across the ocean.

<u>All</u> of the boy are here today.

Taylor loves cat.

SCHOOL

I have two dog<u>s</u> and two cat<u>s</u>.

Three ship<u>s</u> sailed across the ocean.

All of the boy<u>s</u> are here today.

Taylor loves cat<u>s</u>.

THE PATTERN

number words

other signal words

common knowledge

THE PATTERN

noun + s

Figure 15.1 T-Chart contrasting plural patterns in home vs. school English
Source: Wheeler & Swords (2015, p. 60).

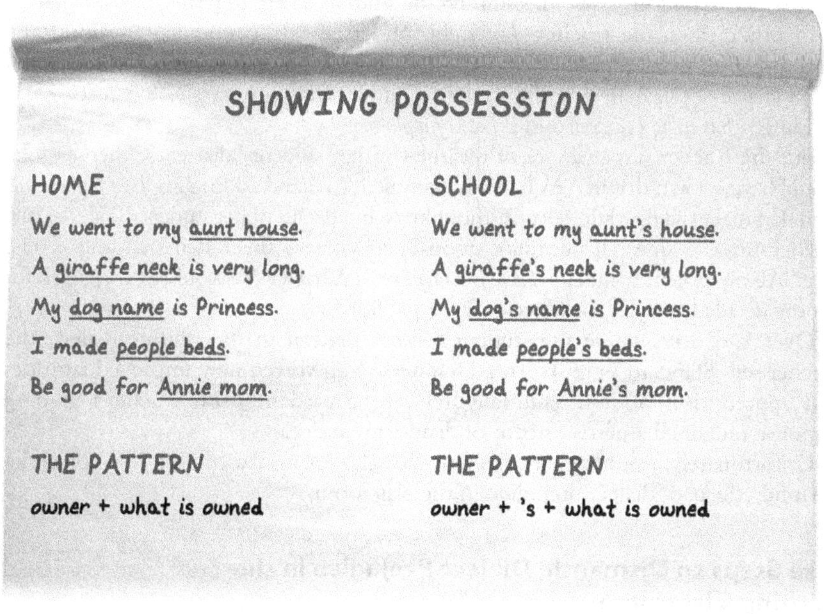

SHOWING POSSESSION

HOME

We went to my <u>aunt house</u>.

A <u>giraffe neck</u> is very long.

My <u>dog name</u> is Princess.

I made <u>people beds</u>.

Be good for <u>Annie mom</u>.

SCHOOL

We went to my <u>aunt's house</u>.

A <u>giraffe's neck</u> is very long.

My <u>dog's name</u> is Princess.

I made <u>people's beds</u>.

Be good for <u>Annie's mom</u>.

THE PATTERN

owner + what is owned

THE PATTERN

owner + 's + what is owned

Figure 15.2 T-Chart contrasting possessive patterns in home vs. school English
Source: Wheeler & Swords (2015, p. 32).

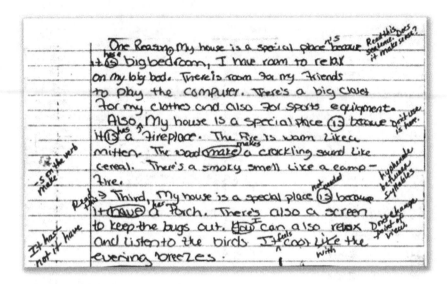

Figure 15.3 Despite new attitudes, English teacher miscorrects the English in an African American student's essay
Source: Wheeler & Swords (2015, p. xiii).

She corrected punctuation and grammar. Seeing "The wood make a crackling sound like cereal," the teacher, true to long-time habit, saw error and responded accordingly, circling and replacing *make* with *makes*. Seeing "my house ... have a porch," the teacher again (mis)assessed, assuming the student had gotten the verb wrong.

In other cases, the teacher *thinks* she understands the student's meaning and structure. Unfortunately, she does not. The student writes *It is big bedroom* (¶1) and *it is a fireplace* (¶2). Believing the student stumbles in grammar, she "corrects" each, yielding *it has a big bedroom* and *it has a fireplace*.

But the teacher was unaware of the rules of her students' dialects. Otherwise, she would have known that in AAVE, *it is* is equivalent to Standard English *there is/there are*. And that makes all the difference. Without knowing details of her students' dialects, "the teacher mis-assesses and hence unintentionally miscorrects the student's writing ... The true SAE equivalent would be *There is a fireplace*." (Wheeler & Swords, 2015, p. 251; for a more detailed analysis, see Wheeler, 2010, p. 957).

Over and over, where the student follows pattern in their home dialect, the teacher sees Standard English error. Despite having voiced new, improved attitudes and appreciation of new culturally relevant approaches, this teacher's grading response remained a perfect storm of dialect prejudice.

Unfortunately, attitude change is not enough, not nearly enough to unbind the harmful effects of dialect prejudice in the classroom.

Five Steps to Dismantle Dialect Prejudice in the Writing Classroom

Our classrooms may feel like war zones for our vernacular-speaking students. Although teachers may have improved their attitudes toward linguistic diversity, old habits of the red pen are difficult to break. When teachers misassess dialectal patterns as errors in Standard English, students' futures are at risk.

Yes, we need deep societal change and acceptance of linguistic diversity. Many scholars and cultural critics are calling for disruption of societal attitudes toward minority dialects.

Concurrently, I call for immediate triage, to arrest the clear and present danger confronting vernacular speakers in our classrooms. To that end, I offer five steps to dismantle dialect prejudice in the grading classroom.

1. Challenge Assumptions: Grammar Difference May Signal Dialect Pattern

Many English teachers are proud of their long commitment to "good and proper English." Some might even pride themselves as "a grammar Nazi." This nose for "error" can be put to good use: it can help us identify dialectal grammar patterns in students' writing. However, when we look for dialectal grammar patterns, we won't *correct* the language. Instead, we use linguistically informed techniques to build on the language of the home in order to add the language of the school. Thus, this deep sense of error can help point toward vernacular *pattern*. But to do so, there must be a commitment to *reflect upon* and *challenge* those feelings of "error."

2. Getting Organized: Mechanics Error Is Not Dialect Pattern

My students ask, "but if *the wood make a crackling sound* isn't error, does that mean that there's no such thing as error?" Not at all.

We can readily identify errors of mechanics—spelling, capitalization, and punctuation. So, when a student writes "Let's go over their" or "I'm going to there house," these are spelling errors, just as "my dog wanted it's ball" illustrates punctuation error. Similarly, if a student writes "We're going to the saturday market," that's a failure of capitalization, of mechanics.

These errors in mechanics represent true errors; they do *not* reflect dialect patterns. Indeed, while "grammar has dialects, spelling does not" (Pullum, 2001). The same is true of capitalization and punctuation. Why does this distinction matter?

Part of being able to dismantle dialect prejudice as we respond to vernacular-speaking students means becoming aware of what is and what is not a dialect pattern. So, we need to separate error in Standard English from pattern in vernacular dialect. We will correct the former and build on the latter with linguistically informed approaches.

Finally, let's look at one more example of error (see Figure 15.3). The student writes, "One reason my house is a special place because it is big bedroom," and later, "my house is a special place is because it have a porch," conflating distinct structures: We can say "One reason that my house is a special place is that" or "My house is a special place because," or perhaps the more casual "The reason is because." The student, confused between these complex Standard English structures, does stumble in error. An appropriate teacher response would be to explain that we use one or the other but do not blend them.

In sum, we need to distinguish error in Standard English from pattern in a different dialect.

3. Become Familiar with Common Grammar Patterns in Students' Community Dialects

We are a big and increasingly diverse nation. Whether a teacher lives and works with students who speak with the grammar and sound patterns characteristic of Bronx English, Appalachian English, Cajun English, Southern English, or any other regional or vernacular English, our task is the same: become familiar with our students' dialects and distinguish error in Standard English from patterns in students' ways of speaking.

In this section, I give examples from AAVE to provide one model for how teachers can learn more about their students' home dialects while helping them differentiate between nonstandard patterns and genuine errors in use of the standard language. I offer two approaches to becoming familiar with AAVE vernacular patterns. First, I point out readily available resources detailing common patterns. Second, I lead us through an analysis of a piece of student writing, showing how to collect examples of patterns relevant to the teacher's own class.

Turning to AAVE, we are fortunate that the dialect now known as African American Vernacular English is perhaps the most deeply studied of all U.S. dialects. Consequently, lists of common AAVE features are readily available to the classroom teacher (Charity Hudley & Mallinson, 2011, 2014; Redd & Webb, 2005; Wheeler & Swords, 2006, 2015). For example, Wheeler and Swords (2015) illustrate eight common grammar patterns, showing the AAVE and Standard English equivalents (Table 15.1).

Some linguists go deeper into the structural detail of the matter, naming the grammatical feature and illustrating with examples from student writing (e.g., Smitherman 1999a, pp. 170–171, reprinted in Wheeler 2016).

Of course, the task is *not* for a teacher to memorize all the grammar patterns found in the many resources available. Indeed, at this point, one doesn't even need to understand the technical linguistic terms used. It's OK to be unfamiliar with technical labels. The point of such lists is to alert teachers to well-known patterns in AAVE so that when they come across similar examples in students' writing, they will think "pattern, not error!" This is a key step in dismantling dialect prejudice in our classroom grading practices.

4. Analyze Students' Writing for Vernacular Grammar Patterns

If we want to build on the patterns of the home to add the patterns of the school, we must first identify what grammar patterns crop up in our students' writing. The most common AAVE patterns in student writing can be found in common feature lists (e.g., Table 15.1). But teachers will still want to look in more particular detail at their students' work.

To do so, first collect a set of student papers. Then read the papers, being alert to distinguish mechanical error (spelling, capitalization, punctuation) and error in sentence boundaries, voice, etc., from pattern in a different dialect. The goal is to develop a list of common vernacular grammar patterns occurring in these students' writing.

To illustrate, let's work with a writing sample from an eighth-grade Virginia student's year-end essay (see Figure 15.4). We will do a needs analysis on this student's essay. Remember, right now we are looking for dialect-related grammar

Table 15.1 Common home and school English patterns

Home vs. School English Patterns		✓
Possessive		
Home	**School**	
The dog tail	The dog's tail	
Plural		
Home	**School**	
Three cat	Three cats	
Showing past time		
Home	**School**	
I finish	I finished	
Subject–verb agreement		
Home	**School**	
She walk	She walks	
Was/were		
Home	**School**	
You was sleeping	You were sleeping	
Am/is/are		
Home	**School**	
They is tall	They are tall	
Gonna/going to, wanna/want to		
Home	**School**	
He's gonna go home	He's going to go home	
I wanna leave soon	I want to leave soon	
Be		
Home	**School**	
He cool with me	He's cool with me	

Source: Wheeler & Swords (2015, p. 233).

issues. To do so, we will first distinguish mechanics issues and issues of sentence boundary, etc.

We easily identify a range of mechanics issues: spelling (e.g., "were" vs. "where," ¶2, lines 3, 9); capitalization (e.g., "First, Imagine," ¶1, line 1; ¶2, line 1); and punctuation (e.g., issues with sentence boundaries, a complex but nondialectal concern). Thus, we see fused sentences ("I would have to keep the light on the bulb would be hot as fire," ¶1, lines 2–3) and stranded clauses ("I wouldn't be able to watch my shows. Such as Girlfriends ...," ¶2, lines 2–3), and so on.

A range of AAVE grammar patterns is also evident:

Verb patterns

Be understood: "Since there no television" (¶1, lines 3–4)
S-V agreement: "Toni ... bring him ..." (¶2, lines 3–4)

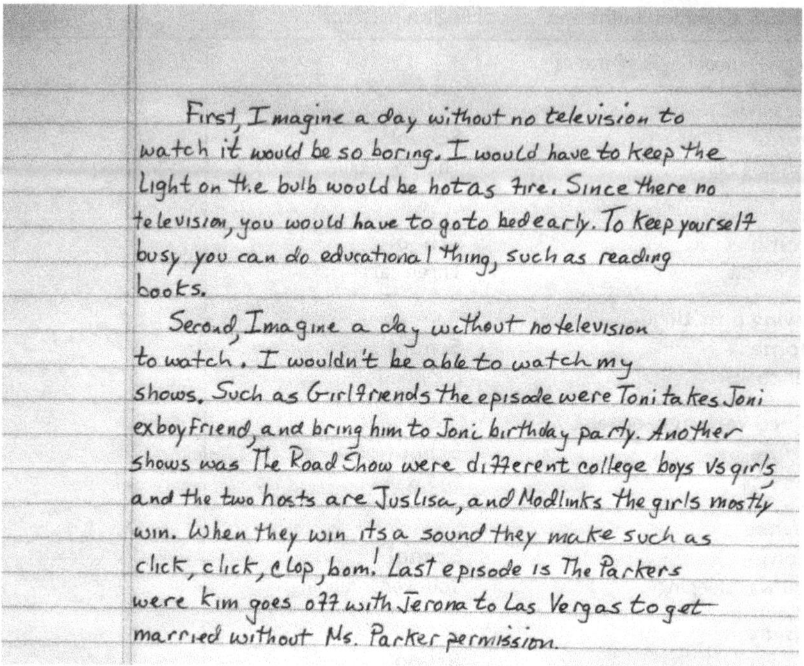

> First, I imagine a day without no television to
> watch it would be so boring. I would have to keep the
> Light on the bulb would be hot as fire. Since there no
> television, you would have to go to bed early. To keep yourself
> busy you can do educational thing, such as reading
> books.
>
> Second, Imagine a day without no television
> to watch. I wouldn't be able to watch my
> shows. Such as Girlfriends the episode were Toni takes Joni
> exboyfriend, and bring him to Joni birthday party. Another
> shows was The Road Show were different college boys vs girls
> and the two hosts are Juslisa, and Modlinks the girls mostly
> win. When they win its a sound they make such as
> click, click, clop, bom! Last episode is The Parkers
> were Kim goes off with Jerona to Las Vergas to get
> married without Ms. Parker permission.

Figure 15.4 Identifying grammar contrasts between home and school English
Source: Wheeler (2010, p. 956).

Noun patterns

Multiple negation: "without no television to watch" (¶1, lines 1–2; ¶2, lines 1–2)
Plurality shown by context: "you can do educational thing" (¶1, line 5)
Possession: "Joni ex boyfriend" (¶2, lines 3–4); "Ms. Parker permission" (¶2, line 10)
"It is vs. There is": "When they win its a sound they make" (¶2, line 7)
Unmarked determiner: "Last episode is The Parkers" (¶2, line 8)

After making a list of common vernacular patterns in their students' dialects, the teacher can begin to add the Standard to their students' linguistic toolboxes. One useful technique is the T-chart, a two-column chart showing the syntactic equivalencies between two dialects (Wheeler & Swords, 2015, p. 32). While T-charts are readily available for working with these AAVE patterns (Wheeler & Swords, 2006, 2015), the teacher can enhance the charts with their own examples or build custom charts for other vernacular dialects relevant to their students' usage.

Once the teacher has practiced distinguishing error from pattern for one paper, they should turn quickly to other papers from the class. What common mechanics errors can be identified? Annotate them so that they can be used as examples for lessons on mechanics. What AAVE grammar patterns can be seen?

Make a list. Collect four to six examples per grammar pattern (i.e., possession, plurality, etc.).

In this way, the teacher can build a needs analysis for the class. From this scouting work, the teacher can then lead lessons in contrastive analysis and code-switching integrated into a writing workshop.[1]

5. Emphasize Code-Switching: A Linguistically Informed Response

Teachers often wonder "but if we don't correct, what *do* we do?"

The brief answer: "We build on the patterns of the home to add the patterns of the school." With this tool, teachers lead students in the scientific method of grammar discovery (see Figure 15.2). Students discover the AAVE pattern for possession: *owner + what is owned*. The apostrophe *-s* is not forgotten; it is not omitted; the student is not confused. They have successfully hit the AAVE pattern. The teacher then asks the students how the examples in the right-hand column differ. Students discover that the Standard English pattern is *owner + 's + what is owned*.

In this way, we add to *all* students' linguistic toolboxes. Adding the patterns of the majority dialect augments the vernacular speaker's linguistic range. And acquainting majority-speaking children with a diversity of dialects fosters a crucial message of social justice—diverse language varieties are neither broken nor partial attempts at Standard English. Instead, acknowledging minority dialects' vitality and viability helps to counter the systemic racism of U.S. society, education, and enterprise.

Attitude Change Is Not Enough: Triage Now!

Attitude change is not enough. If we continue down the path of mistaking AAVE patterns for errors in Standard English, not only do we misassess AAVE speakers but we also inflict dialect prejudice, a racist view of language. When we grade through the lens of dominant language ideology, we assail the human integrity of the student before us. This violence must stop.

We need triage. That's what this chapter has offered: five steps to change classroom grading practice. Once we break the habit of seeing vernacular pattern as mistake, we tangibly crack the cycle of dominant language ideology and dialect prejudice.

Acknowledgments

I thank Michelle Devereaux and Chris Palmer, editors of this volume, for their detailed, insightful, and generous commentary. Their comments contributed greatly to the flow and content of this work. Of course, any limitations or failings remain my responsibility.

---

1 Please see *Code-Switching Lessons* for a full year's worth of support for this work (Wheeler & Swords, 2015).

References

Alim, H. S. (2005). Critical language awareness in the United States: Revisiting issues and revising pedagogies in a resegregated society. *Educational research, 34*(7), 24–31.

Banks, J. A., & Banks, C. A. M. (Eds.). (2010). *Multicultural education: Issues and perspectives* (7th ed.). Hoboken, NJ: Wiley & Sons.

Baratz, J. (1969). Teaching reading in an urban Negro school system. In J. Baratz & R. Shuy (Eds.), *Teaching Black children to read* (pp. 92–116). Washington, DC: Center for Applied Linguistics.

Baratz, J. C., & Shuy, R. W. (Eds.). (1969). *Teaching Black children to read*. Washington, DC: Center for Applied Linguistics.

Charity Hudley, A., & Mallinson, C. (2011). *Understanding English language variation in U.S. schools*. New York, NY: Columbia University Teachers College.

—— (2014). *We do language: English language variation in the secondary English classroom*. New York, NY: Columbia University Teachers College.

Delpit, L. (1995). *Other people's children: Cultural conflict in the classroom*. New York: New Press.

Denham K., & Lobeck, A., (Eds.). (2005). *Language in the schools: Integrating linguistic knowledge into K-12 teaching*. Mahwah, NJ: Erlbaum.

—— (Eds.). (2010). *Linguistics at school: Language awareness in primary and secondary education*. Cambridge: Cambridge University Press.

Fasold, R. W., & Shuy, R. W. (Eds.). (1970). *Teaching standard English in the inner city*. Washington, DC: Center for Applied Linguistics.

Godley, A. J., & Minnici, A. (2008). Critical language pedagogy in an urban high school English class. *Urban Education, 43*(3), 319–346.

Godley, A. J., Carpenter, B. D., & Werner, C. A. (2007). "I'll speak in proper slang": Language ideologies in a daily editing activity. *Reading Research Quarterly, 42*(1), 100–131.

Hancock, C., & Kolln, M. (2010). Blowin' in the wind: English grammar in United States schools. In T. Locke (Ed.), *Beyond the grammar wars: A resource for teachers and students on developing language knowledge in the English/literacy classroom* (pp. 21–37). London and New York, NY: Routledge.

Labov, W. (1969). Some sources of reading problems for Negro speakers of nonstandard English. In J. Baratz & R. Shuy (Eds.), *Teaching Black children to read* (pp. 29–67). Washington, DC: Center for Applied Linguistics.

—— (1972a). Academic ignorance and Black intelligence. *Atlantic Monthly, 6*, 59–67.

—— (1972b). *Language in the inner city: Studies in the Black English vernacular*. Philadelphia, PA: University of Pennsylvania Press.

Lippi-Green, R. (2012). *English with an accent: Language, ideology and discrimination in the United States* (2nd ed.). London and New York, NY: Routledge.

Pullum, G. K. (2001). Grammar has dialects; spelling does not. *Sydney's Child, 12*(3), 30–31.

Reaser, J., & Wolfram, W. (2007). *Voices of North Carolina: Language and life from the Atlantic to the Appalachians*. Raleigh, NC: North Carolina Language Life Project.

Reaser, J., Adger, C. T., Wolfram, W., & Christian, D. (2017). *Dialects at school: Educating linguistically diverse students*. London and New York, NY: Routledge.

Redd, T., & Webb, K. S. (2005). *African American English: What a writing teacher should know*. Champaign/Urbana, IL: National Council of Teachers of English.

Rickford, A. E., & Rickford, J. R. (2007). Variation, versatility and contrastive analysis in the classroom. In R. Bayley & C. Lucas (Eds.), *Sociolinguistic variation: Theories, methods and applications* (pp. 276–296). Cambridge: Cambridge University Press.

—— (2009). From outside agitators to inside implementers: Improving the literacy education of vernacular and Creole speakers. In M. Farr, L. Seloni, & J. Song (Eds.), *Ethnolinguistic diversity and education: Language, literacy and culture* (pp. 241–259). London and New York, NY: Routledge.

Smitherman, G. (1999a). *Talkin that talk: Language, culture and education in African America*. London and New York, NY: Routledge.

Sweetland, J. (2006). *Teaching writing in the African American classroom: A sociolinguistic approach*. Stanford, CA: Stanford University Press.

Sweetland, J., & Wheeler, R. (2014). Addressing dialect variation in U.S. K-12 schools. In M. Bigelo, & J. Ennser-Kananen (Eds.), *The Routledge handbook of educational linguistics* (pp. 446–458). London and New York, NY: Routledge.

Wheeler, R. (2010). Fostering linguistic habits of mind: Engaging teachers' knowledge and attitudes toward African American vernacular English. *Language and Linguistics Compass*, 4(10): 954–971.

—— (2016). "So much research, so little change": Teaching standard English in African American classrooms. *Annual Review of Linguistics*, 2, 367–390.

Wheeler, R., & Swords, R. (2004). Codeswitching: Tools of language and culture transform the dialectally diverse classroom. *Language Arts*, 81, 470–480.

—— (2006). *Code-switching: Teaching standard English in the urban classroom*. Urbana, IL: NCTE.

—— (2015). *Code-switching lessons: Grammar strategies for linguistically diverse writers grades 3–6*. Madison, WI: Ventris Learning.

Wheeler, R., Cartwright, K., & Swords, R. (2012). Factoring AAVE into reading assessment and instruction. *Reading Teacher*, 65(5), 416–425.

Wolfram, W. (1969). *A sociolinguistic description of Detroit Negro speech*. Washington, DC: Center for Applied Linguistics.

—— (2000). Everyone has an accent. *Teaching Tolerance*, 18, Retrieved from www.tolerance.org/magazine/number-18-fall-2000/feature/everyone-has-accent

Chapter 16

Extending the Conversation

Two Teachers' Response to Linguists

Suzanne Loosen and Teaira McMurtry, Milwaukee Public Schools, Wisconsin

In this chapter, we address some of the challenges and solutions described by the linguists in the preceding chapters, discuss some prerequisites needed to implement and expand their recommendations, and consider how linguists and teachers can effectively engage in this work together. We advocate for creating and continuing conversations between linguists, teachers, and students so that we may all learn from each other.

Context

In our work as high school teachers and teacher leaders within the Milwaukee Public Schools in Wisconsin, we see the benefits of studying and teaching linguistics with students and teachers. Since linguistics courses have not traditionally been included in secondary curricula, our work in this field was developed and executed as master's- and dissertation-level research projects. Suzi has taught an elective linguistics English course to tenth- through twelfth-grade students since the 2010–11 school year (Loosen, 2014), a course that was designed as the final thesis project for her master's degree in English with a focus on language and linguistics. Teaira is a teacher and scholar-practitioner who advocates for teaching students about their cultural dialect—specifically, African American English (AAE)—through linguistics lessons that celebrate nonstandard language variations while adding to students' linguistic repertoires. Teaira has also created a sociolinguistically informed professional development series (inspired by the work of many linguists in this volume), which provides teachers with the awareness, knowledge, and tools to embrace and capitalize on their students' cultural dialects.

It is our hope that linguistics content will one day become commonplace in K-12 settings—not as elective, but as integral. The many projects described in the previous chapters demonstrate the value of studying language as key to understanding the human experience.

Common Concerns and Solutions among Linguists

The linguists in Part 2 of this volume affirm that correctionist approaches to dialect variation simply do not work. In fact, they agree that these prescriptive approaches are counterproductive and deleterious to students' identities. Mary Hudgens Henderson, for example, discusses the importance that teachers "move beyond the notion of correct/incorrect grammar" (p. 107). She explains that such binaries simplify language in ways that restrain language and language users. Beyond this, the linguists also note the importance of teacher attitude toward language. Rebecca Wheeler describes her work with teachers who, although able to articulate a new understanding and appreciation of students' language variations, still label dialect patterns as "wrong" (p. 112). How we see our students and their language practices matter. To address this issue, the linguists offer a number of lessons and ideas to help teachers move away from the role of "language guardians."

Anne Lobeck's approach teaches linguistic diversity as a strength, supporting a more inclusive notion of what defines the "language of school" (p. 76). In fact, all of the linguists support the inclusion of various dialects in the language of school because, as they explain, Standard American English (SAE) is only one variety among many. But for teachers to embrace this stance, they also have to understand that SAE, the language of school, must be problematized and deconstructed, which speaks to Mike Metz's fourth principle to "talk explicitly about language, identity, power, and prejudice" (p. 73). This principle is echoed by Jessica Hatcher and Jeffrey Reaser through their lessons with seventh-grade social studies students, and by Kelly Abrams and Trini Stickle through their lessons using audio data from the *Dictionary of American Regional English* (*DARE*).

All of the linguists' chapters provide resources for teachers as they create classrooms conscientious of and celebratory toward linguistic diversity. Such resources include documentaries like *First Language: The Race to Save Cherokee* (Hatcher & Reaser), audio data resources like *DARE* (Abrams & Stickle), linguistic examinations of grammar and usage (Lobeck), core principles of language study (Metz), and step-by-step methods of teaching in linguistically informed ways (Hudgens Henderson; Wheeler).

Another theme of the linguists' discussions is the role of inquiry—from both the students and the teachers. This teacher-as-learner positioning can be frightening at first for teachers used to being the authoritative presence in the room. But in a place where language is being explored as its own fascinating phenomenon, everyone has much to learn together. The language we use is alive and, therefore, changes. Instead of the emphasis of teachers as guardians of the language, we must teach students to become guardians of their own language while expanding their linguistic repertoires at school.

Our Work

In this section, we discuss both the teacher preparation and classroom implementation of linguistically informed teaching. First, Teaira discusses teacher training, detailing two activities that she has done with teacher-practitioners that have affected their attitudes toward standard language ideology (a phenomenon also described in Devereaux and Palmer's introductory chapter in this volume). She also discusses how these activities speak to the ideas shared by the linguists in Part 2. After this, Suzi explains how her linguistics class is set up, detailing connections between her work in the classroom and the methods some linguists have championed.

Teaira: Preparing Teachers

I believe that well-intentioned teachers may *unconsciously* operate from a prescriptivist perspective; linguists such as Wheeler echo this sentiment. In order to implement the descriptive approaches discussed here and throughout this volume, teachers must explore how they might be upholding and enacting Standard English Ideology (SEI)—the belief that there is an ideal variety of English and that this variety is inherently better than nonstandard forms.[1] By exploring and becoming equipped with tools, teachers can make a true pedagogical shift in the classroom away from SEI toward an ideology promoting linguistic diversity. But this is difficult, and teachers need guidance in examining their own commitments to SEI.[2] Metz offers five principles to help teachers begin this journey. Below, I describe two activities that facilitate these sorts of discussions: *The Missing A* and *I Can Go to the Bafroom?*[3] Linguists and other teacher trainers might find these activities useful for pre-service and in-service teachers in their educational linguistics courses and workshops; teachers might find these activities useful for themselves (e.g., during curricular planning).

The Missing A

Overt correction by a teacher (Delpit, 1995) is detrimental, especially when teachers themselves experience it. For this activity, a volunteer teacher stands "in front of the class" and is handed a card that reads: "Tell us what you did today without using words with the letter A." The teacher is instantly tongue-tied. As they try to tell their story, other participants interrupt and correct the volunteer teacher. After this, the activity leader encourages intense *introspection* and *reflection* (Ball, 2009). Teachers who participate in this exercise express their frustration as they know what they want to say but aren't allowed to. Teachers describe the harmful consequences of this experience, ultimately creating more empathy toward and awareness of their students.

I Can Go to the Bafroom?

Inspired by Geneva Smitherman (2000), I created a scenario similar to what I've heard in several classrooms. In this scenario, a student asks to go to the bathroom: "I can go to the *bafroom?*" His well-intentioned teacher publicly interrogates his use of the modal *can* (suggesting that it should be *could*); his use of subject-auxiliary inversion with rising intonation to indicate a question rather than a statement (a feature particularly common in child AAE; see Green, 2002); and his pronunciation of "f" in the middle position of the word *bathroom.* I introduce this scenario after teaching common structural and phonological AAE features (e.g., *copula absence, habitual be,* and *variations on the sounds represented by* <th>) while tracing those linguistic features to their West African origins. Having previously discussed the psychological consequences of overt correction (during activities such as *The Missing A*), participants reflect on the teacher's response to the student's bathroom-visit request.

1 SEI is an English-specific form of the broader phenomenon *standard language ideology*, described in Lippi-Green (2012).
2 To see one example of a teacher moving away from standard language ideology towards an ideology that embraces linguistic diversity, see the chapter by Reed Marshall and Seawood, this volume, pp. 138–146.
3 The two activities described in this section are a part of a larger sociolinguistically informed professional learning series I created and facilitated with high school teachers. Additional activities can be found on the eResources site.

We then discuss how this sort of scenario is in fact an opportunity for a pluralist response to nonstandard language use at school—i.e., advocacy for coexisting language variations.

Such activities not only sensitize teachers to the structural and pragmatic features of their students' cultural dialect, but they also enable teachers to experience the detrimental effects of SEI on a student's personal and academic esteem. To put it briefly, if teachers constantly correct a student's oral expression, it can lead to linguistic insecurity (Harmon & Wilson, 2006), shame (Alim, 2005), and—worst of all—silence (Kirkland, 2013). If students are silenced, they may be hesitant to express themselves and might not engage in opportunities to widen their linguistic repertoire.

Linguists' Strategies for Challenging Standard English Ideology

Conveying goals similar to those in the activities outlined above, many chapters in Part 2 introduce teachers to ways they might grow their linguistic understanding. Explorations in standard grammar ideology (Lobeck) and understanding the five principles of language study (Metz) are important beginnings. Even so, as Wheeler's chapter demonstrates, educators will also need to integrate standard language awareness into their curricula—and not just modify their attitudes—to be the most effective teachers they can be to the diverse language users in their classrooms.

Suzi: Teaching Linguistics

I believe that every student should have the opportunity to study linguistics before they graduate from high school. In the semester-long linguistics course I teach, we study phonetics, morphology, language acquisition, language change, sociolinguistics, and endangered languages.

On the first day, I teach the term *idiolect*, an individual's unique way of speaking, a linguistic fingerprint. This introduces a classroom culture where we are all researchers, with our own first-person data to contribute to class discussion. I also explain the concepts of *prescriptivism* and *descriptivism* to establish that the course will be unlike many of the traditionally prescriptive English classes they have taken in the past. We also learn that every speaker has an accent, that every speaker speaks in a dialect, and that we will study and celebrate this linguistic diversity. Through studying linguistics, students learn new academic vocabulary to describe language features and experiences.

Throughout the semester, I begin most classes by asking students what they have observed about language in the past twenty-three hours since we last saw each other: what have they been hearing in the hall, in biology class, in front of the TV, with their younger sibling, or what has been linguistically interesting in their social media feed or texts? I want students to become keen observers and active listeners to the wealth of language data that surrounds them every day. Such discussions are an easy way to integrate the inquiry stance that the various linguists describe in Part 2. Through doing this work, students become adept at analyzing and critiquing the language use and language ideologies they enact and live every day.

As much as possible, I want my students' learning experiences to be engaging and hands-on. For example, when we study phonetics, students pair up to create linguograms, painting each other's palates with charcoal powder and olive oil and then seeing what imprints they see on their tongues after they pronounce a one-syllable word (see eResources for instructions). When we discuss sign languages, we have a guest speaker come in to tell a story in American Sign Language and then we try to guess what the story is and learn some expressions. For our language-acquisition unit, both of my sons have taken their turns visiting class to "teach" the class about toy trains but really providing rich data of how two- to four-year-olds speak. These activities help create a community—which is particularly valuable when we discuss serious subjects that reflect power, privilege, and identity (see chapters by Abrams & Stickle, Hatcher & Reaser, and Metz for further ideas of bringing these types of discussions into the classroom).

I teach in an ethnically, economically, and linguistically diverse setting and work to navigate differences in our linguistics classroom—an approach that allows us to learn from each other. My students, in their yearly reflections, note the importance of these pedagogical choices, as well as the importance of the course content to their everyday lives. Our students must learn to effectively communicate in a diverse world. They are preparing for adulthood, for self-advocacy, for community. And a linguistics class—or really any class that foregrounds at least some linguistic content—equips them to reflect on the nuances in communication and in the world.

Moving Forward Together: Linguists and Teachers

School is a place where linguistic diversity needs to be embraced and celebrated. Our students seek acceptance and carry with them fragile, forming egos. When we turn to students as experts of their own varieties of language, we empower them to describe, analyze, reflect, and learn from each other. Teachers must be equipped with the pedagogical tools and resources to celebrate and validate students' linguistic identities, as emphasized by all of the linguists in Part 2. Beyond this, teachers must also be equipped and empowered to foster critical conversations about power, privilege, and prejudice in our fraught yet increasingly pluralistic society.

This work is challenging, and none of us can do it alone. Collaboration between linguists and teachers is key: sharing the latest research, co-creating and delivering lessons, and interpreting feedback from students are essential. Teachers benefit from guidance from linguists, and linguists, too, benefit from learning about teacher perspectives and K-12 classroom realities. Suzi's students (and Suzi herself) have benefited from the generosity of linguists in this volume: Anne Lobeck, Kristin Denham, and Dave Pippin have been quick to respond to her emails for the past nine years; Walt Wolfram mailed her a copy of the documentary *Talking Black in America*; Jeff Reaser connected her to Kelly Abrams and Trini Stickle when they were both at the University of Wisconsin, and they visited her students as guest speakers. All of these connections were started through email conversations, and it has been encouraging to talk to linguists at Linguistic Society of America (LSA) conferences. An important takeaway here is that a teacher doesn't have to be in a linguist's university course in order for them to collaborate with one another: linguists can reach out to teachers in their local school district, and teachers can email linguists at the nearest university to ask for guidance.[4]

4 For another example of a teacher seeking out local linguists, see the chapter by Bergdahl, this volume, pp. 11–17.

One initiative working to extend this conversation between teachers and linguists is through the creation of an Advanced Placement (AP) Linguistics course. In 2016, the LSA approved an AP Linguistics committee to research and promote linguistics classes in high schools, eventually leading to an AP class approved by the college board and creating a test that will allow high school students to receive college credit for their coursework in linguistics. To begin the course, 250 American high schools need to agree to offer the class, and the training sessions designed to prepare the teachers opens new opportunities for teachers and linguists to connect. If 250 linguists agree to support the 250 new teachers, we have new partnerships that could support over 6,000 high school students in the first year. And there are of course opportunities beyond AP classes: The LSA, for example, has also recently created a free membership category for K-12 teachers and students as another way of opening the door to these sorts of conversations.

Teachers, linguists, and, ultimately, students have much to gain by working together. The linguists in the preceding chapters describe their work with preservice and practicing teachers in their own college classrooms and with students and teachers in local elementary, middle, and high schools. Through these types of models, we build supportive communities for teachers and students to study linguistic content. By incorporating linguistics more comprehensively into K-12 education, we empower our students to become guardians of their own language varieties and more eager to learn about the language of others.

References

Alim, H. S. (2005). Critical language awareness in the United States: Revisiting issues and revising pedagogies in a resegregated society. *Educational Researcher, 34*(7), 24–31.

Ball, A. F. (2009). Toward a theory of generative change in culturally and linguistically complex classrooms. *American Educational Research Journal, 46*(1), 45–72.

Delpit, L. (1995). *Other people's children: Cultural conflict in the classroom.* New York, NY: News Press.

Green, L. J. (2002). *African American English: A linguistic introduction.* Cambridge: Cambridge University Press.

Harmon, M., & Wilson, M. (2006). *Beyond grammar: Language, power, and the classroom.* Mahwah, NJ: L. Erlbaum.

Kirkland, D. E. (2013). *A search past silence: The literacy of young Black men.* New York, NY: Teachers College Press.

Lippi-Green, R. (2012). *English with an accent: Language, ideology and discrimination in the United States* (2nd ed.). London and New York, NY: Routledge.

Loosen, Suzanne. (2014). High school linguistics: A secondary school elective. *Language, 90*(4), 258–273.

Smitherman, G. (2000). *Talkin that talk: Language, culture and education in Africa America.* London and New York, NY: Routledge.

Part 3

Collaborations between Teachers and Linguists

Using Digital Resources to Teach Language Variation in the Midwest

Amanda Sladek, University of Nebraska at Kearney, Nebraska, and Mattie Lane, West High School, Iowa

It's a common misconception that English speakers from the American Midwest speak without an accent or in a "General American" accent. When discussing models of Englishes, Kachru (1992) explains: "'General American' ... refers to the variety of English spoken ... in the central and western United States and most of Canada" (p. 51), and many non-native speakers attempt to model their pronunciation after this accent. Preston (2011) explores this phenomenon in Michigan specifically, unpacking the "local regard for Michigan as the homeland ... of *normal* and *correct* American English," as well as "Michiganders' lack of respect for English in other areas" (p. 19). This attitude extends beyond Michigan to other areas of the Midwest. Even a web search for the phrase "Midwestern accent" foregrounds a passage from the phrase's Wikipedia page, which reads in part: "may refer to: General American, the most widely perceived 'mainstream' American English accent, which is sometimes considered 'Midwestern' in character" ("Midwestern American English," n.d.).

When living in a linguistically homogenous community, it is hard to acknowledge the uniqueness of one's own language. Some language attitudes are reinforced by negative portrayals of dialect in popular media. For example, *I Love Lucy* and *Modern Family* are two television shows with characters who speak Latinx English. Often, their ways of speaking become punchlines. Such portrayals that criticize diverse speakers for their language use can lead viewers to stereotype all non-standard speakers as silly and unintelligent. Zuidema (2005) explains, "Detrimental portrayals of language variation on the radio, on television, in films, and on the Internet all provide opportunities to cultivate negative attitudes, which can emerge as prejudicial judgments and behaviors when people encounter language variation in real life" (p. 667). As educators, we can use our curricula to deconstruct these stereotypes and promote dialect awareness, especially in areas characterized by the myth of unaccented English.

These goals are even more important in the current political climate in the U.S. Fear of foreigners and minority groups is on the rise, and some government leaders want to close borders, assimilate languages, and erase cultures. If a student's only exposure to diverse languages comes from negative portrayals by certain politicians or media, their perspective on those diverse groups may be skewed. Many students whose language does not align with the idealized "General American" accent will continue to feel frustrated and judged for their difference, especially in areas that consider themselves the home bases of "correct" English.

This feeling of ownership over the English language is misplaced. Crystal (2012) estimates that, globally, people who speak English as a second or foreign language outnumber native speakers three to one. These speakers communicate in a variety of Englishes influenced by culture, native language, and other factors. Considering the dialectal diversity among first-language English speakers, it becomes even clearer that speakers of the Midwestern "General American" dialect comprise a small minority. Given these demographics, the belief that Midwestern American English is the most correct or grammatical seems illogical.

However, this reality is sometimes hard for Midwestern students to accept, especially in areas with limited language diversity. In these cases, digital resources provide what we as instructors cannot. As evidenced by the popularity of language-themed podcasts, infographics, quizzes, and other media, our culture has recently seen an explosion of interest in language issues. Many of these online resources, whether or not they are intended for classroom purposes, can be used to teach language variation and advocate for a more inclusive language ideology in the classroom.

This chapter highlights our experiences using digital media to teach issues of language ideology and variation at the secondary and collegiate level in the Midwest. The Iowa high school we discuss in this chapter is part of a diverse district composed of approximately 50 percent White students. While this classroom represents a variety of demographics, language ideology and variation are not addressed at the school, and students typically do not consider or analyze language and its effects. Standard American English (SAE), or "General American," is promoted through district assessments since it is perceived that this variety leads to academic success. At the Nebraska university discussed in this chapter, classes do typically include students from many different linguistic backgrounds; however, most students have been born and raised in the Midwest. The majority are White and speak some version of the "General American" dialect described above.

While instructors may need to adapt lesson plans delivered in high school vs. university contexts, there are significant similarities as well. For instance, instructors at both levels work toward certain learning outcomes. Secondary teachers must frame their lessons with state standards in mind. For English teachers, the standards address skills for reading, writing, speaking and listening; incorporating dialects and language variation in the curriculum must typically align with these (or similar) standards. It is important to also note that these standards focus on 21st century skills in which students should learn to "communicate and work productively with others, incorporating different perspectives and cross-cultural understanding" (Iowa Core, 2017). As noted in this goal, linguistic awareness is vital in preparing students for post-secondary interactions, both within and outside the university.

Though college instructors often have more freedom than their high school counterparts, they must still keep in mind best practices and their other educational goals. To have the most impact, language variation and linguistic tolerance must be taught to a wide student population in a general education course like introductory composition. The Council of Writing Program Administrators (CWPA) lists twenty-two learning outcomes students should achieve in introductory composition, organized under the headings "rhetorical knowledge," "critical thinking, reading, and composing," "processes," and "knowledge of conventions" (CWPA, 2014). Like high school teachers, then, composition instructors must integrate language issues into a curriculum designed to achieve a range of learning outcomes. While these goals do not mention "dialect" specifically, their emphasis on genre awareness, rhetorical flexibility, and knowledge of linguistic structures complement and reinforce course material related to dialect variation and language ideology. High school teachers should be aware of collegiate differences and expectations to prepare their students for college, while post-secondary instructors should be familiar with high school standards to effectively build on their students' knowledge. In doing so, high school and college instructors can creatively use existing content and materials to embed dialect awareness into their curriculum.

While reading novels, for instance, dialect awareness and language variation can be explored with the aid of digital resources. Mattie teaches English III, a junior-level course with an American literature and composition focus. One of the novels on the curriculum maps is Harper Lee's *To Kill a Mockingbird*. As students read, they analyze the dialects of the characters and the readers' perceptions of those dialects in order to deconstruct stereotypes often associated with them (see eResources for a lesson plan). From Bob and Mayella Ewell to Calpurnia and Atticus, *To Kill a Mockingbird* offers opportunities to explore language variation based on class, race, gender, etc. As characters are introduced, students discuss their opinions of them based on how they speak. Then, "students examine what judgements they make about a person ... based on [their] accent or dialect" (Wolfram, 2013, p. 29). As discussions develop, the instructor introduces digital resources, such as clips from *I Love Lucy* and *Modern Family,* to help the students examine the effects of language variation. For example, *Modern Family* portrays Gloria, the Colombian wife of 65-year-old Jay Pritchett, as a poor speaker of the English language. In Episode 6 of Season 2, Jay corrects Gloria's English: "Last night you said, 'We live in a doggy dog world' ... It's 'dog-eat-dog world'" (Levitan, Lloyd, Richman, & Spiller, 2010). Gloria's response reveals she is oblivious to Jay's chastising tone. Their humorous exchange seems lighthearted, but deconstructing the scene reveals negative representations of diverse speakers. Jay talks to Gloria as if she were a dumb child. In Chapter 18 of *To Kill a Mockingbird,* Mayella Ewell confronts Atticus for "mockin'" her during a cross-examination (Lee, 1982, p. 243). Unlike Gloria, Mayella acknowledges the way people perceive her based on her class and dialect. This lesson meets reading and language standards such as "grasping a point of view," analyzing "impact of specific word choices on meaning and tone," and understanding "how language functions in different contexts" (CCSSI, 2018). Though this activity was initially developed for a high school class, it easily adapts to different texts at various levels. When used in a college composition course, it helps fulfill the Writing Program Administrators (WPA) outcomes related to critical reading, as well as helping students "develop knowledge of linguistic structures" (CWPA, 2014).

Other television clips also provide a framework to encourage linguistic tolerance by building students' understanding of the relationship between language and context. For instance, the Comedy Central show *Key & Peele* often examines code-switching—the use of multiple languages or language varieties in the same utterance, conversation, or text. Lessons related to code-switching fulfill the WPA outcome that students should "develop facility in responding to a variety of situations and contexts calling for purposeful shifts in voice, tone, [or] level of formality" (CWPA, 2014). Similarly, code-switching lessons meet Common Core standards, such as students "apply[ing] knowledge of language to understand how language functions in different contexts" (CCSSI, 2018).

In the "Phone Call" sketch (Comedy Central, 2012), an unnamed character played by Keegan-Michael Key is on the phone with his wife, speaking in a variety that students would likely describe as "standard." When a character played by Jordan Peele approaches, also on the phone, Key's character switches to African American Vernacular English (AAVE). For several seconds, both men carry out their respective conversations in AAVE. When they separate and can no longer hear each other, Peele's character begins speaking in a tone that the video's closed-captioning describes as "effeminate."

Most students initially respond to the humor in the sketch, but there is a lot to analyze in the 47-second clip. In asking students to think about why these characters code-switch, teachers guide students to an understanding of the functions language serves in different situations and communities. While many discussions of code-switching emphasize the need to adjust one's communication to more closely align with the "standard," this example highlights the covert prestige (the positive connotations of a stigmatized language variety among its users) of AAVE and its role in identity expression. Moreover, the sketch speaks to the power dynamics embedded in perceptions of linguistic features associated with ethnicity and sexual/gender identity, laying the groundwork for fruitful class discussions.

Teachers can also use this clip to help students understand how they code-switch, even when they believe they speak "correct" English. Most students admit that they speak differently with their friends than they would at a job interview and, when asked, will identify some of the "nonstandard" features of their casual communication. Not only does this call into question Midwesterners' perceptions of their language variety's correctness, it also acts as a springboard for larger discussions of why some types of language variation are considered more acceptable than others. If everybody code-switches to some extent, why is it that some people go their whole lives believing their language is "standard" while others are ridiculed (or worse) for their language use? While students may not be able to achieve that level of understanding in a single lesson, it does change the way they think and talk about their own and others' language use. It also fulfills the WPA and Common Core goals cited above by helping students make more conscious and purposeful shifts in language and tone for different contexts, particularly if students are asked to practice these skills.

Digital resources like these offer high school and university educators numerous benefits to support what they already do in the classroom. We have provided some resources, but there are many more available. Repositories such as the Digital Archive of Literacy Narratives and the International Dialects of English Archive feature speakers of many language varieties describing their use of and relationship to language. Students can build their understanding of American regional dialects by exploring the *Dictionary of American Regional English* (see Abrams & Stickle, this volume, pp. 84–92) or the many dialect maps available online. Language-themed documentaries and podcasts also supplement instruction when teachers do not have easy access to examples of diverse Englishes. While it is impossible to catalogue all the available resources, we have mentioned some of our favorites above, provided an annotated list on eResources, and shared a lesson plan below to illustrate how digital resources can be used to teach language variation and ideology.

This collaboration highlights the potential for productive exchange between language and literacy educators at the secondary and post-secondary levels. In sharing our ideas and experiences teaching language ideology, we found significant (and perhaps surprising) overlap between our goals for and struggles with teaching language diversity in the "accentless" Midwest. We each benefited from the other's insights, and our combined knowledge painted a fuller picture of where our students come from and where they're going. Our collaboration also helped us explore and better articulate how teaching language diversity enhances curricula at multiple levels and the value of digital resources in providing context, examples, and opportunities for further reflection and application.

Lesson Plan: Exploring Regional Dialects

Recommended Grade Level(s)

Upper-level secondary students and beginning college students

Context

This lesson can be adapted to fit a variety of courses. Mattie has used it in eleventh-grade American literature, and Amanda has taught versions in college-level courses on academic writing and research methods. Because it serves as an introduction to language ideology and dialect variation, it can be placed at the beginning of the term with minimal scaffolding. It can also be adapted to align with other course content and placed anywhere in the curriculum. Amanda has taught this lesson as part of units devoted to literacy narratives, language awareness, and rhetorical analysis. Mattie has taught this lesson to introduce the characteristics of regional literature. Follow-up should relate to the larger focus of the course. Students can be asked to analyze language use in a literary work, compose an autoethnography of their own region's or community's language use, research societal attitudes toward language, or complete any number of follow-up activities.

Objectives

Students will be able to:

*   analyze dialects from a variety of locations;
*   discuss characteristics of dialects and describe how those characteristics impact perceptions;
*   evaluate how their own language use is influenced by geographical and social context.

Common Core and WPA Standards

CCSS.ELA-Literacy.SL.11–12.1

Initiate and participate effectively in a range of collaborative discussions (one-on-one, in groups, and teacher-led) with diverse partners on grades 11–12 topics, texts, and issues, building on others' ideas and expressing their own clearly and persuasively.

CCSS.ELA-Literacy.SL.11–12.1.C

Propel conversations by posing and responding to questions that probe reasoning and evidence; ensure a hearing for a full range of positions on a topic or issue; clarify, verify, or challenge ideas and conclusions; and promote divergent and creative perspectives.

CCSS.ELA-Literacy.L.11–12.3

Apply knowledge of language to understand how language functions in different contexts, to make effective choices for meaning or style, and to comprehend more fully when reading or listening.

WPA-Rhetorical Knowledge-5

Match the capacities of different environments (e.g., print and electronic) to varying rhetorical situations.

WPA-Critical Thinking, Reading, and Composing-1

Use composing and reading for inquiry, learning, critical thinking, and communicating in various rhetorical contexts.

WPA-Processes-3

Experience the collaborative and social aspects of writing processes.

WPA-Knowledge of Conventions-1

Develop knowledge of linguistic structures, including grammar, punctuation, and spelling, through practice in composing and revising.

Procedures

Step 1: Anticipatory Activity (5 Minutes)

Explain that "Most people are shocked when they go to a different region and are told that they speak a dialect, since they take for granted that it is other people who speak dialects. But we all speak dialects, whether we recognize it or not" (Wolfram, 2013, p. 28). Some suggested questions to discuss with students: How would you describe your accent or dialect? What makes it unique? Are there certain words or phrases that you and your family say but others do not? How do others perceive your dialect? Have you ever been in a situation where someone has been surprised or confused by your speech?

Step 2: New York Times Dialect Quiz (10–15 Minutes; Can Be Assigned as Pre-Class Homework)

After this initial discussion, ask students to take the *New York Times* dialect quiz (www.nytimes.com/interactive/2014/upshot/dialect-quiz-map.html). This digital resource asks questions about certain regional words and phrases used in the United States. At the end of the quiz, students will see the location(s) where their way of speaking is most present. It should be noted that this quiz cannot accurately assess the dialect origins of international students. However, it can help them see the extent to which their current surroundings influence their English usage.

Step 3: Small Group Discussion (10 Minutes)

Have students discuss their results with peers in small groups. Were they shocked by their results, or do the results match where they grew up? Then, ask students to share out and discuss with the whole class.

Step 4: Explore IDEA *(5 Minutes; 10 If* New York Times *Quiz Was Assigned as Homework)*

Introduce students to the *International Dialects of English Archive* (www.dialectsarchive.com) and demonstrate how to find dialect samples specific to a country, state, or region. If time permits, listen to and discuss a few examples as a class, asking students to pick the regions where the samples come from.

Step 5: Group Work/Jigsaw (20 Minutes)

Ask students to work with their small groups to explore the dialect samples of a specific state or region (after they choose, ask them to check with you to ensure there's no overlap). Depending on course content and goals, students can limit their focus to the U.S. or another region. Students should listen carefully to the recorded dialect samples (with headphones) and discuss the following questions:

•   What distinctive features did you notice in each of the recorded samples? What makes this person's speech distinguishable from somebody from another region?
•   What similarities and differences did you notice between the dialect samples for your region? What do you think could be the reasons for these differences?
•   Have you heard this or a similar dialect elsewhere? Where? How did you or other people react to it?
•   Have you seen this dialect portrayed in the media? Give specific examples. How is this dialect typically portrayed? What kinds of characters speak using this dialect? What does the audience assume about their education, intelligence, manners, social class, etc.?

After discussion, ask each group to present their findings. If more time is needed, presentations can be carried over to the next class.

References

Arnaz, D. (Executive Producer). (1951). *I love Lucy* [Television series]. Hollywood, CA: Central Broadcasting Service.

Comedy Central. (2012, January 31). *Phone call* [Video File]. Retrieved from http://www.cc.com/video-clips/qvrhhj/key-and-peele-phone-call

Common Core State Standards Initiative. (2018). *English Language Arts standards*. Retrieved from www.corestandards.org/ELA-Literacy

Council of Writing Program Administrators. (2014). *WPA outcomes statement for first-year composition (3.0)*. Retrieved from http://wpacouncil.org/positions/outcomes.html

Crystal, D. (2012). *English as a global language*. Cambridge: Cambridge University Press.

Harker, M., & McCorkle, B. (n.d.). *Digital archive of literacy narratives*. Retrieved from www.thedaln.org/#/home

Iowa Core. (2017). *Employability skills*. Retrieved from https://iowacore.gov/iowa-core/subject/21st-century-skills/11/employability-skills

Kachru, B. B. (1992). Models for non-native Englishes. In B. B. Kachru (Ed.), *The other tongue: English across cultures* (2nd ed.) (pp. 48–74). Champaign, IL: University of Illinois Press.

Katz, J., & Andrews, W. (2013, December 21). How y'all, youse, and you guys talk. *New York Times*. Retrieved from www.nytimes.com/interactive/2014/upshot/dialect-quiz-map.html

Lee, H. (1982). *To kill a mockingbird*. New York, NY: Grand Central Publishing.

Levitan, S., Lloyd, C., & Richman, J. (Writers), & Spiller, M. (Director). (2010, October 27). Halloween [Television Series Episode]. In J. Morton, S. Levitan, P. Corrigan, B. Walsh, D. Zuker, C. Lloyd, … & J. Richman (Executive Producers), *Modern family*. Los Angeles, CA: American Broadcasting Company.

Meier, P., & Paul, D. (2018). *International dialects of English archive*. Retrieved from www.dialectsarchive.com

Midwestern American English. (2017, July 24). In *Wikipedia*. Retrieved from https://en.wikipedia.org/wiki/Midwestern_American_English

Morton, J., Levitan, S., Corrigan, P., Walsh, B., Zuker, D., Lloyd, C., … & Richman, J. (Executive Producers). (2009). *Modern family* [Television series]. Los Angeles, CA: American Broadcasting Company.

Preston, D. R. (2011). Michigander talk: God's own English. In M. Adams and A. Curzan (Eds.), *Contours of English and English language studies* (pp. 17–33). Ann Arbor, MI: University of Michigan Press.

University of Wisconsin-Madison. (2018). *Dictionary of American regional English*. Retrieved from http://dare.wisc.edu

Wolfram, W. (2013). Challenging language prejudice in the classroom. *Education Digest*, 79(1), 27–30.

Zadak, J., Key, K. M., Peele, J., Roberts, R., Atencio, P., & Martel, J. (2012). *Key & Peele* [Television Series]. New York, NY: Comedy Central.

Zuidema, L. A. (2005). Myth education: Rationale and strategies for teaching against linguistic prejudice—literacy educators must work to combat prejudice by dispelling linguistic myths. *Journal of Adolescent and Adult Literacy*, 48(8), 666–675.

Chapter 18

How Power Reveals and Directs Teacher Language Ideologies with High-Achieving African American Students in a Secondary English Classroom

Tanji Reed Marshall, Virginia Polytechnic Institute and State University, Virginia, and Chrystal Seawood, Washington Leadership Academy, Washington, DC

Introduction

Teachers' instructional decision-making and practice reveal a great deal about their educational beliefs. In this chapter, an English education researcher (Tanji) and a high school teacher (Chrystal) have collaborated to explore how teachers' language ideologies and the dynamics of power impact instructional decision-making and instructional delivery with high-achieving African American students (see also Wheeler, this volume, pp. 109–119). Our work is guided by several theories related to language, culture, power, and critical race theory (Delgado & Stefancic, 2012; Freire, 1970; Nieto, 2010; Wilches, 2007); we use these theories as tools to understand how instructional decisions affect (and are affected by) students of color who may speak varieties of English usually not accepted in schools. The lens of language ideology offers a window into examining teachers' thinking about and understanding of the inherent variance in language. We use Chrystal's journey of language discovery as a vehicle to examine language ideologies and instructional power with high-achieving African American students and offer insight into the need for teachers to reflect on their beliefs and hidden biases toward these underserved students.

High Achievement among African American Students

The term "high-achieving" is rarely associated with African American students. There is a pervasive belief that Black students are not as intelligent or academically capable as their White and Asian counterparts. Additionally, African American students are regularly seen through a narrow perspective of anti-intellectualism, behavioral opposition, and economic disadvantage. While teachers espouse beliefs in the potential of all children, research is clear: Many teachers harbor deficit perspectives about Black students, believing they are less capable than White students and students from certain Asian backgrounds (Perry, Steele, & Hilliard, 2003; Sparks, 2015). This deficit perspective is a critical factor in the under-representation of African American students in advanced courses. We focus on high-achieving African American students in this chapter to present a narrative of academic possibility.

There is no definitive way to characterize high achievement. However, in the U.S., standardized tests are the primary tools used to ascribe labels of intelligence and academic achievement. Although high academic achievement is often equated with high intelligence, the two are different. Intellectual giftedness is usually ascribed to individuals who score high on IQ tests (e.g., above 145 on a Binet test), while high academic achievement is used to describe students with higher than a C-grade point average in their coursework (Gould, 1996). Although many states have worked to open access to advanced courses, representational imbalances persist.

While the reasons behind this underrepresentation are complicated, language ideologies are certainly one factor. Teachers' expectations of language and language use influence their ability to see potential in students who do not use school-sanctioned speech—i.e., "Standardized" American English. As Bonner (2000) explains, teachers often use subjective factors associated with White cultural norms to gauge African American students' fitness for advanced courses, regardless of their intellectual abilities. The use of language varieties, or what many English teachers deem as "incorrect English," often signals to academic gatekeepers low intellect and an inability to thrive in an advanced course. Teachers' ideologies about Black language varieties often impede their ability to see the potential in high-achieving African American students.

Power in the Classroom

Power is present in every relationship and interaction, and the classroom is no exception. It creates imbalances and determines whether and how language varieties and cultures move freely or equitably in the classroom. Brazilian philosopher and critical educator Paulo Freire posited it was dishonest and insincere to deny the role of authority that teachers occupy because, as he explained, teachers evaluate students and can influence the trajectory of their education (Giroux, 2011). Freire's beliefs emphasize a need to understand the relationship between teachers and their power. Although power and authority are often used interchangeably, we make a distinction here. Authority exists according to one's role, position, and function—for instance, the difference between a principal's level of authority and a teacher's level of authority. Power maintains the levers of authority. Each exists with the other, and the two are nearly inseparable.

Ask most teachers about power, and these sorts of responses are likely to follow: "I don't see myself as powerful" or "Power is not something I think about in my class." Or even something like, "Well, [students] know that I'm the one in charge and that they will not overtake this classroom. This is a battle you're not going to win, not that they try." These sentiments, from real teachers in real classrooms, reflect a common belief about power and how it operates: Power equates behavior control and force. Teachers rarely think about power relative to how they make instructional decisions. Moreover, many curricular decisions are made outside teachers' control, leaving many to believe they are powerless to exercise their authority beyond corralling, managing, or controlling students. We contend, however, that teachers have more instructional decision-making power than they recognize or are willing to admit. Such power gets wielded in ways that advance teachers' core beliefs about teaching, learning, and their students.

Despite teachers' hesitance to name themselves as powerful, there is a tacit agreement between them and their students about the role each will play. This agreement is an acknowledgment that one will lead the other as the system demands. We thus argue a critical understanding of power and authority are necessary for equitable learning to occur (Pace & Hemmings, 2007).

Intersection of Power and Language Ideologies

Language, culture, and schooling are politically constructed. Each carries the weight of history, and how each manifest in classrooms is directly related to a teacher's ideologies regarding them. In her early years of teaching, co-author Chrystal believed there was a correct and incorrect way to speak and this doctrine needed to be taught most to Black children. She further remembers being so faithful to this belief that her mostly Black students were not allowed to use their home language in her pre-Advanced Placement classroom. Like many teachers, she adopted a correctionist framework (Devereaux, 2015), which reflected her ideologies about the "purity" of "Standard" American English (SAE). In her classroom, there was no room for students to use other varieties of English. Chrystal's insistence on SAE demonstrated her power to force linguistic conformity—by doing this, she revealed a "linguistic inferiority principle" (Wolfram & Schilling-Estes, 2006, p. 6), ultimately uncovering a hidden bias against the use and value of African American Vernacular English (AAVE). Her classroom was an academic space, and, as such, she believed students had to demonstrate they were on the path to becoming "good" students of English. Despite identifying as a Black woman who uses English varieties dexterously, Chrystal held ideologies about language use in the classroom, which led her to demand students communicate only in school-sanctioned structures of English. Herein lies the intersection of power and language: When one's beliefs about the supposed sanctity and purity of "Standardized" American English demands a singular prescribed form of communication, instructional decisions can be made in ways that use power detrimentally.

Classrooms are cultural exchange sites (Reed Marshall, 2017), with language as the primary vehicle for cultural transmission. How teachers and students use language is directly tied to their identity, culture, and social development. Adolescents experiment with language as part of their growth and development (Steinberg & Sheffield Morris, 2001); therefore, language variation is core to racial/ethnic and adolescent culture. When English teachers lack knowledge about and an appreciation for language variety as a means of cultural identification, they use power to make instructional decisions, which force students into "race- and identity-shelving" (Reed Marshall, 2018). *Race-shelving* can be understood as the recognition of race and the use of power to mitigate its presence by requiring the temporary putting aside of behaviors most associated with a particular race—in this case, how language is used in speech and/or writing—and an adoption of behaviors associated with the dominant culture. *Identity-shelving* involves the recognition that individual identity is shaped by factors such as race and the use of power to require a temporary putting aside of racially ascribed elements of an identity believed to be objectionable or personally offensive.

Language is heard and understood through cultural and racial lenses, with value assigned upon hearing. If a student uses what is commonly termed *African*

American Vernacular English or *Black American English*, teachers and other academic gatekeepers may question their intellect and view that student through a deficit lens. In such cases, teachers will make instructional decisions to correct what they believe to be "broken English," thereby requiring students to temporarily put aside the racially associative forms of English, adopting more "acceptable forms" of speech and writing. What is missing from such demands is the recognition students need to learn linguistic flexibility or the language of "best fit," with attention to audience, context, and purpose. This idea is particularly important with high-achieving African American students because language use is often associated with intelligence and academic ability.

Education needs a critical shift in understanding: we must transform instructional power from a weapon advancing institutionalized beliefs about "Standardized" American English to a more inclusive stance allowing language varieties to move freely in classrooms. Sometimes these shifts in understanding can happen by listening to what our students are saying. Chrystal recognized her biased language ideologies only because she listened to her students: They were the ones who pointed out a perceived hypocrisy of her demands for linguistic race-shelving. She remembers talking to her students at lunch one day; one of them noticed and challenged her use of double negatives, *ain'ts*, and subject–verb "disagreement," all vestiges of AAVE. They reminded Chrystal she was speaking "incorrectly." Her response was to tell her students she was speaking in the "normal" way she spoke with family and friends. In that moment, she realized she was not *teaching* anything about the English language but rather reinforcing dominant ideologies about language and using her power to do so. She knew then it was necessary to unpack her thinking about the so-called "correct" way of speaking before she led any more students astray. In reflecting on the relationship between language ideologies and power, Chrystal recalls thinking, *that* moment made her realize she carried a subconscious belief that the vernacular used by her mother and father, her grandmother, her aunties and uncles was a "broken" version of the language and she ought to speak "standard" English. Chrystal quickly realized her instruction about language was problematic; she had been masking the truth about the diversity in the English language and had been implicitly invalidating her students' language use. This incident forced Chrystal to reconcile her language ideologies and consider how her use of instructional power forced her students into a communicative style that fostered a colonizing approach to language.

Chrystal, like many teachers, required an SAE-only classroom with good intentions. However, such intentions may create hostile learning environments as teachers' negative use of power challenges African American students' sense of self. Many teachers believe they are helping their African American students become "better" by requiring only school-sanctioned forms of English and correcting perceived wrongs. These "good intentions" leave many African American students believing their language variety is broken and must be fixed. These beliefs also keep many high-achieving African American students out of advanced courses, as teachers confuse linguistic style with intellect. As Stubbs (2002) notes, "we hear language through a powerful filter of social value and stereotype" (p. 66). Under the guise of good intentions, many English teachers engage in correctionist-inspired strategies designed to teach Black students the "right" way to use English. This is not to suggest students do not need to know the rules of SAE; rather, we must dispel the myth of SAE's purity and sanctity. We must also inform

English teachers about the damaging messages they send by employing such strategies with their students of color.

Language Ideologies, Power, and Lesson Planning

Learning about language involves more than knowing about subject–verb agreement, letter capitalization, or punctuation placement. It is also about meaning-making and the various ways context affects grammar, word choice, and punctuation. In responding to her new perspectives about English and language instruction, Chrystal grappled with how to engage students in language analysis to move their thinking beyond passage-reading and question-answering. She developed a lesson in response to students' struggles with the language of standardized tests (see lesson plan). She recognized her students struggled most with sentence structure because they lacked automaticity and dexterity with the (so-called) SAE sentence structures. Their misunderstandings had become a barrier to their performance on state assessments. Experimenting with sentence deconstruction in a modeled lesson with co-author Tanji provided a strategy for Chrystal to begin shifting her language instruction to help students build bridges between their language and the language of their assessment. As Chrystal applied the strategy, she noticed her students became more adept at analyzing the language of their assessments by connecting it to their own use of language. They also became more confident in their ability to make meaning from and analyze a wide variety of texts.

Conclusion

It can be difficult to teach English since students use language in a variety of ways. Students have their own ideologies about language, which must be understood and appreciated, too. However, teachers become gatekeepers to deep knowledge and understanding when we use our power to maintain comfy falsehoods and fixed notions about what American English is and what it is not. We must shift our understanding and appreciate that there is no absolute "best" way of using language, and language use is not a signal of academic potential or intellect. We must be aware of how we use power to make decisions about language use, especially for high-achieving African American students. We must also be sure our own language ideologies are not sending the message that any language variety outside the school-sanctioned variety equals low academic ability.

Lesson Plan: The Language of Testing

Recommended Grade Level(s)

Ninth grade through twelfth grade

Context

This lesson addresses the language of standardized tests and can be leveraged to help students make sense of and discuss possible conflicts among the intersections of language, society, culture, and identity. This lesson can serve as an introduction to or continuation of learning about language ideologies.

Objectives

Students will be able to:

- analyze and discuss the language varieties between their speech and writing and language on standardized test questions;
- describe and identify language diversity and flexibility within the parameters of language and identity and language and society.

Common Core Standards

CCSS.ELA-Literacy.L.9–10.3

Apply knowledge of language to understand how language functions in different contexts, to make effective choices for meaning or style, and to comprehend more fully when reading or listening.

CCSS.ELA-Literacy.SL.9–10.1

Initiate and participate effectively in a range of collaborative discussions (one-on-one, in groups, and teacher-led) with diverse partners on grades 9–10 topics, texts, and issues, building on others' ideas and expressing their own clearly and persuasively.

Procedures

Step 1: Warm-up (10 Minutes)

Provide students with no more than two sample test questions from a standardized test. Have students independently analyze and make sense of the test language to explore and identify their beliefs about language diversity and flexibility. Use the following questions to frame their thinking:

- What do you notice about the way the test questions are written? (*This question will help you understand the way they create language on standardized tests.*)
- How does the test language compare to the way you write and speak? Based on this comparison, what ideas do you have about the different ways people use language in

society? (*This question will help you understand how students understand their language in comparison to standardized English.*)

• Pick one question to translate into your own words. Write the question using your most commonly used form of speech and writing. (*This question will help you identify variations in student language, as well as struggles with student comprehension.*)

Step 2: Pair and Share (2 Minutes)

Have students share their translated questions with a partner.

Step 3: Identifying Language Diversity (10 Minutes)

The following activities will help students identify and discuss diversity in language.

Option 1: Gallery Wall and Walk

Step 1: Gallery Wall
Have students transfer their question translations onto chart paper. (Note: To save time, you may want to spread large post-its around the room to give students space to write their sentences at the same time.)

Step 2: Gallery Walk
Have students analyze the various question translations in the following ways:

> **Compare and contrast:** Pick two to three question translations to analyze. List one similarity and one difference you notice between yours and your peers' translations.
>
> What does this comparison tell you about how people use language?

Option 2: Think. Link. Sync.
Have students write their question translations onto an index card. Students will share their question translations using the following format:

> **Think:** Walk around and think about how you will "pitch" your question to a classmate as the "correct" interpretation.
> **Link:** Find a partner with whom to share your translated question. Discuss and determine the best use of language to convey the meaning of the question.
> **Sync:** With your partner, determine the best language to use, combine your linked ideas, and construct a new question that best conveys your understanding of the question.

Have students consider the following:

> **Compare and contrast:** Discuss the similarities and differences you notice about your and your peer's question translations.
> Discuss what the comparison can reveal about the various ways people use language.

Step 4: Discussion (15 Minutes)

At this point, students have begun to sense what it means to be linguistically diverse. The classroom discussion will help students formally define language diversity and flexibility. Ask students the following: Based on your and your peers' question translations, complete this sentence: Language diversity and flexibility can be defined as _____.

Expect students to debate about "correct" and "incorrect" ways to use language as they share their ideas. Here are a few "listen-fors" as students begin to flesh out their ideas about language: *That's the way that White people talk. You're talking "proper" if you're speaking like that. I didn't understand the question/answer. That's the "right" or "incorrect" way to talk.*

The following prompt will guide student understanding about language diversity and flexibility:

- Think back to how you understood your peers' question translations. How did they use language to convey meaning?
- How did the test language compare to your speech and writing? Under what circumstances do you write or speak in a manner similar to the test language? Why? How do you make decisions about your language use?
- What does your language decision-making reveal about how context influences language use, form, type?

Step 5: Closer, Exit Ticket (5 Minutes)

How does your understanding about language variety and context impact your ability to make meaning from standardized questions and respond more accurately?

References

Bonner, F. (2000). African American giftedness: Our nation's deferred dream. *Journal of Black Studies, 30*(5), 643–663.

Delgado, R., & Stefancic, J. (2012). *Critical race theory: An introduction.* New York, NY: New York University Press.

Devereaux, M. (2015). *Teaching about dialect variations and language in secondary English classrooms: Power, prestige, and prejudice.* London and New York, NY: Routledge.

Freire, P. (1970). *Pedagogy of the oppressed.* New York, NY: Continuum.

Giroux, H. (2011). *On critical pedagogy.* New York, NY: Bloomsbury.

Gould, S. J. (1996). *Mismeasure of man: The definitive refutation to the argument of the Bell Curve.* New York, NY: W.W. Norton.

Nieto, S. (2010). *Language, culture, and teaching: Critical perspectives.* London and New York, NY: Routledge.

Pace, J. L., & Hemmings, A. (2007). Understanding authority in classrooms: A review of theory, ideology, and research. *Review of Educational Research, 77*(1), 4–27.

Perry, T., Steele, C., & Hilliard, A. (2003). *Young, gifted, and Black: Promoting high achievement among African-American students.* Boston, MA: Beacon Press.

Reed Marshall, T. (2017). Influences of language, culture, and power on instructional decision making with high-achieving African students in advanced secondary English classrooms (doctoral dissertation). Retrieved from VTechWorks database.

—— (2018). To correct or not correct: Confronting decisions about African American students' use of language varieties in the English classroom. *English Journal, 107*(5), 51–56.

Sparks, S. D. (2015). Unequal access to advanced courses targeted. *Education Week, 35*(10), 12–14.

Steinberg, L., & Sheffield Morris, A. (2001). Adolescent development. *Annual Review of Psychology, 52*, 83–110.

Stubbs, M. (2002). Some basic sociolinguistics concepts. In L. Delpit & J. K. Dowdy (Eds.), *The skin that we speak: Thoughts on language and culture in the classroom* (pp. 63–86). New York, NY: The New Press.

Wilches, J. (2007). Teacher autonomy: A critical review of the research and concept beyond applied linguistics. *Ikala, Revista de Language and Culture, 12*(18), 245–275.

Wolfram, W. & Schilling-Estes, N. (2006). *American English: Dialect and variation.* Hoboken, NJ: Blackwell Publishing.

Chapter 19

Sustained Linguistic Inquiry as a Means of Confronting Language Ideology and Prejudice

Kristin Denham, Western Washington University, Washington, and David Pippin, Young Achievers Science and Math Pilot School, Massachusetts

The flexibility of elementary classroom teachers to teach across subjects makes it possible to develop a rich program of linguistic inquiry in multiple subjects, and such a program can be successfully adapted and implemented by teachers even at the middle and high school levels. We have worked for years to teach scientific inquiry through the domain of language, building on work by Honda (1994) and Honda, O'Neil, and Pippin (2004, 2010). In the process we offer students the tools they need to confront linguistic ideology and prejudice, maybe even before they have directly encountered it. In this chapter, we demonstrate how developing one key topic throughout the year and in multiple domains gives students the opportunity to apply their reasoning to the linguistic phenomena all around them.

Consider the Syllable

If upper-elementary or middle school students have encountered the idea of a syllable before, it's likely to have been connected to the teaching of reading, spelling, or the writing of poems with a certain syllabic pattern, such as haiku, limericks, or cinquains. Awareness of syllables and their structures is very much a part of the foundational knowledge associated with literacy, and features in the Common Core standards from kindergarten on.

In our work, we start with the basic structure of syllables in general. Instead of asking students to memorize a new set of jargon in isolation, we use their knowledge of syllables, both learned and unconscious, and give them a reason to inquire about the structure of a syllable. Because the lesson deals with an engaging language game, students are also motivated to delve into the meanings of concepts that they've long heard about but never fully investigated—the basic components of words and linguistic questions like "What is a vowel? What is a consonant?"

Pig Latin

The lesson plan we provide at the end of this chapter is on a "language" called Pig Latin (Denham, 2005). Children all over the world invent or pass on *ludlings* (from Latin *ludus* 'game' and *lingua* 'tongue' or 'language'). These ludlings, also called *language games* or *secret languages*, distort the native language in some way, usually to prevent understanding by those who have not learned the language game. Some examples include the Gibberish family, prevalent in the U.S. and Sweden, and Verlan, spoken in France. Pig Latin, which is used all over the globe, is one of the most common games based on English. In this lesson, we consider the rules that govern the language of Pig Latin by adopting a "garden path" approach to inquiry, an easy entry into a situation where competing hypotheses exist. In this case, the beginning sounds of the words are the relevant features. As we introduce more data, students learn that they probably have to revise their hypotheses.

The basic rule of speaking Pig Latin is to remove the first sound of a word, move it to the end of the word, and then add "ay"—so the term *Pig Latin* would become *Igpay Atinlay*. When students consider words that start with a single consonant, this hypothesis emerges easily. However, when words begin with vowels or consonant clusters, it becomes less clear how to construct the Pig Latin versions of English words. Is the English word *oak* pronounced *oakay* in Pig Latin? Is *tree* pronounced *reetay* or *eetray*? Is *spruce* pronounced *ucespray* or *prucesay* or *rucespay*? Along the way, students may revise their own hypotheses, and they may also have different opinions on the "correct" versions of Pig Latin words, thereby discovering dialectal variations of Pig Latin. Students start to think about consonants and vowels as categories of sound as opposed to just letters, as when they encounter a word like *honest*, which starts with a consonant in spelling but a vowel in pronunciation. If they defined the problem in terms of spelling, and not sound, then this would be a good time to revise their hypothesis. In fact, distinguishing between spoken and written language features is found in the Common Core State Standards (CCSS), as is recognizing language variation.[1]

This introductory linguistics lesson draws students into the scientific process. They get experience with observation, hypothesis formation, collaboration, and, by checking for counterexamples to their arguments, the flexibility that is needed to revise one's theories. When students arrive at a hypothesis that stands up to all of the data thus far presented, it's possible to make an idea even more parsimonious by introducing some linguistics. Having the satisfaction of successfully working through the lesson using their own student language, they should be open to the expert take on the problem presented below. Giving students opportunities to see how expert language can sometimes be simpler and clearer than generalist language is an important goal of reading programs and of the CCSS.[2]

The Universal Structure of Syllables

Languages have varying syllable structures. The group of consonants at the beginning of a syllable is called the onset, and the vowel and any consonants following it at the end of the syllable are called the rime (or rhyme), a term which will be familiar to everyone in the class from the rhymes they've explored in poems. The rime can be further divided into a nucleus, a vowel (typically), and a coda, the consonant(s) at the end of the syllable. Figure 19.1, for instance, is a visual representation of the syllabic structure for the word *dog*.

---

1 For example, consider CCSS.ELA-Literacy.L.5.3.B: "Compare and contrast the varieties of English (e.g., *dialects, registers*) used in stories, dramas, or poems" (2018).
2 See, for example, CCSS.ELA-Literacy L.5.6: "Acquire and use accurately grade-appropriate general academic and domain-specific words and phrases, including those that signal contrast, addition, and other logical relationships" (2018).

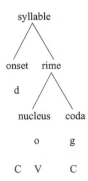

Figure 19.1 Syllable structure for *dog*

The capital letter "C" appearing at the bottom of the figure stands for any consonant sound; similarly, the "V" stands for any vowel sound. Thus, the word *dog*, which has three consecutive sounds, can be described as having a CVC or consonant–vowel–consonant structure.

Working with this new information, students form a new hypothesis for the Pig Latin problem that goes something like this:

To form words in Pig Latin, move the onset to the end of the word and add "-ay."

Such a hypothesis is both accurate and economical, and students feel empowered by the use of linguistic vocabulary rather than intimidated by it.

Syllables in English vary considerably in the details of their structure, compared to other languages. They can have a cluster of up to three sounds at the beginning— consider words like *splat*, *strap*, and *sprig*, all of which have three consonants as the onset—and a cluster in the coda as well—consider *barks* or *bands*. A fun extension of this work is to encourage students to find examples of all twenty-two syllable types that are possible in English, from CV—like the word *do*—to CVC—as in *bag*—to CCCVCCCC. Students will need to be reminded that letters do not correspond directly to sounds, so a word like *psychology* starts with just a single consonant /s/, and *thick* is a syllable with only three sounds—CVC—since <th> represents a single sound, just like <ck>. For yet another extension, have them try to figure out the math themselves by calculating the number of combinations. Wondering what kind of word has a CCCVCCCC pattern? You can find an example of this last structure (or CCCVCCC, depending on one's dialect) and read a good poem by checking out Galway Kinnell's "Blackberry Eating" (1980).

Once students have an understanding of basic syllable structure, it becomes possible to compare across languages. In many other languages, including Hawaiian and Japanese, an onset can have only a single consonant, and a rime must be just a vowel, so the basic structure of the Hawaiian syllable is simply a consonant plus a vowel, or just a vowel all by itself. A so-called "CV" syllable is the most common type of syllable in the world's languages. Providing students with data to let them figure this out for themselves is a satisfying endeavor, and teachers can bring in data from languages that students in the class know or are familiar with.

When a word is borrowed from one language into another, speakers will make that word conform to the syllable structure of their own language. Consider the English word *strike*, which, when borrowed into Japanese, conforms to the CV syllable structure of Japanese, thus turning a one-syllable English word into a five-syllable Japanese word: su-to-ra-i-ku. Likewise, in Hawaiian, the English loanword *aunty* becomes 'a-na-kē. Each syllable of 'a-na-kē is CV (the mark ' represents a glottal stop, a consonantal sound that can be heard in the middle of *uh-oh*), and the word also includes a replacement of /t/, which is not part of the Hawaiian sound system, with /k/, which is a close relative of /t/. The all-time favorite English word to explore in Hawaiian with fifth-graders, though, is *cow*, which becomes *pipi wahini*. The borrowed word *beef* becomes *pi* and then doubles. This process of reduplication is also present in languages in a different part of the Pacific Rim, the Pacific Northwest.

Languages of the Pacific Northwest and Reduplication

In the Pacific Northwest, as in many parts of the country, young students, or even college students, typically know very little about the Native languages of their home region. In a survey of his fifth-grade class in Washington State, Pippin found that while most said that they didn't know anything about languages in the area, some students had both good insights and understandable misconceptions. One mentioned that there was more than one language in the region; another connected the language to the Salish people; and another knew that Native languages of the region had almost died out and were being revived. One person's views parroted negative stereotypes of Native American languages as portrayed in the media—"Some talk like this: wooo calla mella wooo mee saaa," but at least she could identify the source—*Night at the Museum* (2006). There are two ideologies to confront then by introducing students to scientific inquiry into Native American languages: negative portrayals of Native languages in general, and lack of knowledge of any sort about the languages of the First Peoples to inhabit the region in which contemporary Americans live. Confronting such ideologies is a critical component of social studies classes, and so linguistic inquiry can easily be folded into curricula about Native people and state history.

Lushootseed/dxwəlšucid is one of the indigenous languages of the Salish Sea and a member of the Salish language family. One of the features of Lushootseed is the process of reduplication. Lushootseed has several distinct reduplicative processes; one is illustrated in Table 19.1, where speakers modify one word by doubling a piece of it to create an "out of control" version of that word.

You can offer students a prompt to describe the process that forms the words in B from those in A:

"My hypothesis is that in order to make the 'out of control' form of a word, you ..."

Table 19.1 Examples of Lushootseed reduplication

A		B	
ʔáɬ	'fast, quickly'	ʔáɬáɬ	'hurry up'
dᶻáq'	'fall, topple'	dᶻáq'áq'	'stagger, totter'
čəx̌	'split'	čəx̌əx̌	'cracked to pieces'

Table 19.2 Additional examples of Lushootseed reduplication

yubil	'starve'	yububil	'tired out, sick'
gʷədil	'sit down'	gʷədədil	'sitting for lack of anything else to do'
saxʷəb	'jump, run'	saxʷaxʷəb	'scurrying about ineffectively'

There are other words that employ the "out of control" reduplicative affixation process (see Table 19.2). We ask students if these words, which are all word pairs, conform to their previous hypotheses. If not, they revise to account for these new pairs.

The reduplication lesson (see Denham & Pippin, 2018; and eResources) raises for the students more questions about the nature of syllables—what syllables are, how we know what they are, and how they vary across languages. This particular problem also might motivate them to ask about syllable boundaries. Does the break come at *yu • bil* or *yub • il*? Most importantly, inquiry of this sort exposes students to languages of their region and allows them to discover and become experts on a feature of language they likely were not familiar with.

Syllables under Stress

The verbal prefix *a-*, as in *a-singing* or *a-running*, provides another opportunity to explore syllables. This prefix is typically associated with Southeastern speech and may also be considered somewhat archaic. In the book *Our Only May Amelia,* the author, Jennifer Holm, makes use of this prefixing. In one section, May Amelia says she was just "a-planning." In the Appalachian Mountain region and, perhaps, the Shoalwater Bay area of Washington at the turn of the century, some words that end in *-ing* take the *a-*, pronounced as [ə] (similar to the word *uh* or the first sound in *again*) in front of the word, as in "She went *a*-fishing." But not every *-ing* word can have an *a-* prefix. There are patterns or rules that determine when the *a-* prefix can be used and when it cannot be used: it has to be in front of a verbal participle. (But students don't need to have that language about language—"verb-like thing" works just fine.) The word the prefix attaches to also has to start with a consonant, and finally, the *a-* prefix must adhere to a particular rule about stress. Consider the following data (where the syllable that receives the most stress is marked with ´) taken from a lesson plan found in Reaser and Wolfram (2007):

> She was discóvering a trail.
> She was fóllowing a trail.

> She was repéating the chant.
> She was hóllering the chant.

In both cases the *a-* prefix works with the second item in the pair, alike in terms of word class and in having an onset, but different when it comes to stress. The *a-* prefix can attach only to words that have stress on the first syllable, so here again syllables come into play. Students have intuitions about which of the two examples in a pair is a well-formed expression of the prefix, and if this lesson comes on the heels of a discussion of stress, they are likely to figure it out. When students encounter dialect in literature, exercises like this one help them to examine the features of a dialect, as conveyed by the author, and what those features might suggest about the character's class, race, ethnicity, or level of education.

The Benefits of Such Investigations

We have provided here several very different kinds of examples of the ways we use the syllable as a jumping-off point for linguistic inquiry. There are many more such opportunities. For example, U.S. history classes can study the Cherokee syllabary as they learn about the government's removal policy of the nineteenth century. Lessons on the collapse of unstressed vowels to schwa answer questions that students and teachers have about spelling, such as the difference between the pronunciation of *moral* and *morality*. The doubling of consonants in spelling also involves stress of syllables, as in *benefited* compared to *omitted*, where consonant doubling occurs with stress on the final syllable of the root.

How do such discussions and investigations help students confront language ideology and linguistic prejudice? Confronting linguistic discrimination can happen in a variety of ways, and, importantly, the knowledge builds throughout the year as students gain exposure to a wide variety of languages and dialects and their linguistic features. Students' home languages other than English should be brought in as examples, and these then become not burdens to overcome but critically important language data that students are the experts on. In addition to studying directly the languages of students and their families, investigation of the languages of the Native peoples of a region goes a very long way toward understanding the interconnectedness of history and culture with contemporary attitudes—that linguistic discrimination has as its roots colonialism and racism. Whether these topics are addressed directly or not, exposure to the languages themselves and to the people who speak them helps students understand that language and identity are intimately intertwined. Moreover, the rules of other dialects—including variations of English learned as a second language and even Pig Latin's dialects—can and should be studied, not as an attempt to eradicate "nonstandard" features but to understand their rules and to learn from them.

We have used syllables as an example of how investigation into language can be incorporated into existing studies, alongside lessons on spelling, poetry, fiction, or social studies. While investigating Pig Latin or Lushootseed or *a-* prefixing may seem like a diversion from the more important topics, we firmly believe that the benefits are real and broad. Such an approach showcases language as an object of study and demonstrates how students can practice scientific methodology. Investigating an unfamiliar language variety can be intimidating to teachers and students alike, and that's where the teacher–linguist partnership can be important. But it can also be important to jump in right alongside the students, conveying to them that linguistic knowledge is something to be discovered. It's okay not to have all the answers, but it's not okay not to even ask the questions.

Lesson Plan: Parsimonious Pig Latin

Recommended Grade Level(s)

Elementary through high school

Context

This is an introductory lesson on syllable structure that can connect to inquiry in literature study—both poetry and prose—as well as spelling, science, and social studies.

Objectives

Students will be able to:

- develop a hypothesis about language;
- identify the components of a syllable;
- use a feature of language to explore linguistic variation.

Common Core Standards

CCSS.ELA-Literacy.RF.K.2

Demonstrate understanding of spoken words, syllables, and sounds (phonemes).

CCSS.ELA-Literacy.RF.4.3.A

Know and apply grade-level phonics and word analysis skills in decoding words.

CCSS.ELA-Literacy.RF.5.3.A

Know and apply grade-level phonics and word analysis skills in decoding words.

Procedures

Step 1: Data Analysis, Part 1 (10 Minutes)[3]

Consider the following data, where the Standard English word is transmogrified into Pig Latin:

English	Pig Latin
madrone	adronemay
hemlock	emlockhay
cedar	edarcay
fir	irfay

Formulate a hypothesis that accounts for Pig Latin formation.

3 See eResources for student handout and teacher notes.

Step 2: Data Analysis, Part 2 (10 Minutes)

Now consider the following additional data. Do these words challenge your hypothesis? If so, talk to your classmates and revise your theory:

English	Pig Latin
oak	oakay
ash	ashay
alder	alderay
osoberry	osoberryay

Do you have to revise your theory? If so, what is your revised theory?

Teacher Notes

After working through the lesson, the class should have come up with a hypothesis that looks something like the following:

If the word starts with a consonant, move all the letters from the first part of the word up to the vowel to the end of the word and add -*ay*. If it begins with a vowel, just add -*ay* to the end of the word. Or, more parsimoniously: Move all the consonants up to the first vowel to the end of the word and add -*ay*, otherwise just add -*ay*.

Step 3: Data Analysis, Part 3 (10 Minutes)

Finally, consider this data:

English	Pig Latin
tree	eetray
shrub	ubshray
spruce	ucespray
quercus	ercusquay

Does your theory account for this data? If not, what is your revised theory?

Teacher Notes

Challenging the group with an apparent counterexample such as the word *honest* forces the class to think about consonants and vowels as categories of sound as opposed to just written letters. It turns out there are variations of Pig Latin that would or wouldn't include the [h] in the final pronunciation. Thus, Pig Latin has dialects. When words start with vowels, there are several ways to form the Pig Latin word. Here are four of them:

		Dialect 1	Dialect 2	Dialect 3	Dialect 4
(a)	*eat*	eat-may	eat-hay	eat-way	eat-ay
(b)	*art*	art-may	art-hay	art-way	art-ay
(c)	*honest*	onest-may	onest-hay	onest-way	onest-ay

Step 4: Hypothesis (10 Minutes)

Use the model of a syllable to arrive at a more parsimonious hypothesis.

Teacher Notes

After exploring the universal structure of syllables with the class, ask students to use the language of *onset*, *rime*, *nucleus*, and *coda* to develop a parsimonious hypothesis about the rules of Pig Latin.

References

Common Core State Standards Initiative. (2018). *English Language Arts standards*. Retrieved from www.corestandards.org/ELA-Literacy/L/5

Denham, K. (2005). Ludlings teach language diversity and change: From Pig Latin to Ubby Dubby, National Council of Teachers of English Annual Convention, Pittsburgh, PA, 2005.

Denham, K., & Pippin, D. (2018). *Voices of the Pacific Northwest*. Retrieved from www.voicesofthepnw.net

Hammel, T. M., & Levy, S. (2006). *Night at the museum* [Motion Picture]. USA: 20th Century Fox.

Honda, M. (1994). Linguistic inquiry in the science classroom: It is science, but it's not like a science problem in a book. *MIT Occasional Papers in Linguistics 6*. Cambridge, MA: MITWPL.

Honda, M., O'Neil, W., & Pippin, D. (2004). When Jell-O meets generative grammar. Linguistic Society of America Annual Meeting, Boston, MA, 2004.

—— (2010). On promoting linguistics literacy. In K. Denham & A. Lobeck (Eds.), *Linguistics at school: Language awareness in primary and secondary education* (pp. 175–188). Cambridge: Cambridge University Press.

Kinnell, G. (1980). Blackberry eating. In *Moral acts, moral words*. Boston, MA: Houghton Mifflin Harcourt. Retrieved from www.poetrysociety.org/psa/poetry/poetry_in_motion/atlas/chicago/blackberry_eating

Reaser, J., & Wolfram, W. (2007). Voices of North Carolina: Language and life from the Atlantic to the Appalachians. Retrieved from https://cdn.chass.ncsu.edu/sites/linguistics.chass.ncsu.edu/documents/teacher_hi-res.pdf

Chapter 20

"Standard" English, "Classic" Literature

Examining Canonical and Linguistic Ideologies in *Huck Finn*

Jeanne Dyches, Iowa State University, Iowa, and
Cameron Gale, West Des Moines Community Schools, Iowa

Scholarship has long examined language and dialect variation, finding that language practices and ideologies both generate and reproduce power imbalances between mainstream and stigmatized speakers (Wolfram, 2000). However, these iterations of privilege and marginalization are not confined to the field of linguistics: the literature canons found in our secondary English classrooms, and the texts at their foundation, also perpetuate the dominant ideas of what is "proper," "traditional," and "acceptable" in secondary English classrooms (Bissonnette, 2016; Dyches, 2017; Morrison, 2007). Yet these conversations have largely been isolated from each other and rarely found in secondary English classrooms.

Equipping teachers and students with the knowledge and skills necessary to grapple with the oppressive literacy structures present in both their classrooms and their social worlds helps increase student and teacher agency (Dyches, 2018; Godley & Minnici, 2008). This chapter introduces new strategies for increasing student and teacher agency by detailing a collaboration between a linguist, Jeanne, and a high school English teacher, Cameron, as they designed lessons intended to open conversations around linguistic and canonical systems of power.

The Researcher: Jeanne

A woman who identifies as White, middle-class, cisgender, and heterosexual, I was born and raised in the southeastern U.S. For five years, I taught juniors and seniors at a large urban high school in Raleigh, North Carolina, where the vast majority of my students identified as persons of color. That my students' bodies, lived experiences, and realities contrasted so strikingly with the state's and district's required curricula became increasingly clear to me the longer I taught. Over time, I became more intentional in designing culturally responsive canonical instruction. These same topics—disrupting the problematic ideologies imbued throughout curricula and other staples of the secondary literature classroom—have continued to drive my intellectual pursuits as a researcher at a large university in the Midwest.

I met Cameron in the fall of 2016 after accepting an invitation from his English department to discuss the intersections between social justice and English instruction. Throughout the department-wide conversation, I was struck by Cameron's willingness to explore his own sociocultural identities and how they influenced his teaching. That spring, we met to discuss the potential of a collaboration. This chapter is the product of work with someone who I believe teaches in critical, socially just ways.

The Teacher: Cameron

More and more, I realize ways that my identity as a White, middle-class, cisgender male affords me privileges across nearly all areas of life. My only claim to diversity might be that I grew up in extremely rural areas of the Northwest, Northeast, and Mountain West. I found my first teaching job at a large suburban school in Iowa and have been teaching there for fifteen years.

My school is over 70 percent White and, starting a couple of years ago, has been working hard to address both hidden and obvious inequities within our school system and the larger community. I see this as our most important work and have sought ways to tackle issues both within and beyond the classroom. To that end, my department's partnership with Jeanne has been fortuitous. We are lucky to collaborate with a researcher who loves to work with high school students and pushes teachers who too often fall victim to curricular and pedagogical inertia.

Participatory Action Research

Our collaboration channeled participatory action research (PAR), a model for researchers attempting to co-design research projects *with* participants rather than *for* participants (McIntyre, 2007). PAR invites teachers to identify issues in their classrooms; design interventions; collect, assess, and draw conclusions from data; and reflect on the experience in order to modify their practices for students' increased success (James, Milenkiewicz, & Bucknam, 2008). We settled on this approach organically given our desire to craft an experience tailored to meet the needs of Cameron's students. We also wanted to locate the synergies between Jeanne's research agenda and Cameron's professional agency and identities. PAR allowed us to meld all of these ambitions.

Lesson Overview

In the following sections, we discuss the planning and implementation of our co-constructed unit that focused on critical race theory to help students better understand and identify connections between the canon and language ideologies through their reading of *Adventures of Huckleberry Finn* (1996, referred to as *Huck Finn* hereafter).

Planning

In the spirit of PAR, Jeanne wanted Cameron to lead the work as much as possible; therefore, he picked the focus of the collaboration. Jeanne admits that she stifled a groan when Cameron said *Huck Finn*. But as we worked through the particulars of the collaboration, the potential for our work crystallized. He shared his previous approaches to teaching the novel, which included having students apply critical inquiry during their study. Cameron's students generated and investigated the novel-influenced questions of their choice, which increased his students' engagement with and comprehension of the book. As a result, he wanted to continue using an inquiry approach to teaching *Huck Finn*.

Wishing to honor and build on these positive instructional experiences, Jeanne proposed a shift to a critical inquiry model—one that positions students to "question the everyday world and consider actions that can be taken to promote social justice" (Lewison, Leland, & Harste, 2008, p. 8). Understanding that social justice involves the disruption of systems of oppression, including sexism, racism, heteronormativity, and classism (Dyches & Boyd, 2017), we decided to focus on critical race theory (CRT) since *Huck Finn* naturally opens up conversations around racism, Whiteness, and oppression. Our goals for students included (a) to understand CRT; (b) to apply CRT as we examined notions of "canonical" American literature; (c) to apply CRT as we problematized "Standard American English" practices and the ways that dialects shape readers' engagement with *Huck Finn*; and (d) to begin to notice the parallels and intersections between these oppressive systems of both the literary canon and "Standard American English."

Implementation

To begin our novel study, we first familiarized students with CRT, asking them to consider the following elements (Bell, 1995; Delgado & Stefancic, 2001), which we worded using student-accessible terms:

1. Race is (and has historically been) everywhere and is threaded throughout American society.
2. Experiences and stories of persons from nondominant groups matter and are important.
3. In American society, people who identify as White often enjoy benefits they aren't even aware of.
4. Race is experienced through various lenses (gender, class, religion, sexuality, etc.)—it can't be experienced in isolation.
5. CRT requires action.

Wanting to make sure that students understood the role Whiteness plays in racial construction and stratification (Omi & Winant, 2014), we paid particular attention to exploring the notion of Whiteness as the dominant story. We also wanted students to understand that Whiteness behaves as a seemingly neutral phenomenon that in fact confers privileges to those who identify as White (Harris, 1993). To highlight these ideas throughout the unit, we asked students to also consider the following tenets of Critical Whiteness Studies (CWS):

1. Whiteness is a modern invention; it has changed over time and place.
2. Whiteness often isn't questioned or noticed and frequently provides people with certain benefits they don't realize.
3. In understanding and unpacking Whiteness, we can improve our society.
(Nayak, 2007, p. 738)

Over the course of the unit, we implemented a variety of lessons designed to help students notice and respond to elements of CRT/CWS. In one activity, Jeanne took students on a "critical literacy walk" during which the group attempted to identify ways in which CRT/CWS manifested in the normalized structures of the school. For example, the group noticed that the school's movie-night line-up involved production posters with entirely White casts and talked about how these selections reinforced Whiteness as the dominant narrative. In another hall, students had created posters for Hispanic Heritage Awareness month. The posters listed a stereotype (such as one that read "All Hispanics are illegal"), a student-drawn image, and a response to the stereotype. This example provided the opportunity to discuss counterstories (stories that speak against those that may be accepted in mainstream spaces) and how these counterstories help us understand different perspectives.

Using CRT to Problematize Canonical Literature

Next, we moved into a conversation about how CRT/CWS helps explain and complicate the underpinnings of texts deemed "canonical" literature. During this portion of the unit, we (instructors and students) read an assortment of materials, including excerpts from Applebee's (1974) *Tradition and Reform in the Teaching of English: A History*; key national studies of secondary literature curricula spanning 1907–2010; a *New York Times* news article on the canon wars of the 1980s/1990s; and portions of the Common Core State Standards and its text exemplars. We discussed the notion that *Huck Finn* has been lauded as "the great American novel," and how CRT/CWS might help us dissect the underlying messages of whose voices, bodies, and experiences count, particularly when considering the "classic" literature that secondary students have historically read, and continue to read, in their literature classes (Bissonnette & Glazier, 2016; Schieble, 2014).

Using CRT to Problematize Language

Having forged conversations with students about CRT, canonical literature, and *Huck Finn*, we then moved into a two-day lesson in which we explored how conversations of CRT/CWS could help us make sense not only of the ideologies driving the literary canon but of language itself. The lessons draw on pedagogical materials created by linguists Jeffrey Reaser, Walt Wolfram, and Jessica Hatcher (Reaser, Adger, Wolfram, & Christian, 2017; Reaser & Wolfram, 2007) and on research these linguists cite in their own work (Baugh, 2003; Rickford & King, 2013). In addition to using a template that we created to help students process and think through the various materials of the unit, students engaged in quick-writes as well as small-group and whole-class discussion. For full lesson plans, see eResources.

During this portion of the lesson, students began by responding to the question "What is the right way to speak?" Next, they read an excerpt titled "The Right Way to Speak" from Woodson's (2016) *Brown Girl Dreaming*. Following discussion of these materials, we moved into unpacking what a *dialect* is, a conversation undergirded by our reading of Wolfram's (2000) "Everyone Has an Accent." Next, we examined materials from the George Zimmerman case, focusing on the testimony of Rachel Jeantel, the last person to speak with Trayvon Martin. Jeantel's fluent use of African American Vernacular English (AAVE) during her questioning sparked a national conversation around AAVE and Standard American English. We then discussed with students the ways in which language impacted how Jeantel was treated both by the public and by the court. Lastly, we asked students to think about dialect in *Huck Finn,* reflecting specifically on how our lessons on language and power shaped how they thought of Jim's and Huck's dialects.

Following the lessons on language, which served as the final segment in the *Huck Finn* unit, students completed a survey, reflecting on their engagement with the unit. We asked them to consider our conversations around CRT, canonical literature, and language practices, and how their perceptions had shifted throughout the experience. We also wanted to know how these conversations shaped their experience reading *Huck Finn.* We believed this reflection was important for the students—and for us—to perform. Below, we detail these reflections.

Reflections

In the following sections, we untangle Cameron's perceptions of the unit—that is, how students engaged with conversations on CRT, the canon, and language awareness. We then move into how the unit influenced Cameron's own thinking and future practices. For full interview transcript, see eResources.

Critical Race Theory

Following the unit's completion, Jeanne asked Cameron to reflect on the ways in which conversations about the canon helped students understand critical race theory. Cameron offered that, "I actually think it's the other way around: I think our work with CRT set students up to view the canon more critically when we discussed it with them." Cameron believed that beginning the unit with CRT "primed" students to think through the lens when we discussed the canon, *Huck Finn,* and discriminatory language practices. Discussions about the canon, Cameron shared, gave students another way to see how race affects society. Students used information about the canon in their visual essays at the end of the unit, a finding that showed students were making important connections between race and the canon.

Problematizing the Reverence of Huck Finn

The unit also helped students think differently, and perhaps more deeply, about their reading of *Huck Finn.* Cameron believed that our conversations around CRT, and how the secondary literature reflects many of its tenets, encouraged students to see *Huck Finn* in a "more complex way." Students understood Twain's criticisms of racism, and the novel's prominence in the tradition of American literature. But students also began to consider the nuances of the book more deeply, and the role authorship plays both in the narrative and in its preservation. Cameron shared that by the end of the unit he believed students were beginning to think about Twain as "another White male author" and about how these facets of authorial identity might have impacted the narrative *and* historical reverence of the book.

Language and CRT

Cameron was pleased with how quickly students grasped the privileged nature of language use and how open they were to the connections between language and power. As with conversations around the canon, he believed that discussing language and linguistic ideologies "gave students another tool in their CRT belt." During the lessons, students engaged readily with the materials and enjoyed rich, lively discussion. While Cameron was pleased with students' willingness to discuss language and its connections to CRT, students largely left out any mentions of linguistic practices/discrimination in their visual essays. Cameron wondered if the timing of the lesson's implementation influenced their experiences discussing language and their understanding of how language works in *Huck Finn*. Cameron shared that, "in the future, I hope to place the [language] lessons earlier in the unit so as to better leverage them in our reading of the novel."

Cameron's Self-Reflections

While Jeanne was interested in Cameron's perceptions of students' engagements with the unit, she also wanted to understand how the experience altered Cameron's thinking about race, language, and the canon. Cameron mused that "these lessons certainly nudged me into a more acute awareness of my own reactions to the speech of others. I think this awareness will serve me well as our school and district gradually work deeper into addressing our race and inequity issues." He noted that he had begun to find himself more aware of the speech he heard in the school hallways. Cameron ruminated on a conversation in one of his social-media circles in which older generations were criticizing a younger person about his use of slang. He recognized the conversation as one that showed the intersection of privilege as it plays out racially, culturally, and generationally. He noted that "without … my students, I'm not sure I would have been attuned to this important and problematic situation."

Cameron realized also that he wished to locate new ways to help students push back against curricular traditions and expectations. Respective to his literature curriculum, Cameron shared that

> I'd like students to question our own curriculum more. We have yet to read much this semester by female authors or authors of color. That's a problem, yet not a single student has brought it up. Obviously, I'm aware of it and know the need to address it, but I should also be finding ways to help students question it as well.

The unit helped Cameron see his students' lack of curricular resistance; he began to think of ways in which to position students to investigate, and push back against, curricular boundaries.

Looking Ahead: Forging Connections between CRT, Huck Finn, and Language

Even with discussion on CRT, the canon, and language practices, and how the entities can help students complicate their reading of *Huck Finn*, Cameron believed that, overall, students struggled to connect the novel to the present day. He felt that facilitating conversation about language and linguistic ideologies earlier in the unit could help with this issue. He reflected:

> We had some interesting discussions about characters and power, and the dialect piece will further those discussions in the future. I also think that giving language

more prominence in the unit will lead to deeper discussions of code-switching, which I see as incredibly relevant to students' own lives. Huck as a character is incredibly adept at code-switching, adapting to many different circumstances. Maybe that will help students find further connections to the present day.

Cameron also wished that we had asked students which authors we should be reading in addition to Twain. This shift is critical for us to make in the future: by providing students a voice in the curriculum-making process, we will help them develop and hone a discipline-specific form of student agency, itself a marker of social-justice teaching (Dyches & Boyd, 2017).

Significance

Our co-constructed researcher/teacher narrative aims to show the possibilities for partnerships not only between language and canonical ideologies but between researchers and secondary teachers as well. The unit positioned students—and the two of us—to question the ways in which Whiteness acts as the traditional standard in both language and canonical literary representations.

As we conclude this chapter, we hope readers will see our partnership as one that reveals the powerful possibilities available when teachers and researchers work together, and that these partnerships, at their best, can better position students to recognize—and resist—the systems of power that permeate the secondary literature classroom.

References

Applebee, A. N. (1974). *Tradition and reform in the teaching of English: A history*. Urbana, IL: National Council of Teachers of English,

Baugh, J. (2003). Linguistic profiling. *Black linguistics: Language, society, and politics in Africa and the Americas, 1*(1), 155–168.

Bell, D. A. (1995). Who's afraid of critical race theory? *University of Illinois Law Review*, 893–910.

Bissonnette, J. D. (2016). Privileged pages: Contextualizing the realities, challenges, and successes of teaching canonical British literature in culturally responsive ways. Doctoral dissertation, University of North Carolina, Chapel Hill. Available from ProQuest Dissertations and Theses (10119821).

Bissonnette, J. D., & Glazier, J. (2016). A counterstory of one's own: Using counterstorytelling to engage students with the British canon. *Journal of Adolescent and Adult Literacy, 59*(6), 685–694.

Delgado, R., & Stefancic, J. (2001). *Critical race theory: An introduction*. New York, NY: New York University Press.

Dyches, J. (2017). Shaking off Shakespeare: A White teacher, urban students, and the mediating powers of a canonical counter-curriculum. *Urban Review, 45*(3), 1–26.

—— (2018). Investigating curricular injustices to uncover the injustices of curricula: Curriculum evaluation as critical disciplinary literacy practice. *High School Journal, 101*(4), 236–250.

Dyches, J., & Boyd, A. (2017). Foregrounding equity in teacher education: Toward a model of Social Justice Pedagogical and Content Knowledge (SJPACK). *Journal of Teacher Education, 68*(5), 476–490.

Godley, A. J., & Minnici, A. (2008). Critical language pedagogy in an urban high school English class. *Urban Education, 43*(3), 319–346.

Harris, C. (1993).Whiteness as property. *Harvard Law Review, 106*(8), 1707–1791.

James, E., Milenkiewicz, M., & Bucknam, A. (2008). *Participatory action research for educational leadership: using data-driven decision making to improve schools.* Los Angeles, CA: Sage Publications.

Lewison, M., Leland, C., & Harste, J. C. (2008). *Creating critical classrooms: Reading and writing with an edge.* New York: Erlbaum.

McIntyre, A. (2007). *Participatory action research* (Vol. 52). Los Angeles, CA: Sage Publications.

Morrison, T. (2007). *Playing in the dark.* New York, NY: Vintage.

Nayak, A. (2007). Critical whiteness studies. *Sociology Compass, 1*(2), 737–755.

Omi, M., & Winant, H. (2014). *Racial formation in the United States* (3rd ed.). London and New York, NY: Routledge.

Reaser, J., Adger, C. T., Wolfram, W., & Christian, D. (2017). *Dialects at school: Educating linguistically diverse students.* London: Taylor & Francis.

Reaser, J., & Wolfram, W. (2007).Voices of North Carolina dialect awareness curriculum. Retrieved from https://linguistics.chass.ncsu.edu/thinkanddo/vonc.php

Rickford, J., & King, S. (2013). Justice for Jeantels: Fighting linguistic prejudice and racial inequity in courts and schools, after *Florida* v. *Zimmerman. New Ways of Analyzing Variation.* Paper Presented at *New Ways of Analyzing Variation* Conference, Pittsburg, PA.

Schieble, M. (2014). Reframing equity under Common Core: A commentary on the text exemplar list for grades 9–12. *English Teaching: Practice and Critique, 13*(1), 155–168.

Twain, M. (1996). *Adventures of Huckleberry Finn.* New York, NY: Random House.

Wolfram, W. (2000). Everyone has an accent. *Teaching Tolerance, 18*, 18–23.

Woodson, J. (2014). *Brown girl dreaming.* New York, NY: Penguin.

Index

Note: Page numbers in *italics* refer to figures, while those in **bold** refer to tables and boxes. References to notes are given as the page number followed by "n" and the note number.

We use both "in classrooms" and "teaching" purposefully in this index. "In classrooms" denotes how to bring ideas into the classroom on an ideational level. "Teaching" denotes practical instructional ideas. This distinction is applicable throughout the index.

accent: ideologies of 8, 12, 23, 74, 83, 135; Midwest 129, 133; Southern 3, 18, 74; Valley Girl 5
Advanced Placement (AP) Linguistics 43, 48, 125, 140
African American English (AAE): grammatical patterns of 71, 73, 80, 96, 110, 114, **115**; ideologies of xviii, 5, 35, 73, 80, 94, 109, 140, 160; registers 20, 23; teaching xviii, 5, 35, 120, 132
African American naming traditions 5
African American Vernacular English (AAVE) *see* African American English (AAE)
Appalachian English *see* regional dialects
assignment(s) xxi, 4, 12, 13, 14, 64, 85, 87, 90, 91
authority xi, xx, 76, 77, 79, 95, 97, 139–140

bilingualism 5n2, 98, 101–102, 107
borrowings *see* loanwords
Boston accent *see* regional dialects

calque 105, 105n3, **106**
canonical literature and the canon xx–xxi, 54, 63, 75, 88, 97, 157–164
capitalization xviii, 50, 113, 114, 115, 142
charged language: cracker 90–92; N-word 25–30, 63; swear words 83; taboo words xviii, 26–27

Cherokee 95, 97, 99, 152
Chicanx English *see* Latinx English
clause 40–43, 77n1, 77n2, 78, 80–81, 81n4, 115
code-switching: characters' use of 163; identity and 20; language and 20, 105, 106, 163; literature and 83; media and 131; privilege and 76, 82, 132; students and 20, 55, 105; teaching 19, 20, 22 23, 48, 56, 110, 117, 131
colonial period 95, 97, 98
colonizing as language discrimination 95, 97, 141, 152
Common Core State Standards *see* standards
consonant 69, 147–152, 154
consonant doubling 152
contrastive analysis 102, 104–106, **105**, **106**, 110, 117
correctionist framework 120, 140, 141
counterstories 93, 98, 160
creole 34
critical discourse analysis 93
critical inquiry *see* inquiry
critical language pedagogy 93, 105
critical race theory 138, 158, 159, 161
Critical Whiteness Studies 159
culturally relevant teaching 97, 143
culture: classroom and school 19, 25, 47, 50, 54, 123, 140; cultural change and language xviii; language and xvi, xvii,

11, 109, 130, 138, 139, 140, 143, 152;
literature and 18, 55, 96; mainstream
(dominant) 84, 107, 129, 140; teaching
55, 97, 107
curriculum: English or language arts xi, 18,
21, 131, 162, 163; inclusive (integrated)
xii, xxi, 83, 130, 134; linguistically
informed (language-focused, dialect
awareness) xii, 18–21, 61–66, 130–131;
literature 18, 131, 162; required 65;
revision 18, 19–20; social studies 66, 109

descriptivism: prescriptivism and 4, 7, 11,
13, 14, 62, 63, 123; teaching 4, 9, 12–13,
14, 15–16, 123
dialectology 4, 94
dialect respelling 84, 85, 85n3, 89, 91
dialects: awareness 62, 109, 129, 131;
definition 71, 87n4, 160; diversity
110, 130; eye see eye dialect; grammatical
patterns of 113–117, 121; literature and
13, 55, 63, 84, 85, 85n3, 97, 131, 152,
159, 161, 162; maps 132; media and 4,
5, 20, 64, 129; Pig Latin and 152, 154;
prejudice 109, 110, 112, 113, 117;
regional xvi, 34, 35, 39, 71, 88, 91, 95,
132, 134–136; standard 76, 101, 101n1,
102, 107, 109, 117, 130; teaching 4–5,
8–9, 19–20, 23, 39, 62, 63, 66, 85–92,
96–97, 109, 110, 130, 123, 129, 130,
134–136, 152, 160; variation xi, xx, 18,
34, 39, 43, 55, 70–71, 109, 110, 117, 120,
130, 148, 157; vernacular (nonstandard,
non-mainstream) xvii, xviii, 92, 109; see also
regional dialects; Standard(ized) English
dictionaries xii, 4, 8, 33, 44–45, 84–92,
121, 132
Dictionary of American Regional English
(DARE) see digital resources
digital media see media
digital resources: Dictionary of American
Regional English (DARE) 84–92,
121, 132; Digital Archive of Literacy
Narratives 132; Do You Speak American?
4, 12, 20, 96; International Dialects of
English Archive (IDEA) 95, 132, 136;
Speech Accent Archive 34
diphthong 85
discrimination 61, 73, 82, 83, 96, 109,
152, 162

diversity: in classrooms xxi, 47, 54, 76, 95;
institutional 76; in the curriculum 83,
109; see also dialects; linguistic diversity
Do You Speak American? see digital resources

Ebonics xviii, 35; see also African American
English
emoji 33, 83
engagement: critical 95; educator 62, 65;
ethical 28; reader's 159; student 18, 158,
161, 162
English as a Second Language (ESL) 102
English Only 95, 98
eye dialect 18, 19, 84–87, 85n3, 89, 91, 97

formal English see Standard(ized)
English

games see language games
grammar xi, 3, 5, 8, 12, 13, 15–16, 21,
33, 39–43, 70, 73, 76–79, 82–83, 85,
96, 101–107, 110–117, 142; see also
descriptivism; lexical categories;
prescriptivism; syntax

history (of language) 5n2, 25, 32, 35, 39, 70,
82, 95, 97, 98, 140
hypothesis: formation 4, 7, 148, 149,
153, 154; parsimonious 155; revising 148;
testing 4, 153

identity: curriculum and 18, 55, 56, 73, 161;
cultural and social 54, 73; expression 132;
features of 47; language and xix, xxi, 5,
19, 21, 55, 56, 73, 74, 76, 99, 143, 152;
power and 74, 99, 124, 132; shelving 140;
student xv, 140; teacher 158; teaching
58n1, 58–59, 73
ideology see language ideologies
idiolect 33, 123
inquiry: critical 158, 159; in classrooms 69,
71–72, 79, 121, 123, 148, 151,
153–155, 159; linguistic 83, 102–104,
106, 147, 150, 152; scientific 147, 150;
student 20, 62; tools 78
International Dialects of English Archive
(IDEA) see digital resources

language acquisition 3, 123, 124
language and media see media

language and music 47–53, 63, 83
language awareness 39, 61, 62, 64, 65, 109, 123, 134, 161
language diversity *see* linguistic diversity
language games xii, 33, 147–148
language ideologies: authority and xx; in education 61–66, 91n8, 138; linguistic diversity ideology (definition) xvii; standard language ideology (Standard English Ideology, dominant language ideology, prescriptive ideology) xvii, 3, 70, 76, 93, 109, 110, 117, 121, 122, 122n1, 147; teaching xvi, xviii, xxi, 4, 7–9, 27, 32, 79, 82, 91n8, 123, 130–133, 152
language policy 20, 95
language (linguistic) prejudice 19, 21, 23, 73, 92, 152
language prestige 19, 23
language (linguistic) profiling 19, 23, 96
language variation: definition xvi; in classrooms xv, 18, 19, 20, 39, 48, 55, 61–66, 69, 75, 99, 107, 120, 121, 129, 130, 132, 140, 148; teachers and 20–21; teaching xv, xvi, xviii, xx, xxi, 3, 18, 20, 22–23, 32–34, 48, 56, 79, 82, 91, 96–97, 130, 131
languages: Fijian 19; French 98; German 98; Hawaiian 149–150; Japanese 149–150; Korean 98; Latin 147; Lushootseed 150–151, 152; Tagalog 19, 98; Tongan 19; *see also* Cherokee; Spanish
Latinx 93, 94, 107
Latinx English 129
lexical categories 40, 40n1, 41n2; adjective 40–41, 44, 77, 81, 95; adverb 40–41, 63, 69, 72; conjunction 40n1, 41, 81n4; determiner 40–41, 77, 116; noun 40–41, *42*, 44, 77–78, 80, *111*, **115**, 116; preposition 32, 33, 40n1, 41, *42*, 81; pronoun xixn5, 29, 41, 63, 101n1; verb xix, 40–41, *42*, 72, 77–80, 77n1, 85, **89**, 102–106, 112, 115, **115**, 141, 142, 151
lexicography 32
lexicon (lexical) 32–33, 85, **86**, **89**, 91; *see also* vocabulary
linguistic assimilation 18, 129
linguistic diversity: ideology xvii; in classrooms and schools 6, 50, 54, 62–64, 72, 76, 82, 112–113, 122, 123, 124, 141;

limited 130; sociolinguistic diversity 94; teaching xxi, 4, 33, 34, 35, 54, 62–64, 82, 97, 98, 121, 133, 143–145; value of xviii
linguistic inquiry *see* inquiry
linguistic prejudice *see* language prejudice
Linguistic Society of America (LSA) 124
linguograms 123
literature: *Adventures of Huckleberry Finn* by Mark Twain 34, 63, 158–163; *The Adventures of Tom Sawyer* by Mark Twain 42–43; "A Bit of Shore Life" by Sarah Orne Jewett 88; "Blackberry Eating" by Galway Kinnell 149; *Def Poetry Jam* 35; "Dry September" by William Faulkner 27–30; "Gal Young Un" by Marjorie Kinnan Rawlings 90; *The Great Gatsby* by F. Scott Fitzgerald 35, 36–37; *The House on Mango Street* by Sandra Cisneros 97; *Into the Wild* by Jack London 44–45; "Mother Tongue" by Amy Tan 19, 20, 22; *The Narrative Life of Frederick Douglass* by Frederick Douglass 97–98; *Our Only May Amelia* by Jennifer Holm 151; "Spanglish" by Tato Laviera 35; *Their Eyes Were Watching God* by Zora Neale Hurston 18, 20, 22, 63; *To Kill a Mockingbird* by Harper Lee 27, 131; *When My Name Was Keoko* by Linda Sue Park 97
loanwords xviii, 32, 33, 105, 150
ludling 147; *see also* language games

mainstream English *see* Standard(ized) English
maps 4, 94, 95, 96, 97, 98, 98n2, 131, 132
math/mathematics 11, 12, 13, 14, 70, 101n2, 149
mechanics 113, 115, 116; *see also* capitalization; punctuation; spelling
media: and its influence xvi, xxv, 3, 8, 9, 129, 130; digital media and language 130; language and 3–5, 129, 136, 150; social media and language 26, 32, 33, 55, 76, 91, 123, 162
Midwestern dialect *see* regional dialects
morphology xi, 11, 12, 40–41, 44–45, 77–80, 77n3, 85, **87**, **89**, 91, 102–106, 111, 115–116, 123, 150–152; *see also* words

Native American languages and cultures 95, 150, 152
New York City dialect *see* regional dialects

nonstandard *see* vernacular
Northern Cities Vowel Shift 35
N-word *see* charged language

Outer Banks English *see* regional dialects

participatory action research 158
parts of speech *see* lexical categories
perceptual dialectology 4
phonology and phonetics xi, 3, 11, 19,
    85, **86**, **89**, 91, 122, 123–124, 147–150,
    151–152, 153–155; *see also* consonant;
    pronunciation; syllable; vowel
phrase (syntax) 40–43, 77n1, 77n2, 78,
    80–81, 84
pidgin 34
Pig Latin 147–149, 152, 153–155
power: canonical literature and 157;
    classrooms and 18, 54, 138, 139–140, 163;
    identity and 55, 99, 124; language and
    xii, xviii, xix, xx, 3, 18, 19, 20, 34, 55, 56,
    70, 71, 73, 77, 90, 94, 96, 97, 98, 99, 132,
    138, 140–142, 157, 161–162; mainstream
    xvi, **xvii**, xix; political 95, 97; prejudice
    (discrimination) and 26, 93, 124, 157;
    privilege (prestige) and 8, 77, 124; society
    and xix, xxi, 26, 27, 55, 56, 64, 73, 93;
    teaching 19–20, 26, 28–30, 55, 56, 58–59,
    73–74, 138, 142, 162
predicate 41, 41n3, 78; *see also* lexical
    categories: verb
prejudice 73, 74, 85, 92, 110, 124; *see also*
    dialects; language prejudice
prescriptivism: critique of 13, 32, 63;
    descriptivism and 4, 7, 11, 13, 14, 62, 123;
    four strands of 62–63; ingrained 3, 12;
    teaching 4, 7–9, 12, 14, 15–16, 123
pronunciation 5, 39, 85, 85n3, **89**, 96, 97,
    122, 129, 148, 152, 154
punctuation xix, 50, 52, 112, 113, 114,
    115, 142
purpose (linguistic instruction) xiii, xix–xx,
    xxi, 26, 55, 63, 72, 74, 97, 101, 106, 130,
    132, 141

race: canonical literature and 161, 162;
    classroom or school demographic
    22, 76; critical race theory *see* critical
    race theory; language and 73, 84, 131,
    140, 152; race-shelving 140; racism

and 96; society and 159, 161; teaching 3,
    18, 19, 22, 74, 91n8, 131
racism 117, 152, 159, 161
r-dropping xvi, 5
reduplication **150**, 150–151, **151**
regional dialects: Appalachian English
    23, 48, 80, 95, 151; Boston xvi, 5;
    Bronx English 114; Cajun English
    34, 114; California 5, 23; Illinois 39;
    mid-American 71; mid-Atlantic xvi;
    Midwestern xvi, 129–133; Montana 39;
    New York City xvi, 5, 85; Outer Banks
    Brogue 95; St. Louis corridor xvi;
    Southern English (Southeastern) 3, 5, 18,
    20, 34, 71, 72, 73, 74, 85, 94, 114, 151;
    Western Pennsylvania xvi
register: academic 13, 71, 101, 101n2, 107;
    definition 71; formal 20, 71; of Standard
    English 19; teaching 19, 20, 23, 35
repertoire (linguistic) xiii, xx, xxi, 71, 75,
    91, 101, 102, 104, 106, 107, 120, 121, 123

schwa 152
slang xii, xvi, 4, 5, 12, 13, 32, 33, 34, 73, 162
social justice 35, 62, 76, 117, 157, 159, 163
social media and language *see* media
social studies 65, 66, 93–100, 109, 121,
    150, 152
Southern English *see* regional dialects
Spanglish 32, 35, 102, 105, 106, 107
Spanish 18, 34, 71, 98, 99, 101–108
Speech Accent Archive *see* digital resources
spelling xii, xvii, 19, 35, 85, 85n3, **89**, 97,
    113, 114, 115, 147, 148, 152, 153; *see also*
    dialect respelling; eye dialect
Standard English learners 94, 99
Standard(ized) English (Academic English,
    General American, Standard written
    English, Standard(ized) American
    English, school-sanctioned forms of
    English): and ideology 19, 21, 54, 73, 76,
    109, 110, 113, 139, 140, 141, 159, 160;
    as a dialect 71, 71n1, 101, 101n1, 121;
    grammar of 71, 72; in classrooms and
    schools xv, **xvii**, 32, 39, 54, 73, 112, 113,
    114, 130; regional standard Englishes xvii;
    registers of 3, 19, 20, 71; Standard English
    learners 94, 99; teaching xii, 12, 20, 39,
    42, 43, 48, 50, 74, 82, 85, 88, 117, 153,
    159; *see also* language ideologies

Standard(ized) Spanish 101, 101n1, 104–107
standardized testing and assessment xv, xxi, 8, 26, 27, 139, 142, 143–145
standards (Common Core State Standards and other state and federal standards): in curriculum decision-making xii, xv, xxii, 25, 26, 63, 94, 130, 131, 147, 148, 160; in lesson plans 7, 15, 22, 28, 36, 44, 51, 58, 134, 143, 153
stereotypes 5, 6, 74, 84, 85, 90, 91, 92, 93, 95, 129, 131, 150
stress (syllables) 151–152
subject (grammar and syntax) 41, 77n1, 78, 80, **115**, 122, 141, 142
surveys 3–4, 8–9, 14, 64, 102–104, **103**, **104**
syllable (syllabary) 69, 124, 147–152, 153–155
syntax xi, 3, 33, 36, 37, 40–43, 41n2, 77–78, 77n2, 80–83, 85, **87**, **89**, 91, 116

taboo words 55; *see also* charged language
Talking Black in America 124
T-chart *111*, 116
teacher training 20, 56, 121–123, 122n3

vernacular (nonstandard): grammatical patterns of xvii, xviii, xix, 110, 113, 114, 115, 152; ideologies of xvi, xvii, xviii, 3, 4, 18, 35, 48, 79, 84, 85, 92, 109, 110, 112, 122, 123, 129, 132, 141; teaching xx, 8, 19, 27, 114, 116, 117, 120
vocabulary 14, 19, 20, 26, 37, 40, 71, 85, 87, 90, 95, 96, 101n2, 105, 123, 149; *see also* lexicon
vowel 5, 35, 85, 96, 147–149, 152, 154

words: creation of xi, xiii, 77n3, 95; dictionaries xii, 8, 45, **89**; meaning 25–27, 29, 33, 40, 44–45, 71, 77n3, 95; nonsense 40, 77–78; origins of xii, xviii, 39, **89**; prescriptivism and 8, 12, 32, 39, 48, 57, 82, 122; reduplication 150–151; syllable structure 147–150; syntax and 40, 77n2, 78; word choice (diction) 12, 33, 34, 36–37, 49, 64, 85, **89**, 96, 131, 142; *see also* charged language; lexical categories; lexicon; loanwords; morphology; slang; vocabulary

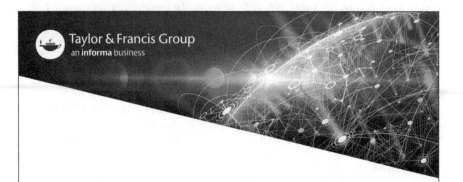